Psychological Foundations of Education

Psychological Foundations of Education

ISMAIL THAMARASSERI

KANISHKA PUBLISHERS, DISTRIBUTORS
NEW DELHI 110002

KANISHKA PUBLISHERS, DISTRIBUTORS
4697/5-21A, Ansari Road, Daryaganj
New Delhi -110 002
Phones : 2327 0497, 2328 8285
Fax : 011-2328 8285
E-mail : kanishka_publishing@yahoo.co.in
kanishkabooks@gmail.com

Psychological Foundations of Education
Edition: 2022

PRINTED IN INDIA

Published by Madan Sachdeva for Kanishka Publishers, Distributors, 4697/5-21A, Ansari Road, Daryaganj, New Delhi-110002, Typeset by Sunshine Graphics, Delhi, and Printed at G.S. Printers, Delhi.

Preface

There have been inormous new trends and developments in the field of educational psychology. The study of human behaviour and its dimensions is indispensable for every aspiring teacher. With the recent increase in the tempo of educational expansion in the country the value and importance of educational psychology for the prospective entrants to the teaching profession is being increasingly recognized and the subject is very popular with students offering psychology and education for their under graduate and post-graduate study.

The book *Psychological Foundations of Education* deals with the most of the areas of educational psychology. The utility of the book enhanced by the 'Model Questions' in the end of each chapter. It also meet the further quest of the reader via 'References' in the end of each chapter.

The objectives of the book are:

The Student/Reader Understands

- The contributions of the various schools of psychology to the theory and practice of education.
- The various methods and techniques of educational psychology.
- The nature and process of child development.
- The developmental needs and developmental tasks of various stages.
- The theories of personality, factors influencing personality and individual differences in areas like intelligence, aptitude, learning disability, creativity, etc.
- The process of learning, theories of learning, the factors influencing learning and strategies to facilitate learning.

- Process of remembering and forgetting and methods to ensure good memory.
- Importance of transfer of learning and need for teaching of transfer.
- The psychological bases underlying the methods, models and techniques of teaching.
- The basic assumptions of psychological evaluation of personality, attitude, aptitude, intelligence, etc.
- The theoretical assumptions and techniques of guidance and counselling.
- The role of the teacher as a manager and the psychological bases of classroom management.
- The student-teacher acquires positive attitude towards the students and teaching profession.
- The student-teacher becomes sensitive towards the psychological problems of students.
- He appreciates his roles as a counsellor and a facilitator.
- The student-teacher develops skills to cope with the developmental needs of children and to devise suitable instructional strategies.
- To motivate the learners.
- To provide appropriate learning experience and to develop positive attitude, concepts, skills, values, etc.
- To improvise and administer test items to measure intelligence, attitude, personality, anxiety level and other psychological constructs and to interpret the observed data.
- To conduct case studies and action researchers for solving psychological problems of the needy students.
- To render guidance and counselling to the needy students.

The author extremely indebted to various authors, educationists, psychologists, research workers, whose views and opinions have been incorporated in the text. The author grateful to his colleagues, friends, family members and students who offered suggestions,

Guidance and assistance. The author wish to express thanks to M/s Infratec Computer Systems, Calicut University for the computerization of the work.

Finally, the author great thankful to M/s Kanishka Publishers, Distributors, New Delhi for the meticulous process and publishing of the work.

All the suggestions, comments for the improving of the work will be accepted with thanks.

Kottakkal, Kerala **Ismail Thamarasseri**
January, 2008

Contents

1
Introduction to Educational Psychology

Psychology is a combination of two words psych means soul and logos means science. During the development of psychology it go through different meanings like science of soul, science of mind, science of consciousness and science of behaviour.

Psychology as a Science of Soul

Greek philosophers Plato and Aristotle considered psychology as a science of soul. During these time psychology is one of the branch of philosophy. The nature of soul couldn't be defined in this time.

Psychology as a Science of Mind

Immanuel Kant, a German philosopher one of the proponent of this view. He failed to give an exact description to mind. Therefore, this view didn't get acceptance for long.

Psycholcgy as a Science of Consciousness

During 19th century, William Wundt and William James, argue that psychology is a science of consciousness. But if we consider psychology as a science of consciousness we neglecting the other parts of mind i.e., sub-conscious and unconscious.

Psychology as a Science of Behaviour

During 20th century psychology deemed in the place of a pure science. J.B. Watson is one of the major contributor for the same. R.S. Woodworth commended on the changes of definitions of psychology: "First psychology lost its soul, then it lost its mind, then it lost its consciousness, it still has behaviour of a sort."

Definitions

Educational psychology deals with the problems, process and products of education:

Skinner : "Educational psychology is that branch of psychology which deals with teaching and learning."

Crow and Crow : "Educational psychology describes and explains the learning experiences of an individual from birth through old age."

Peel : "Educational psychology is the science of education."

Ausubel : "Educational psychology is an amalgam of all branches."

NATURE OF EDUCATIONAL PSYCHOLOGY

Educational psychology, the applied behavioural science, uses the principles and techniques of psychology and employs scientific methods and scientific approaches. It influences all the theories and practices of education, hence it is "the science and technology of education."

Kurt Koffka: "Psychology is the scientific study of behaviour of living creatures in their contact with the outer world."

SCOPE OF EDUCATIONAL PSYCHOLOGY

(*a*) the learner;
(*b*) learning experiences, the learning process; and
(*c*) learning situation or environment and the teacher (strategies).

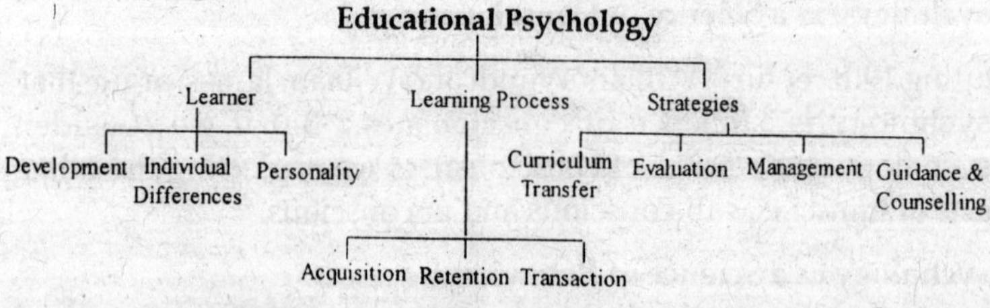

Fig. 1.1: Scope of Educational Psychology.

The scope of educational psychology is very wide with includes the learner, learning experiences, the learning process and the learning situation or environment and the teacher (strategies). Under the learner it consists learners development, individual differences and personality. The learners developments includes its stages factures, aspects and needs. The individual difference includes the intelligence, aptitude, creativity and disability. The area of personality including both theories and measurements. The learning process consisting the acquisition, retention and transaction it deals with its theories and factors. The strategies considering curriculum transfer its models and methods, evaluation both personal and academic achievement, the micro and the macro management and educational, vocational and personal guidance and counselling.

MEANING OF EDUCATIONAL PSYCHOLOGY

Psychology is intimately connected with education. It is inseparable. Psychology is the study of human behaviour and education is the process of modifying human behaviour. Educational psychology deals with human behaviour and its modification through learning. Educational psychology is concerned with the application of principles and techniques of psychology to solution of the problems confronting the teacher.

BRANCHES OF PSYCHOLOGY

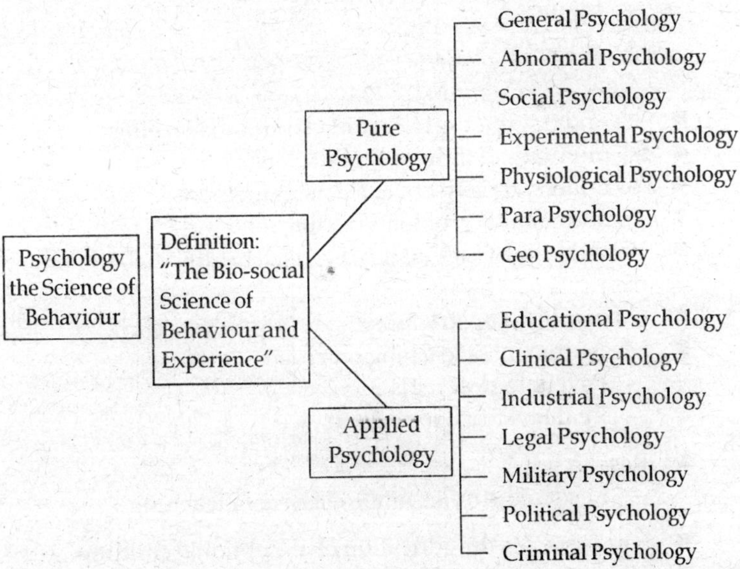

Fig. 1.2: Branches of Psychology.

General Psychology deals with behaviour of normal and adult human being. Abnormal Psychology deals with abnormal behaviour of the individual. Developmental psychology deals with the developments of human beings birth to old age and growth and development. Social Psychology deals with social behaviour and inter relationship of people themselves. Experimental Psychology deals with psychological experiments along scientific lines under laboratory situations for the mental processes and behaviour. Para Psychology deals with extra sensory perception, pre-cognition and re-birth. Educational Psychology is one of the applied psychology deals with the human behaviour. Clinical Psychology deals with clinical methods and behavioural disorders. Industrial Psychology deals with business environment. Criminal Psychology deals with criminal behaviour. Military Psychology deals with military activities. Political Psychology deals with the art of diplomacy and deriving political gains.

CONTRIBUTIONS OF EDUCATIONAL PSYCHOLOGY

Contribution to Theory of Education

- To understand developmental characteristics:
  - Infancy
  - Childhood
  - Adolescence.
- To understand the nature of classroom learning
- To understand individual difference
- To understand effective, teaching methods
- To understand problems of children
- Knowledge of mental health i.e., ill health, mal-adjustment etc.
- Curriculum construction
- Measurement of learning outcome
  - Psychological tools
  - Evaluate teacher performance.
- Research
  - Research studies in the classroom teaching.
- Guidance for the education of exceptional children
- Helps to develop positive attitude
- Understanding group dynamics

Contribution to the Practice of Education

- Problem of discipline
- Use of AV Aids
- Democratic administration
- For scientific time-table construction
- Co-curricular activities
- Use of innovations like activity centred, learner centred teaching
- Production of textbooks.

OBJECTIVES OF EDUCATIONAL PSYCHOLOGY

- To provide teachers with some basic skills related to teaching
- To give teacher's guidelines to solve problems of teaching/ learning process
- To help teachers to understand the scientific knowledge
- To instill in teachers a spirit of inquiry for their professional growth.

LIMITATIONS OF EDUCATIONAL PSYCHOLOGY

- Not a accurate/pure science
- Individual difference – not practicable to all situations/ individuals
- Performance of human beings varies from time to time
- Most of the psychological experiments conducted in animals
- Success of teachers work depends on natural aptitude and experience e and personal interaction.

Science is a systematized body of knowledge and it applicable for further research.

Psychology is not a pure science. It is a positive science. It's a behavioural science. Only scientific methods are adopted in psychology. The selection of a particular method depends upon.

1. Nature of the problem.
2. Orientation and resourcefulness of the investigator.
3. Availability of the materials, subject, time and financial resources.

METHODS OF EDUCATIONAL PSYCHOLOGY

Case Study

Case study is an in depth study of any social unit – a person, family, institution or community – it is a longitudinal or life long study.

Making and using a case study involves the following steps:

1. Collection of information regarding pupil.
2. Conduct interview.
3. Observation of tests, if necessary.
4. Documentation.
5. Diagnosis and plan for treatment/remediation.

Suggestions for Studying a Case

1. Identify a pupil from your own class (either deviant child or an outstanding child).
2. Try to plan the case in a small way.
3. A rapport is established in interview.
4. Use plain and simple language in report writing.
5. Not to attempt treatment which is beyond his/her experience.

Steps in Case Study

1. Determination of the problem.
2. Determination of the most probable antecedents of the case.
3. Formulation of the hypothesis.
4. Collection of data from all possible sources.
5. Verification of the hypothesis.
6. Remedial steps for removing the cause of mal-adjustment.
7. Follow-up of the case.

Experimental Method

Experimental method is the most precise, systematic and controlled observation. It is an attempt to establish cause—effect relationship.

Features

1. Experiments performed essentially require two persons—the experimenter and the subject or person whose behaviour is observed.
2. These experiments are always conducted on living organisms.
3. The main factor in the method is the controlling of the conditions or variables. Variable is an event or condition which can have different values; can be measured and varies quantitatively.

Experimental/Scientific Method/Designs

Steps

- problem, hypothesis, test, reject/accept hypothesis.
- most scientific and objective method for studying behaviour.
- tries to study cause and effect relationship.
- objective observations under rigidly controlled conditions.

For example, "Effect of anxiety on scholastic achievement." Here anxiety independent variable and it stands for a cause. Scholastic achievement is dependent variable and it stands for the effect. The independent variable stands for the cause and the consequent change in the dependent variable is effect of that cause. The other factors that influence the cause and effect of relationship are called intervening/controlled variable. For example, Socio-Economic Status, Education of the parents. Single group design and parallel group designs are the types of experimental designs.

Merits

Objective, Systematic, getting reliable data, findings are open to critical examination and verification.

Demerits

Mental process are fluctuating, costly, time consuming, difficult to control all factors.

Variables in Experiment

(*a*) Independent (e.g:- intelligence).
(*b*) Dependent (e.g:- academic achievement).
(*c*) Intervening (e.g:- social factors).

Case History/Clinical Method/Case Study/Clinical Study

Case study/clinical method is used for studying the behaviour problems of a mal-adjusted/deviant individual (case).

A case is "An individual facing problems that could be solved only on the basis of detailed study".

A child who is socially mal-adjusted or emotionally wrecked or is experiencing difficulty in a school subject is a clinical case.

Case study is an indepth study in all details. It aims at studying everything about something rather than something about everything.

It is detailed, realistic, concrete description and explanation of a case. For this, various tools and techniques are used. Information from all sources is pooled together in a sequential order to prepare a comprehensive case—history and locate the cause of mal-adjustment.

Merits

1. It considers all aspects of the child. Hence it highly reliable and can be used as a tool of evaluation.
2. To helps to understand the root causes of mal adjustment and suggesting remedial measures for rehabilitation.

Demerits

- Time consuming, wants of lot of efforts.
- Only for individual case and ends it.
- Requires technical proficiency and experience.

Differential Method—Statistical Method

Survey Method

The purpose of survey method is to obtain information from a large number of subjects in an efficient manner. A questionnaire, or inventory, containing structured or open–ended items, issued to obtain information on a wide variety of personal traits, and the results provide norms, indicating what is normal or expected for a certain group–observation and interview are involved in the process.

In this details of the phenomena are entered in opinionnaires/ questionnaire.The data are analyzed and interpreted. It gathers data from a relatively large number of cases at a time. Using statistics for analyzing the data. Use of various techniques—tests, questionnaire, observation, interview are general in survey methods. There are various types of survey methods, i.e., historical survey (relevant factors about past from various sources), sample survey (representation 'sample' of the 'population') and population survey (details regarding all the members of the group—e.g.: census). These are very popular in social science and education. In these, if the sample increases validity and reliability also increase.

Merits

1. It is useful in determining the present trends and solving current practical problems.

2. It provides 'suggestions for further research'.

Demerits

1. Focuses on existing condition, it pays little attention to the past-condition which might have caused the present problem.
2. Possibility of 'manipulation' of data by the surveyor.
3. 'Sampling error'. Sometimes 'samples' are not true representative of the population.

TOOLS AND TECHNIQUES OF EDUCATIONAL PSYCHOLOGY

Anecdotal Record

It is the reports of informal teacher observations regarding his pupils either in the classroom or outside. It contains a description of the students conduct and personality in terms of frequent, brief, concrete observations of the student made a record by the teacher. Two column-description of the incident, interpretation of the incident are included in this. It is not considered a tool complete itself only a supplement.

For example: The response of a child while his/her friend asking help in malpractice, the behaviour of a child when a gold ornament found, behaviour of a child when his/her friend meet a problem during a tour/camp.

Merits

- Helpful to understand the child's behaviour in diverse situations.
- They provide data for pupils to use in self-appraisal.

Demerits

- Careless recording more harm than good.
- Observer may project his own feelings or subjectivity.

Cumulative Record

It is the confidential and systematic accumulation of significant factual information about an individual student while at school. It is the readily available permanent data about a child. It progressively develop and maintained. It contains information about the health, family, school, performance on psychological tests and their vocational goals. It helps the teacher in appraising the child assets and liabilities and to guide the child. It give a very comprehensive picture of the past and present career and help in making prediction.

Merits

- It helps the teacher to identify the needs and problems of each student.
- It will help to asses pupils occupational insight.
- It useful for guidance and counselling.
- It helpful for rejoining in another educational institutions.
- New school get a comprehensive – idea about the entrant.

Demerits

- Inefficient and lack of punctuality of teachers.
- Subjectivity of teachers.

Check List

Check list is developed by Hartshore and May (1929). It is a laundry type of device. It is easy to make and easy to use. In this prepared a list of items like behaviour, sequence of skills, etc. The observer records a check (✓) to denote the presence/absence of whatever being observed.

Rating Scale

It is the judgement of one person by another. Individuals personality is assessed by the impressions he makes upon others. There are 3 point scale (Good, Average, Poor), 5 point scale (Excellent, Very good, Good, Average, Poor) and 7-point scale (Excellent, Very good, Good, Average, Below average, Poor and Very poor) such scales are prevalent. Number of point fixed is an odd number for convenience in statistical manipulation. Traits like generosity, co-operation, punctuality, honesty are rated.

For example: In class how have you been? Talkative, easy talker, when necessary, listening, retained from talking.

Merit

Simple and less expensive.

Demerits

- Subjective bias

- The person doing rating is not well-informed and experienced the data collected will be invalid.

Questionnaire

Questionnaire is a device for securing answers to questions by using a form which the respondent fills in himself.

Types

There are two types of questionnaires

1. *Closed/structural/Fixed Response*
   It is short, check responses or provides for making just as 'Yes'/'No' response. Example: "Are you satisfied with the library facility of your college?" – (Yes/No)
2. *Open End/Unrestricted/True Response Type*
   It requires a free response in the respondent's own words. Example: "Why did you choose to do your B.Ed. degree at this centre?"

Characteristics

Its importance should clearly stated

- as short as possible.
- arranged in categories.

Merits

- Most popular and quite useful in collecting information.
- Data could be collected from a large mass of subject at a stretch.

Demerits

- May not respond all questions.
- Expected number of scripts may not be received back.

Techniques of Educational Psychology

Interview

Interview is a process of communication or interaction in which the subject or interviewee gives the needed information verbally in a face-to-face situation. It gives an opportunity for mutual exchange of ideas and information between the subject and the psychologist.

Interview broadly divided into two i.e., structured and unstructured interview. In structured interview questions are planned sufficiently earlier. Unstructured interview is more flexible and questions are decided according to the situation. It is not pre-planned.

Types of Interview

Interview again divided into three, based on its functions it classified into diagnostic interview, clinical interview and research interview. Based on role of participant it divided into individual interview, group interview, single interviewer interview and panel interviewer interview. Based on the roles they divided into two i.e., non-directive interview and focused or depth interview.

Observation

The literary meaning of observation is "looking outside". It is the examination of something especially for the collection of data. It is the inspection of overt behaviour of a person in appropriate situations. To get reliable results, it should be repeated in a number of times.

Types of Observation

1. *Participant Observation*: In this observer become the part of the group. Observer freely mingles with the members of the group. Here observer plays a double role. The advantages of participant observation is, it is more reliable and very flexible but it time consuming and sometimes observers presents create problems. Example: Observing childrens in the classroom.
2. *Non-participant Observation*: The observer observes the group under the study with actually participating in its activities. It is used for infants, childrens and abnormal persons. The position of observer here least disturbing the subject. For example: Observing the childrens while they playing.
3. *Controlled Observation*: It made under controlled conditions. Observer may equip an experimental laboratory with manifold objects. Example: Observing via CCTV.
4. *Uncontrolled Observation*: It is done in natural settings as they occurred spontaneously. Example: Observing the behaviour of boys during play.

Merits of Observation

- It is useful for all age groups.
- Not require any tool.
- Adaptable both individual and group(s).

Demerits

- Possibility to personal prejudice.
- It reveals only overt behaviour.
- The time lag of recording observation.

SOCIO-METRIC TECHNIQUES

Socio-metry

It is the measurement of social relationship that exists among the members of a group. It attempt to describes attractions/repulsions between group members by asking them to indicate whom they would select/reject in various situations. Study of social adjustment, group dynamics, learning, motivation, discipline and other problem areas are involve social relations. The technique is generally traced by J.L. Moreno's work entitled "*Who shall Survive,1934*". Socio-metry developed by Moreno and Jennings in 1946.

Socio-gram

In this socio-metric choice may be represented graphically.

'Guess Who' Techniques

It is developed by Hartshorne and May (1929). In this a student is asked to read each statement and write the name who best fits that description. Example: "The person is always happy.........", "the person is always worried....."

Advantages of Socio-Metric Techniques

- Easy
- Less expensive
- Less time consuming.

Limitations

- Individual do not reveal the reason why they choose or reject some members.
- Results not suggest how the social structure of the group can be changed.

PROJECTIVE TECHNIQUES

In projective techniques the testee unconsciously unknowingly projects his own desires, hops, fears and repressed wishes.

Thematic Apperception Test (TAT)

It is developed by Murray and Morgan in 1935, it includes 20 vague and infinite pictures showing one or more human figures in different poses and actions. The respondent is asked to narrate the story centered around the picture. The narration may be feelings, emotions, motivations, desires, frustrations to express voluntarily. In this 10 cards are common and each 10 cards exclusively for both men and women.

Rorschach Ink-Blot Test

It is developed by Hermann Rorschach a Swiss psychologist in 1921. It consists 10 standardized cards, 5 in black and white and 5 in multi-colour. If one interpret the picture as animal shape that indicates narrow thinking. Those who interpret it is a bear that indicate strong degree of emotional control. The movement of the picture indicating the introvert behaviour.

Children's Apperception Test (CAT)

Dr. Leopold Ballack developed this projective technique for children between 3-10 years. It includes 10 cards of pictures of animals in various life situations. The counsellor as to make story himself based on the cards and the counselee projects himself.

Other important projective techniques are Word Association Test (WAT) by Carl Gustav Jung, Picture Association Test and Man Drawing Test.

Advantages/Merits of Projective Techniques

- There is no danger of giving response by the individual.
- Not possible for the individual to give readymade habitual or stereo typed pattern of responses.
- No demand of literacy/academic skills.

Demerits

- Time consuming for both administration and scoring.
- Only a well trained-experienced person can administer.

Techniques and Tools for Data Collection – A Comparison

Techniques	Tools
1. *Testing*—It is a process which is either oral, written or performance.	1. *Tests*—A psychological test is an instrument used to measure a sample of certain aspects of behaviour, quantified by numerical scores.
2. *Interview*—Interviews are used to gather information in a face-to-face session regarding an individual's experiences and knowledge; his or her opinions, beliefs and feelings; and demographic data–the clinical interview and other major types–merits and demerits of the method.	2. *Anecdotal record*—It is a record of anecdotes or a casually observed significant behaviour of the pupils. It is a record of observations either in the classroom or outside.
3. *Socio-metry*—A technique used for describing the social preferences of individuals in a group. Socio-metric choices may be represented graphically it is socio-gram.	3. *Cumulative record*—This is a progressive record of pupil's educational history dealing various aspects like physical, intellectual, morals, social and academic achievement.
4. *Projective technique*—Used togather data which cannot be collected directly from the individual. Here the individual responds to a vague stimulus unconsciously projecting his inner experiences - For example: Rorsochach's ink blot test, Thematic Apperception test, Word Association Test, etc.	4. *Check-list*—It is a prepared list of behaviour or items. The behaviour may be indicated by checking yes or no type or number of items may be indicated by inserting the appropriate word or number.
5. *Observation*—Direct, indirect or participation observation.	5. *Rating scale*—Involves qualitative description of a limited number of aspects of a thing or of traits of a person. The subject can be respond to an item in the scale according to the degree of acceptance or rejection. Example: Strongly agree, agree, undecided, (neutral) disagree, strongly disagree.
	6. *Questionnaire*—It is a device used togather information through which respondents answer questions or respond to statement in writing. It may be Yes or No type or structured or unstructured type.

MAJOR APPROACHES TO EDUCATIONAL PSYCHOLOGY

A group of psychologists having similar points of views and making similar approaches to study human mind or behaviour constitute a school of thought in psychology.

Table–1.1
Major Approaches to Educational Psychology

Major Approaches	*Behaviourism*	*Cognitive*	*Psychoanalytic*	*Humanistic*	*Neurobiological*
Chief Exponents	John. B. Watson, Skinner, Pavlov, Thorndike, Guthrie, Hull	Jean Piaget, Bruner, Ausubel, Wertheimer, Kohler, Lewin, Tolman	Sigmund Freud, C.G.Jung, Adler, Erikson	Carl Rogers, Abraham Maslow, Combs.A, Glasser.W	Ramony Cajal, Mc.Connel, Hyden, Flexner
Focus	Overt Behaviour & S – R Conditioning	Cognitive Process & Schemata Development	Unconscious Motivation & Libidinal Orientation	Personalised Experience & Self Actualisation	Nervous System & Structure and Functions of Brain

Neurobiological Approach

Nervous system forms the base of human behaviour. All the modern theories of learning, intellectual functions and emotional reactions are based on neurobiological researches. The basic unit of our nervous system is *neuron or nerve cell.* Endless neurons are present in our nervous system. Between Neuron are small gaps called synapse. Impulses (electro chemical) are transmitted along the neurons and across the neurons. As the impulses reach terminal button of a neuron, a transmitter substance (e.g. Acetyl cholene) is released, which inturn is attached to a receptor site on the neighbouring neuron. Then the second neuron gets excited and thus impulse travels along and across neurons. In this way messages are transmitted from the body surface to the brain and vice versa.

Let us examine the structure of Neuron/Nerve Cell.

Structure of Neuron/Nerve Cell

In an average brain there are about 12 to 15 billion neurons in the cerebrum, about 70 million neurons in the cerebellum and one billion in the spinal cord (James W. Kalat–Biological Psychology–V. Edition p. 27). Imagine the multitude of inter-connections and pathways!

Outline–Nervous System

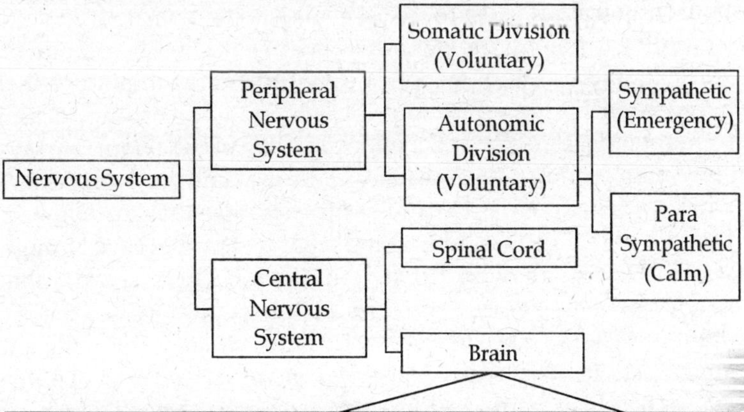

Parts	*Functions*
Two Cerebral hemispheres, each of which is divided into 4 lobes	
■ Frontal	Cognition i.e., thinking, reasoning, etc.
■ Parietal	Somato sensory
■ Temporal	Smell and Hearing
■ Occipital	Vision
Corpus Callosum	Joins two cerebral hemispheres
Cerebellum	Co-ordinate body movements
Medulla	Repetitive process, viz., breathing, heart beat, etc.
Reticular Activating System (RAS)	Keep awaken even during sleep
Pons	Connection to cerebellum and involved in dreaming.
Hypothalamus	Homeostasis, Control eating, drinking, sex
Thalamus	Relay station of impulses
Pituitory	Master gland (Control hormone secretions)
Hippocampus	Memory
Amygdala	Emotions.

Fig. 1.3: Outline – Nervous System.

Behaviourism

Behaviourism given importance to overt behaviour and S-R conditioning. J.B. Watson popularized this school of psychology. Watson an American Psychologist made a revolution in psychology. According to him psychology is the objective study of behaviour. He was extremely environmentalist. Environment is important than heredity in the determination of behaviour according to him. Conditioning is the key to the understanding of behaviour. He says, "give me a dozen healthy infants, well-formed and my own specified world to bring them up in and I will guarantee to take any one at random and train him to become any type of specialist, I might select—Doctor, Lawyer, Artist.... and Yes beggar man and thief regardless of his talents, tendencies, abilities, vocations and the race of his ancestors." The subject-matter of psychology is human and animal activity which can be observed and measured in an objective way. The chief method of learning is conditioning. There is an immediate response of some sort to every effective stimulus: Every response has some kind of stimulus.

Later Behaviourists Clark L. Hull (1884-1952)

Hull, the Professor of Yale University he called the straight of association between stimulus and response is *Habit Strength.* Habit strengthened by practice and repetition.

Burrhus Frederick Skinner

According to him *Operant Conditioning* is a type of learning process by the process of rewarding. He conducted experiment on rats, pigeons. His major ideas are *shaping, reinforcement* and *punishment* is according to him the teachers can able to shape the students in a desired manner via rewards, reinforcement and through motivation.

Edward L. Thorndike

He was one of American Psychologist. The proponent of S–R Bond Theory. Trial and error is a method of learning in which various responses are tentatively tried and some discarded until a solution is attained.

It is a S–R theory, which assumes that through conditioning specific responses (R) came to be linked with specific stmuli (S). The base for learning is the linking between S–R. According to him learning is a mechanical process. His learning theories are:

1. *Law of Readiness*: "When a conduction unit is ready to conduct for it do so is satisfying. When a conduction unit is not ready to conduct, for it to conduct is annoying. When a conduction is ready to conduct not to conduct is also annoying."
2. *Law of Effect*: When a modifiable connection between S and R is made and is accompanied by a satisfying state of affairs, of that connections strength is increased. When it is accompanied by an annoying state of affairs, its strength is decreased.
3. *Law of exercise.*
4. *Law of Use.*
5. *Law of Disuse.*
6. *The principle of multiple response.*
7. *The principle of analogy.*

Educational Implications of Thorndike S–R Theory

- Given Importance to motivation.
- It strengthens the importance of mental readiness.
- More and more opportunities given to the learner to use and repeat knowledge.

Psycho-analytical Approach to Psychology

Sigmond Freud (1856-1939), Viennese physician was the major proponent of psycho-analytical school. Psycho-analysis is a method for understanding behaviour and for treating mental illness. His school of thought is known as *psycho-analysis*. The approach he adopted understanding human behaviour and personality is known as psycho-analytical approach.

REFERENCES

1. S.K. Mangal, *Advanced Educational Psychology*.
2. Arnowitting, *Introduction to Psychology*.
3. Benjamin B. Lahey, *Introduction to Psychology*.
4. Clifford T. Morgan, *Introduction to Psychology*.
5. Edward E. Smith, *Introduction to Psychology*.
6. N.L. Munn, *Introduction to Psychology*.
7. Dr. R. N. Sharma, *Methodology of Educational Research*.
8. Rama, S., Anandan, Anil, R. & Nambiar, B. (2005, July). *Psycho-*

pedagogy. Paper presented at the Seminar on Psychological Foundations of Education, DAMTEC, Calicut.

9. John W. Best & James V. Khan, *Research in Education.*
10. S.S. Chauhan, *Techniques and Principles of Guidance.*

MODEL QUESTIONS

1. Give an acceptable definition of psychology. Explain the major terms in the definition.
2. Elaborate the term behaviour ?
3. Who is exponent of Psycho Analytic Theory? What are the major assumptions?
4. Who is the exponent of Humanistic Theory? What are the major assumptions?
5. Who is the exponent of Cognitive Theory? What are the major assumptions?
6. Differentiate between direct and indirect observation.
7. Define case study and explain its procedural steps.
8. "Experiment is observation under controlled conditions". Explain the statement and explain the process?
9. What do you mean by survey study?
10. Explain the importance of neuro-biological process in the study of human behaviour.
11. Explain an anecdote that throws light to any significant behaviour of child.
12. What are the difference between direct and indirect observation?
13. List the uses of cumulative record.
14. Write any two merits of interview.
15. What is a sociogram? What are its uses?
16. Why are some tests called projective techniques? Give an example.

2

Developmental Psychology

DIFFERENT PHASES OF DEVELOPMENT

Introduction

The human being is never static. From the moment of conception to the time of death, the person is undergoing changes. Development may be defined as a progressive series of orderly, coherent changes. The various developments that take place during the life time of an individual are physical, motor, social, emotional, intellectual, aesthetic and moral.

Physical Development

Physical development refers to the physical changes in the size, structure and proportion of the parts of the body that take place at the moment of conception. Directly physical development determines what children can do at a particular age. Indirectly, it influences their attitude toward self and others. As the child grows physically, the range of his experiences increases. The increase in his experience contributes to the developments in cognitive, emotional, social and moral areas.

Studies show that growth comes in cycles. The term 'cycles' means that physical growth does not occur at regular rate rather in periods or phases, sometimes rapidly and sometimes slowly.

During the early childhood years, the growth in slow. Height and weight increase at the lower rate during this period. During early childhood all the parts of the childs body grow, but at different rates. During early childhood, the forehead area develops faster than the lower part of the face. This is due to rapid growth of the brain. The trunk grows longer and broader in the early years of childhood. *Arms* grow much longer between babyhood and age 6. Arms are thin and straight because the muscles grow at a very slow rate. Legs grow at a slower rate than the arms. Teeth – most of the baby teeth have cut through the germs shortly after babyhood ends. The baby teeth will be fall between 5 and 7. The process of loosing baby teeth and replacing them with permanent teeth goes on until the child is 12 or 13 years.

Bones: Bone development consists of growth in bore size, change in the number of bones, and change in their composition. Bone development is most rapid during the first years of life, then relatively slow up to the time of puberty and one again more rapid.

Muscles and Fat: Fatty tissues develop faster than muscle tissue during early childhood. Children who eat too much carbohydrates and too little protein will develop too many fat cells.

Nervous System

At birth brain weight is one-eighth of total weight, at 10 years, one-eighteenth, at 15 years, one-thirtieth, and a maturity one fortieth.

Sex Differences

- At birth girls tend to be shorten than boys.
- Boys are generally taller than girls at all ages except 10, 11 and 12 years as girls tend to reach puberty earlier.
- Boys tend to be heavier than girl right through the first nine years. Between ten to fourteen years the girls have a tending to shoot ahead.

Factors Affecting Physical Development

Heredity and environment are the two main factors that affect physical development. The environment factors include pre-natal and birth conditions, socio-economic status, nutritions, physical exercises etc.

Motor Development

Motor development means the development of control over bodily movements through the co-ordinated activity of the nerve centres, the nerves and the muscles.

Significance

Motor development is of greater significance for the total development of the child.

1. Good health which is vital to the child's development and happiness is partly dependent on exercise.
2. *Emotional Maturity*: Once the child develops his motor skills adequately he starts participating in team games and sports and learn to control his emotions, show sportsmanship etc.
3. *Independence*: Motor development gives the child a sense of independence and with it a feeling of security since he can learn to tackle things on his own.
4. *Self-entertainment*: Motor control enables children to engage in activities which give them enjoyment even in the absence of playmates.
5. *Socialization*: Good motor development contributes to the child's acceptance and provides opportunities to learn social skills.
6. *Self-concept*: Motor control leads to feelings of physical security, which are soon translated in to psychological security.

Gross and Finer Motor Skills

Motor skills can be roughly divided into two main types.

1. The gross muscular skills like jumping, hopping, running, lifting and climbing.
2. The finer muscular skills like drawing, painting and writing.

Special Skills – Hand Skills

- *Self-feeding*: During the latter past of the first year of life, babies try to hold a bottle or cup and reach for the spoon with which they are being fed.
- *Self-dressing*: By the age of 5 years a child manages to dress entirely by himself, except for tying his shoe laces.
- *Writing*: At one year of age a child can just bang and scribble with his pencil. A three year old tries his hand at some kind of symbol formation, though not exactly letters. It is only by the age of approximately 5 or 6 years that a child is ready to write.
- *Ball Throwing and Catching*: Some babies roll and may even attempt throw balls before they are two years old. At four,

few can throw well. By six years, most children are proficient though there are marked variations at every age.

Leg Skills

- *Standing and Walking*: After babies reach 18 months of age, motor development in the legs consists primarily of the perfection of Walking and the acquisition of related skills.
- *Running*: By the age of 5 or 6 years the child is able to run smoothly and with speed, and play regular running games.
- *Jumping*: By 2½ to 3 years a child can jump from a height of about 40 cms.
- *Skipping*: Girls of 5 years of age are able to skip but boys of this age are not able to skip.
- *Hoping*: By 8 years children are able to hop like a frog, and hop on both feet and in another year they even learn to hop backwards.
- *Tricycling and Bicycling*: By the age of 2 years, a few toddlers can ride tricycles. Between 3 and 4 years, all young children who have had an opportunity to learn to ride tricyles can do so.

Sequence in the Development of Major Skills

Motor development follows a definite sequence starting with the head and moving downwards, and from the centre to the sides. At various stages of development the children learn to combine the new skills that they have learnt with those learnt previously. In this way co-ordination occurs, and more complex tasks become possible.

Factors Influencing Motor Development

Heredity, maturation, readiness and learning are the major factors influencing motor development.

EMOTIONAL DEVELOPMENT

'Emotional development' refers to the emergence of emotions like anger, joy, delight, happiness, fear, anxiety and sorrow and the socially acceptable ways of expressing them. As the child grows up and becomes aware of acceptable ways of behaviour, a variety of emotions also emerge. As an infant he expresses only discomfort and delight. As he grows older expressions of joy, happiness, fear, anger and disappointment appear. He learns to express these emotions in a healthy manner.

From the simple emotional states present at birth, new and more complex emotions develop. This development comes partly from maturing but mostly through learning. By the end of the first year, the baby feels fear, anger, jealousy, envy, curiosity, joy and affection.

Common Emotions of Childhood

1. ***Affection***

Anything that gives the young child pleasure a person, a pet or a toy-becomes the object of the child's affection.

2. ***Anger***

Anger has a very bad influence on the personality of the individual and hence is called a negative emotion.

3. ***Curiosity***

Things that are new and different may make children want to explore them. Later, when children can ask questions, they add facts given the answers to what they learned from exploring.

4. ***Envy***

The usual causes of envy in young children are the things other children own or can do.

5. ***Fear***

Is a form of self-protecting flight from any dangerous situations. The child is frightened by loud noises, animals, strange persons, high places, darkness, loneliness, pain and falling down.

6. ***Grief***

The loss of anything important to children a family member, a pet or a loved toy-makes them cry and they refuse to do what they usually do.

7. ***Jealousy***

Jealousy is an attitude of resentment directed towards people. Whenever, a parent or other adult shows more interest in, and gives more time and attention to another child, young children may resent it.

8. ***Joy***

Anything that makes a young child feel satisfied and important, such as doing something well and winning praise for it, gives rise to an overall feeling of happiness known as joy.

Patterns of Emotional Development

The ability to respond emotionally is present in the new born infant. Even before babies are a year old, emotional expressions are recognizably similar to those of adults.

In the developmental pattern, some periods are characterized by "equilibrium" and other by "dis-equilibrium". In equilibrium the child is making goal adjustments and is easy to live with. Between 6 years and the onset of puberty, equilibrium prevails. During the periods of equilibrium children are "In focus" and show signs of good adjustment. In disequilibrium adjustment appear to be disrupted by conditions within or by environmental factors, there are tensions, indecisions, insecurities and other behaviour problems.

Factors Affecting Emotional Development

Emotional problems show up in many warp. Failure in school work may leads to depression or angry outburst at home.

Emotional Disturbance

Moodiness, substitute responses, displacement, regression, emotional outburst etc., are the major symptoms of emotional disturbance.

Steps to Avoid Emotional Disturbance and Maintain Mental Health

1. Some strenuous physical exercise daily, through either play or work, and an understanding of how this aid physical and emotional well-being.
2. The development of a sense of humour so that one can laugh even at onself.
3. A close and affectionate relationship with at least one family member, a parent can help a child to develop a more mature perspective on his problems.
4. A willingness to talk over one's problems with a sympathetic person.

SOCIAL DEVELOPMENT

Social development implies the development of an individual in such a way as he becomes a useful member of society or the group to which he belongs. Social development begins with the infant's first contact with other people and continues throughout life. It is the net result of the child's constant interactions with his social environment. Social development helps in learning and acquiring social qualities of character. Social development enables the child to adjust himself to his social environment and to maintain social relationships.

Social Development During Early Childhood (2-4 Years)

During early childhood, the social behaviour of the child exhibits a progressive change from individualization towards socialization. During three and four years child is completely ego-centric. That is in this period he is unable to identify his self with others. He has no social insight. He is unable to accept the point of view of others. He thinks all is based on himself. As the child approaches his fourth year, he comes to realize that 'what is mine is yours' also and likes to share or exchange toys with his playmates.

Factors Affecting Social Development

The main socializing agents are home, peer group, school and community. These agencies are responsible for socialization of a child.

(a) *Home:* Is the first socializing agent. The congenial home environment has a positive and socializing effect on the child. The positive reinforcements that the growing child receives in the home helps his social development.
(b) *Parental Attitude and Social Development:* Children from autocratic homes are more quarrelsome, more unstable emotionally, more daring and uninhibited more sensitive to praise and blame and less considerate to other than children from democratic homes.
(c) *Child Rearing Practices:* Optimal child rearing practices should help the child to develop social needs which are in harmony with social values of his culture.
(d) *Relation with Siblings:* The first child in the family is a responsible type. He takes life seriously and shows some tendency to be dominant and 'bossy' towards siblings. The youngest child in the family may expect and secure much attention and may be highly dependent and accustomed to extra privileges.
(e) *Socio-Economic Status (SES):* The family members of high SES

have the opportunity of moving about in a higher and wider circle of society. This naturally helps them in their socialization.

(f) *Influence of Peer Group:* Peer group introduce the child to the social world outside the family mainly for play purposes. The peer groups satisfy various needs of the children like acceptance, achievement, affection, approval, belongingness, fame, recognition, expression of thought and opinion etc.

(g) *School:* The school life plays an important role in the social development of the child. The curricular, co-curricular activities and teachers have a great hearing on the social development of the child.

Self-Concept and Social Development

When a child recognizes and identifies with his ways of growing, behaving and thinking he is strengthening his awareness of himself. This awareness of self-attributes as he sees and believes them be, constitutes his self-concept. The self-concept is developed from comments made by others and from inferences from experiences the child has had in his life. The child reaches middle childhood with a self-concept derived through his parents immediate family and a limited number of peers. His life concept is likely to be distorted or incomplete.

COGNITIVE DEVELOPMENT

Thinking, perceiving, remembering, forming concepts, generalizing, abstracting and creativity as well as other general intellectual activities are the areas of cognitive development. Cognitive development refers to the orderly changes that occur in these areas of cognition at specific time.

Many psychologists have made attempts to study the nature and sequence of cognitive development. Jean Piaget and Jerome S. Bruner are the two prominent psychologists among them. They help us understand a child's cognitive development a great deal.

Piaget's Theory of Cognitive Development

Jean Piaget studied how children think and develop intellectually. His cognitive theory deals with acquisition of knowledge and the comprehension of what is acquired. The major concepts of his theory are schema, operation, assimilation, accommodation, disequilibrium, equilibrium and equilibration. According to Piaget, cognitive development is a result of what he calls 'equilibration', the search for equilibrium, constantly makes use of assimilation and accommodation. According to Piaget there are four main stages of intellectual development:

1. The sensory motor stage (Birth to 2 years).
2. The pre-operational stage (2 to 7 years).
3. The concrete operational stage (7 to 11 years).
4. The Formal operational stage (11 to 16 years).

Children of early childhood education are in Piaget's pre-operational stage. During the end of the second year, the child is capable of representing experiences mentally. Child's play, during this period is more imaginative than full of motor activities. In this stage the child is influenced by the externally significant characteristics of objects like size, colour, length and shape, whether the object is manipulable, turnable, throwable and so on. His thinking is abstract.

In the concrete operational stage the child can deal with concrete problems, visual problems are solved more rapidly than verbal problems.

Burner's Theory of Cognitive Development

Jerome S. Burner believes that in each stage of development the individual may represent his experiences enactively, iconically and symbolically.

In *enactive* mode of representation action is the way the child understand his environment.

In *iconic* mode of representation the information is carried by imagery.

In *symbolic* mode of representation the child can translate his actions and images to symbols.

AESTHETIC DEVELOPMENT

Aesthetic development refers to a sense of appreciation in seeing, hearing and doing. Every child possess a sense of appreciation towards objects, colour, sounds etc. But its degree varies from child to child. Aesthetic development ensures best use of sense organs. Child sees objects of different shapes, child matches, sorts and compares them.

Children love deep colours, red, yellow, blue and green in the order of preference. Observation of sky at night, rainbow, dust etc., stimulates children's appreciation of beauty. Sensitivity to sounds of birds, animals, music, rhythm, etc., develop appreciation of nature and environment.

For aesthetic development, different types of hand work activities such as brush painting, finger painting, clay work, play with newspaper cuttings, music, dance, rhythmic movements etc. are introduced.

MORAL DEVELOPMENT

Moral development of a child implies inculcation of a number of qualities such as honesty, truthfulness, self-respect, self-control, compassion, duty consciousness and righteousness in children. According to Piaget there are four stages in the moral development of a child.

1. *Anomy* (first-five years): It is the stage without law. Pain and pleasure are the only regulation of behaviour at this stage.
2. *Heteronomy* (5-8 years): It is external authority that controls moral conduct. 'Do that', 'don't do that', rewards and punishments regulate moral development.
3. *Heteronomy* (reciprocity) (9-13 years): At this stage there is a morality of co-operation. With peers or equals. This stage is regulated by reciprocity which implies we should not do to others what will be offensive to us.
4. *Autonomy* (13-18 years): The individual at this stage is fully responsible for his behaviour. The rules governing moral behaviour come from within the individual.

Factors Affecting Moral Norms of Children

Children always imitate. Hence good models are very helpful for moral development. Children must learn what is right and what is wrong. These can be accomplished most successfully by associating pleasant reaction with what is right and unpleasant reactions with what is wrong. Social norms, beliefs customs, policies and religion too influence moral development.

During pre-school years children do not have their own concept of morality and possess no clear understanding of social rules, except for the regulations laid down by the adults.

Later Childhood Period

This stage is reflecting the nature of whole life of the child. Co-curricular and extra-curricular activities must be integrated with educational programme, well-organized physical activities and athletic events may be provided for wholesome development of the body and mind.

Health and hygiene of the children at this stage must be properly attended. Play way methods and activity oriented educational programmes must be emphasized. Educational arrangements of scouting, guides, debates, school assemblies, exhibitions, excursions etc., should be properly organized for the right physical and mental development. Emotional integration for balanced personality development should be well-established. Democratic ways of life and social values should be inculcated through school activities. He must be provided suitable environments for developing desirable behaviour that are socially accepted.

EDUCATIONAL IMPLICATIONS OF DIFFERENT PHASES OF DEVELOPMENT

Early Childhood Period

1. Parents should take care of the education of the child. They should lay foundations for all improvement in different dimension of developments.
2. A sound mind has to built in this early stages. Physical activities should be an integral part of education. Proper nourishing food should be given. Protection from epidemic diseases must be carefully attended.
3. Mother-tongue should be taken as the medium of instruction since mother-tongue has an emotional attachment by being early understood.
4. There should be associated with good environments that may keep themselves away from various deeds.
5. The instincts of curiosity should be developed. Their questions must be properly answered. They should broaden the mental horizon of the child.
6. Group playing, peer group relations should be encouraged. Education should find provision for such developments of social qualities.
7. Some interesting and entertaining activities such as music,

fine arts etc., should be the essential part of education at this stage.

8. Play way method in education is the essential psychological approach at this stage of education. Scientific and attractive toys, models etc., should be freely displayed to their access for releasing then innate and dormant qualities.

Conclusion

Development in each area affects development in other. Development of physical skills makes the infant mobile, increases, his range of activity and helps him to explore his surroundings. This also helps in cognitive development. Language development helps the child to communicate better. It also allows him to interact with more people. This interaction has a significant influence on this social development. The child is a complete person with the experiences and skills in one area influencing the development in others. The effect of each area of development cannot be separated out easily. Thus development is a holistic process.

DEVELOPMENTAL TASKS

In every cultural group experience has shown that people learn certain behaviour patterns and certain skills more easily and more successfully at some ages than at others. The group then comes to expect each individual to perform according to this come table of development. People of all ages are well-aware of these 'social expectations'. Social expectations are known as developmental tasks.

Havighurst has defined a developmental task as a task which arises at on about a certain period in the life of an individual, successful achievement of which leads to his happiness and success with later tasks, while failure leads to unhapphiness in the individual disapproval by society and difficulty with later tasks. Some developmental tasks arise mainly as a result of physical maturation others are developed mainly from the cultural pressures of society clearing to read as learning appropriate sex roles. Still others grow out of the personal values and aspirations of the individual. (choosing and preparing for a vocation). Most developmental tasks arise from all three of these forces working together. The major developmental tasks for childhood (Havighurst's developmental tasks for childhood).

Birth to Six Years

- Learning to walk.
- Learning to take solid foods.
- Learning to bath.
- Learning to control the elimination of body wastes.
- Learning sex differences and sexual modesty.
- Achieving psychological stability.
- Forming simple concepts of social and physical reality.
- Learning to relate oneself emotionally to parents, siblings and other people.
- Learning to distinguish right and wrong and developing a conscience.

Six to Twelve Years

- Learning physical skills necessary for ordinary games.
- Building wholesome attitudes towards oneself as a growing organism.
- Learning to get along with age mates.
- Learning an appropriate masculine or feminine sex role.
- Developing fundamental skills in reading, writing and calculating.
- Achieving personal independence.
- Developing fundamental skills on reading concepts necessary for everyday living.
- Developing conscience, morality, and a scale of values.
- Developing attitudes toward social groups and institutions.

Purposes of Developmental Tasks

Developmental tasks serve three very useful purposes. First, they act as guidelines to help parents and teachers to know what children should learn at a given age.

Second, developmental tasks sense as motivating forces for children to learn what the social group expects them to learn at that age. Children quickly learn that social acceptance depends on their being able to do what their age-mates do. The stronger their desire for social acceptance, the greater will be motivation to learn to do what their age-mates do.

Third, developmental tasks tell parents and teachers what will be expected of children in the immediate and remote future. As such they alert them to the necessity of preparing children to meet these new expectations. When children begin to play with their age-mates of alerts parents.

FACTORS INFLUENCING MASTERY OF DEVELOPMENTAL TASKS

A number of factors influence the mastery of developmental tasks. Some acts as obstacles to this mastery and some aid it. Some of this factors are controllable, as in the case of opportunities to learn. Others is axis true of body build and intelligence are either not controllable only within narrow limits.

Aids to Mastery

- Accelerated physical development.
- Strength and energy above average for age.
- Above average intelligence.
- An environment that offers opportunities for learning.
- Guidance from parents and teachers in learning.
- A strong motivation to learn.
- Creativity accompanied by a willingness to be different.

Obstacles to Mastery

- Retardation in developmental level, whether physical on mental.
- Poor health resulting in low energy and strength levels.
- A handicapping physical defect.
- Lack of opportunity to learn what the social group expects.
- Lack of guidance in learning.
- Lack of motivation to learn.
- Fear of being different.

IMPORTANCE OF MASTERING DEVELOPMENTAL TASKS

In spite of the importance of mastering the developmental tasks appropriate for the childs age and level of development, not all children do so. This failure has these serious consequences. First, it makes the child feel inferion, and this leads to unhappiness. Second, of result in social disapproval, which is often accompanied by special rejection. The child is considered immature and babyish. Third, it makes the mastery of new developmental tasks difficult. Each year the child will lag further and further behind because the necessary foundations on which to build will not be present.

By contrast, children who are precocious in mastering the developmental tasks set by the social group are rewarded by social approval and self-approval. Both of these contribute to happiness. Social approval puts children in line for leadership roles because they are judged by their age-mates to be superior in skills and general maturity. Self-approval contributes to self-confidence and provides a strong motivation to live up to social and self-expectations.

PROBLEMS CONFRONTED BY ADOLESCENCE AND ITS REMEDIAL MEASURES

Adolescents, their interests and problems have been intriguiting parents, teachers and counsellors for scores of years. A number of studies in a bid to identifying and quantify there interests and problems revealed interesting facts.

Indian adolescents obviously have problems and interests similar to those of the American adolescents of Minnesota study.

A Study of Problems of Youth

Procedure

To help the adolescence adjust better to their problems, these is the need of bringing the problems of the individual into the open and in apprising the major concerns of the group.

A Search into the Adjustment Problems of Students

One of the vital functions of the school is to assist the students in adjusting themselves to their problems. This function can legitimately start after having probed in to those problems which hinder the students from adjusting to the demands of day-to-day life.

Sample

In this study an attempt was made to survey the problems of girl students of a local higher secondary school for girls. The sample was on the whole representative of just average socio-economic stratum.

Procedure

A new approach to elicit their problems was made. The usual test situation which encourages inhibition, was avoided is that an informal students investigator relationship was created by talking to the students as student welfare activities for about half an hour preceding the actual study.

Results

A quantitative analysis of the problems of thus revealed is given below. This chart provide a clear idea bout the common problems of the adolescence.

Table–2.1

Problems Common to the Adolescents

Sl. No.	*Problem*	*Total % Having this Problem*
1.	Cannot keep mind on studies	8.3
2.	Problem with a particular subject	5.0
3.	Too much emotional attachment with school mate	5.7
4.	Unable to stick to time schedule for study	5.7
5.	Not interested in certain subjects	5.3
6.	Trouble with same subjects	5.3
7.	Getting low marks in scholastic achievements	4.0
8.	Not knowing how to be popular	3.0
	Percentage having Adjustment Problems	42.3

Remedial Measures for Adolescents Problems

Good Effects of Emotions

Emotions work as motives which drive the organism for an action. Love, fear, anger and curiosity, may help to achieve our goal.

Control and Training of Emotions

Developing proper emotions and controlling them is very essential objective of education during adolescence

- proper training,
- development of resistance,
- guidance and counselling, and
- proper understanding.

Conclusion

The teacher and school can encourage the development of affective maturity in adolescence. School should provide identification of proper model and constructive ways of expressing feelings. An important method which a classroom teacher can encourage is to help the students to express their emotions in constructive ways.

Table-2.2
Area-wise Distribution of Problems and Comparison of Problem Areas

Sl. No.	*Problem Areas*	*No. of Problems Checked*	*Rank in Present Study*	*Rank in Able and Ruby's Study*	*Rank in Mooney's Study*
1.	Adjustment to school	1012	1	1	3
2.	Personal psychological relations	941	2	3	4
3.	Social Recreational Reactions	847	4	2	7
4.	Health and Physical Development	798	5	4	6
5.	The future: Vocational and Educational	702	7	7	5
6.	Curriculum and Teaching Procedure	688	8	8	1
7.	Home and Family	592	9	10	–
8.	Courtship, Sex and Marriage	562	10	11	8
9.	Morals and Religion	469	11	6	9
10.	Social Psychological Relations	924	3	5	7
	Total	**793**			

LANGUAGE DEVELOPMENT

Theory of Lev Vygotsky

Lev Vygotsky (1896-1934) a Russian psychologist and educationalist who became known to the world of education and psychology after 1980; had given many important theories including language development theory. His most important contribution to learning is the idea and theory of 'social constructivism' or socio-cultural theory. This importance writings includes, thought and language. Thinking and speech, mind in society, the development of higher psychological process, school instruction and mental development etc. Vygostsky's theory of language development is given below:

Language and Thought

Vygotsky identified two separate roles for knowledge, as a means of communication and as the basis of thought. In his view the two roles were initially separate. Infants were said to have non-language-based means of thought which co-existed with a form of language whose purpose was to regulate the infant's social world. Vygotsky took the view that language and thought came together at the end of the second year when children were able to use words as symbols for thoughts. After this time language and thought become closely interrelated and mutually supportive.

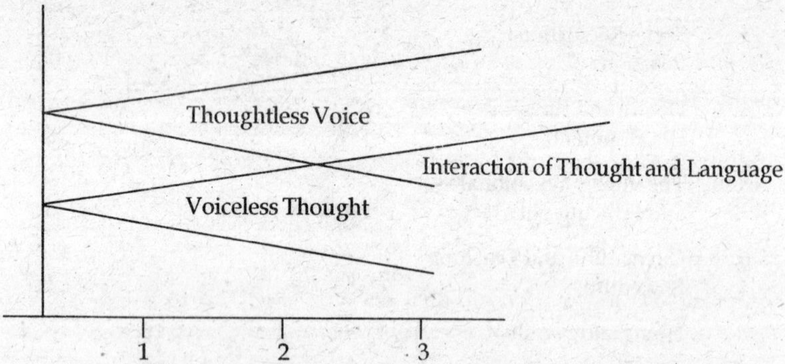

Fig. 2.1: Pictorial Representation of Vygotsky's View on Thought and Learning.

Stages of Language Development

Language is tool to organize thought (Vygotsky, 1962). He says that language is very important for the development of thought (cognition). He says that language develops from, social speech (external idea exchange speech) then to private speech and last to inner speech. It can be said as stage of language development.

First Stage (Social Speech)

Here the child interact with the society (outer environment) through meaningless general verbal prompts and body actions. Social speech increases when there is someone to hear him/her, and reduces when there nobody and the social speech is acquired from society.

According to Vygotsky, children's skills and personalities develop as they take part in co-operative dialogue with skilled parents on tasks that are within their zone of proximal development.

Zone of Proximal Development: It is Vygotsky's term for the range of tasks that are too complex to be mastered alone but can be accomplished with guidance and encouragement from a more skillful partner.

Second Stage (Private Speech)

Vygotsky says that private speech is self-directed speech that children use to plan and guide their own behaviour. It is children's frequent talks to themselves as they play and explore the environment.

If the task is difficult or complex the intensity of private speech increases. He reasoned that children speak to themselves for self-guidance and self-direction. Because language help children think about their own behaviour and select course of action Vygostsky Regarded it as the foundation for compelx cognitive skills such as controlled, sustained attention, deliberate memorization and recall, categorization, planning problem solving and self-reflection. Here the child gives to sound to the acquired social speech.

Third Stage (Inner Speech/Verbal thought)

As children get older and tasks become easier, their self-directed speech declines and is internalized as salient, inner speech. It can be said as the verbal dialogues we carry on with ourselves while thinking and acting in everyday situations.

Meaning of Words

Meaning of words, says Vygotsky, are the smallest element of thought and language. Word's meaning is active and changing according to circumstances word meaning is only a part of word consciousness. Word consciousness includes all mental actions in our cognition produced by a word. The relation between moral thought goes on changing. Thought get stability through words by fixing connection with matter (things).

Main Points

- Development of thought and language is from society to person.
- Private speech is self-directed and self-guided speech that children use to plan a guide their own behaviour and utterances that is connected with any activity.

- At first, it is social speech, which is acquired from society and not private speech. Private speech is giving voice (speech) to it.

PIAGET'S THEORY OF COGNITIVE DEVELOPMENT

Jean Piaget (1896-1980) was born in Newchatel, Switzerland at an early age he showed a keen interest in observing animals in their natural environment. At the age of 10, he published his first article, a description of an albino sparrow which he had observed in the park; before he was 18 years old, journals had accepted several of his papers on the subject of molluses. During his adolescent years a second major intellectual interest grew from his study of philosophy, in particular the branch of philosophy concerned with knowledge – *Epistemology*. His undergraduate studies however were in the field of biology and his doctoral dissertation was on molluses.

After his doctorate degree in Zoology he proceeded to Vienna to join Freud's Psycho-analytic institute to learn the technique of psycho-analysis. It could not hold his interest beyond a year. He took a train for Paris to join the Institute of Intelligence Testing founded by Alfred Binet. He wanted to master the technique of administering intelligence tests and computing intelligence quotients. He kept wondering why a child found it difficult to answer some test-items while young, but could easily do so at an advanced age. He wanted to find out what makes an individual 'know' what he comes to know. Piaget resigned the job and shifted to Geneva to set up an institute for child study of his own. His subjects for his longitudinal study were his own kinds. This led him to embark on a life long quest known as *Genetic Epistemology*, which means the origin and Growth of knowledge. How does knowledge originate? How does it develop? Are there distinct stages in cognitive development? Is it possible to quicken the pace? Would it be beneficial or harmful to a child? Does it have a bearing up on child up brining. Is it relevant to curriculum–framing? Piaget was obsessed with these queries and his search for answers resulted in a theory of Cognitive Development. No other thinker has revolutionized psychology and education in the 20th century the way Piaget did.

Jean Piaget stressed the importance of biological maturation in the thinking process. He saw human being as an integrated whole and assumed that there must be some common denominators in biological and mental functioning. One of these, he suggested, is the concept of *adaptation*. The human body adapt to its environment in the process of intellectual growth. The whole sequence of change that Piaget saw in a child's cognitive development is the result of a gradual process of adaptation to experiences. In this way Piaget emphases the role of learning as well as biology. He viewed the development of cognitive skills as an interaction between the child's maturational level and its learning experiences.

Piaget viewed the child as an active ingredient in the process of learning and development. Children interact with the environment. They examine, explore match sort, look at, classify and compare experiences, objects and events. The environment does not simply mould their response. Piaget saw the child as an inventor or a theoretician. Each child over the course of the first 10 or 15 years of life must discover basic principles of nature and devise basic theories about how the world works and how objects relate to one another.

Piaget introduced a number of concepts in order to explain the cognitive development theory. These include:

1. Schema

Piaget used the term 'schema' (plural, 'schemas' or 'schemata') to mean a component of the cognitive structure or the pattern of behaviour used by individuals while dealing with objects or situations in the environment. This is the result of the individuals forming a mental image of experiences and registering it in their cognitive structure. As development proceeds each pattern enlarges and changes in accordance with the nature of the mental images formed. A 'schema' is something like a computer programme that people construct for dealing with complex problems. Just as a particular programmes in a computer provides the same response in different situations, each specific schema in the cognitive structure of an individual leads him to similar responses on different occasions. Babies learn about objects by sucking on them, biting them, banging them and throwing them. when the infant encounters a new object how are they to know what the object is all about? According to Piaget they will use the schema they have developed and will find out whether it gives milk, whether it moves or makes a land or soft sound.

Schemas are mental images developed from experience or behavioural pattern formed from an experience. Different types of schemas are:

1. *Physical Schema:* Idea of physical object. Object based – Early childhood is the best stage to develop physical schema.
2. *Social Schema:* schemas developed from social experience is through interaction with society.
3. *Physiological Schemas*: bodily related schemas.
4. *Language Schema:* Cognitive structure is the totality of schemas.

2. Organization

Piaget used this term to refer to the inborn capacities to co-ordinate existing cognitive structures or schemas and combine them into more complex systems. Example: the infant of 3 months has learned to combine, looking and grasping with the earlier reflex of sucking. She can do all three together when feeding, an ability which the new born baby did not have.

3. Adaptation

By adaptation Piaget means the striving of the organism for balance or equilibrium with the environment, which is achieved through the complimentary processes of assimilation and accommodation.

Assimilation

Assimilation means "taking in" or incorporating new experience (schema) and fits into an existing schema. In other words, it is "the fitting in" new schema with already existing cognitive structure or making unfamiliar to familiar. It is similar to putting a new data into a computer as part of an existing programme. Example : a child may have learnt the words 'dog' and 'car'. For a while all animals are called 'dogs' (i.e., different animals take into a schema related to child's understanding of dog or all four-wheeled vehicles might be considered as 'cars'). This process is balanced by accommodation.

Accommodation

Accommodation means a change or modification in a person's concepts or strategies because of the new information that has been assimilated or accommodation is the process by which one's thought patterns are modified in order to fit himself into the environment.

Piaget uses the term accommodation to describe the changing of an existing schema to fit it with new experiences. Thus a baby assimilates when he internalizes and perceives the new experience in the light of his old perceptions. But when a baby forms a new schema by modifying or changing his old perceptions with a view to adjust with the new experience it is a process of accommodation. In this way a baby forms new structure or new schemata and consequently develops cognitively.

From experience the child begins to perceive that cats can be distinguished from dogs (and he may develop different schemas for these two types of animals) and that cars can be discriminated from other vehicles.

4. Equilibration

The cognitive structure which is built up with schemata changes from one developmental stage to another by the process of equilibration i.e., maintaining balance between the child and his changing environment. A baby who hangs an egg has to deal with a situation that cannot be fully handled by existing schemata. This creates a state of disequilibrium or an imbalance between what is understood and what is encountered. This results in distress. In such as case the individual tries to avoid the distress by reducing such imbalances. This is done by focusing attention on the stimuli that have caused the disequilibrium and by developing new schemata or adopting old one until equilibrium is restored. This is achieved by assimilation and accommodation. This process of restoring balance is called *equilbration*. Piaget believes that learning depends on this process.

Equilibration is the main part of Piaget's cognitive development theory. Equilibration is attained by assimilation, accommodation, reversibility and operation. *Reversibility* is a ability of shuttling the schemas to and fro in the thought process in order to solve a problematic situation. In order to locate the schemas which are appropriate for the present situation is called shuttling. Operation in the process of meaningful correlation of schemas or it is the process of manipulating schemas in order to establish new relations.

In short through the twin process of assimilation and accommodation the child achieves a new state of equilibrium (equilibration). This equilibrium, however, is not permanent. The balance will soon be upset as the child assimilates further new experiences or accommodates his existing schemas to another new idea. In a sense equilibrium only prepares the child for disequilibrium that is further learning and adaptation, the two cannot be thought of separately. Assimilation helps the child to consolidate mental structures, accommodation results in growth and change.

Piaget's Stages of Cognitive Development

According to Piaget human development is the result of continuous interaction between the organism and the environment. He describe four major stages in the continuous process of growth and change in the cognitive development during childhood. Each stage is marked by the emergence of new intellectual activities. Piaget believes that all children pass through these segmental stages and no child can skip a stage, although different children pass through the stages at some what different pace.

1. The Sensory-motor Stage (0-2 Years)

This pre-language period is marked by motor actions and sensations. The child will be engaged mostly in the acquisition of motor skills. Simple learning occurs but the child does not think at this stage. But the early sensory-motor experiences of the child have a great bearing on the development of his later intellectual abilities. In the world of the child an object exists when it is physically present. He them gains some consciousness about the stability of the object.

He starts comprehending casually. It is sometimes said that the child's mental development at this stage is equal to that of an intelligent animal. The development of the concept of object permanence is one of the major accomplishments of this period and is not fully complete until the child is about 18 months of age. By the end of 2 years the child develops a sense of the relationship among objects and between objects and his own body.

During this period, the intellectual development is characterized by four fundamental constructions.

- *(a)* *Object Concept Formation:* Here children comes to realize that objects occupy space but it is concerned with present.
- *(b)* *Co-ordinated Space*: The child acquires the special concept. He learns to grasp objects and thus becomes aware of the special relations between objects.

(c) *Objectified Casuality:* Any action of the child brings about an effect is taken as the cause of that event. Examples: when the child kicks a ball, it, rolls off, then he realize kicking casuality with the effort produced.

(d) *Objectification of Time:* The child gets the perception obtained but it is concerned with the present. The child also acquire the ability to represent objects or events with the few words in their vocabularies.

2. *Pre-Operational Period (2-7 Years)*

Piaget divided this stage into the pre-conceptual period (2-4 years) and the intuitive period (4-7 years).

(a) *The Pre-Conceptual Period (2-4 Hours)*: The pre-conceptual period builds on the capacity for internal or symbolic, thought which was developed in the sensory-motor period. There is a rapid increase in children's language which results from the development or symbolic thought. His triangle may be used as racing car, a stick may be used as a gun and so on. The child now becomes ego centric that is primarily concerned about oneself.

(b) *Intuitive Stage (4-7 Years)*: During this period, cognitive behaviour of the child is still controlled by perception. The thinking of the child is not logical; it will be based mostly on intuition. Intuitive thought is primarily concerned with static conditions, but the child is able to use concepts as stable generalizations of his past and present experiences. He however cannot adequately link a whole set of successive conditions into a integrated totality. The child can grasp only one relationship at a time because he has not developed the ability for reversibility. While, thinking i.e., in the thinking process, the child is unable to lecture to his starting point.

3. *The Concrete Operational Period (7-11 Years)*

This, is the stage when child develops logical thought Piaget uses the term operational thought to indicate this change. Operation investment to represent action which can be manipulated in the mind, which are reversible and which form part of an integrated system of mental actions. The child develops logical operations from simple associations.

He learn to add, substract, multiply and divide. He is in a position to classify concrete objects. These operations are called *concrete* because they relate directly to objects. Then these operations do not involve abstract thinking Piaget has coined a new term '*grouping*' to describe a set of operations. He has given a long list of operations which make it possible to handle numbers in tune with various relations to each other, to group objects into classes and sub-classes and to seriate objects according one or more attributes.

4. *Formal Operational Stage (After 11 Years)*

At this stage the thought process of the child becomes quite systematic and reasonably well-integrated. The individual no longer requires concrete material for thinking for he has required a capacity for abstract thought and he can reasoning using hypothesis. They begin from observations and figure out some theory or system, but until they are about 12 or 13, they cannot reverse the process and go from the theory to hypothesizing something that ought to be seen beyond their own specific, concrete observations. By about 12 years, the child starts to employ a form of hypothetic deductive reasoning. Now he can approach problems by reflecting and determining. All possible solutions before testing to see which of them is correct. He shows particular orientation to problem solving. He isolates and controls the relevant variables and seeks logical justification and verification of his solutions.

5. *Educational Implications*

1. It provides a broad development perspective to the educator for building a curriculum for the children.
2. The description of developmental stages and qualitative aspects of intellectual growth is very useful in providing suitable educational practices.
3. The cognitive theory states that the child is to be actively involved in the teaching-learning process for his intellectual growth.
4. Piaget based curriculum requires that children should not skip any stage.
5. The pre-school child is at the pre-operational level. The educational programme at this stage should provide concrete operations.

6. Educational programme should enable the child to integrate the information.
7. A child should be helped to develop internal consistency of the system.
8. Drilling unskills us to be avoided.
9. Teaching-learning situation should be geared to a point where the child is neither too familiar nor too unfamiliar with the objects and ideas.
10. Variety of cognitive activities like story and telling, rhymes signing etc., are included in the programme in a systematic manner. There is a deliberate attention of developing cognitive growth.
11. A child's development is retarded if he is not allowed a fairly wide sensory and motor experience in his early years.
12. Real events and concrete objects play an important role in learning.
13. In science and mathematics learning from physical environment is more important than what is learnt from people, books or television.
14. A teacher should arouse curiosity of the child through planned activities.

Criticism of Piaget's Theory of Development

Several psychologists do not agree with Piaget's theory of cognitive development. According to R.M. Gagne (1968) stages described by Piaget are not necessarily the inevitable result of a inborn time-table. Instead they are a consequence of children having learned sets of rules that are progressively more complex and these rules are taught by their physical and social environment. Gagne thinks that Piaget was indifferent to the role of learning in developmental changes.

Some psychologists do not agree with the view of Piaget that infants are born with some elementary mental structures that are starting points for their attempts to deal with their environment.

More recent researchers have found that child can perform tasks either earlier than Piaget predict (for concrete operations) or only later than he predicted (for formal operation). His stage model has clearly been "stretched" well away from its original periods.

Table-2.3
Sub-Stages of the Sensori-Motor Period-Piaget

Substage	*Age (months)*	*Characteristics*
Reflex Activity	0-1	The infant practices the inmate reflexes leg sucking, looking. Behaviour largely but not entirely, assimilative.
Primary Curricular Reactions	1-4	The behaviour is primary in the sense that it is basically made up of reflexes or motor responses; it is circular in the sense that the child repeats it. These appears to be no differentiation between self and outside world.
Secondary Circular Reactions	4-10	The infant now focuses on objects rather than on her own body. They begins to make interesting things happen e.g. Moving a hanging toy by hitting it. It has begun to change her surrounding intentionally.
Co-ordination of Secondary Circular Reactions	10-12	She begins to combine schemas in order to achieve goals or to solve problems in new situations. Example: she will use the hitting schema, in order to knock down a barrier between herself and a toy.
Tertiary Circular Reactions	12-18	She actively uses trial and error methods to learn about objects. Increased mobility enables her to experiment and explore. Learns new ways of solving problems and discovers more about properties of the environment.
Internal Representation	18-24	The beginning of mental action and insightful solutions to problems objects and people can be represented symbolically. Behaviour can be imitated from previous observations.

Conclusions

According to Piaget, just as the body has physical structures that enable it to adapt to the environment, so the mind build psychological structures organized ways of making sense of experience (schemas) that permit it to adapt to the external world in the development of these structures children are intensively active. They select and interpret experience in terms of their current structures and they also modify those. Structures so that they take into account more suitable aspects of the surrounding world. For Piaget, each child's mental reality is his or her own unique construction. But since all of us possess the same biological equipment for interpreting experience, the course of cognitive development is the same for all human being.

Piaget believed that children more through four stages of development-sensory-motor, pre-operational, concrete operational and formal operational-during which the exploratory behaivour of infants are transformed into the abstract, logical intelligence of adolescence and adulthood.

BIOLOGICAL BASES OF BEHAVIOUR

In 1848, a 25-year old Philippinee, a rail road construction crew met an road accident. It didn't affect his speech, intelligence, ability to move but dramatically changed his personality. He become being polite, conscientious and hardworking. This indicate a relationship between brain and behaviour. We will organize our discussion of the biological processes that underlie behaviour around fundamental concepts in these three areas:

- The structure and function of the nervous system, whose basic units are nerve cells/neurons.
- The endocrine system which is composed of glands that manufacture and secrete chemical substances called hormones in the blood stream.
- Behavioural genetics which is concerned genes and heredity.

The Human Nervous System

At every moment of everyday even when you are sleeping, your nervous system is active, exchanging millions of signals that correlate with thoughts, feelings and actions. Example: recognizing a friend coming towards you. In this example, the processes of information about the person sent brain (female, heights, brown hair, glasses), information interpreted ("hey! that s Babu"), translated into a signal for action, finally brains sends a command, "Hello, how are you Babu?."

All this happens in a second of fraction. Our nervous system makes this rapid and automatic recognition possible. In human beings the nervous system is the primary information processing and communication system, creating and carrying messages from one location to other over a network of interconnected neurons.

Neurons are the key biological elements for information transmission in the nervous system. They are organized into neural circuits, also called *pathways*. Which controls the direction, speech and destination of message travelling through the nervous system.

The nervous system is by far the most compelx biological system of the human body. The human brain alone consists of at least 10 billion and possibility as many as 100 billion neurons, each of which directly connected to some 100 to 10,000 other neuron.

There are three general functions of the nervous system in human beings and other animals. They are:

1. Sensing specific information about external and internal conditions (input).
2. Integrating (processing) that information.
3. Issuing commands, for a response from the body's muscles or glands out put.

Thus, nervous system is the foundation for our ability to perceive, understand and react to our environment.

Neurons

A neuron is the biological cell, consisting of a cell body, an axon, and dendrites specialized to carry "information" from one place to another.

The typical neuron consists of three base parts:

1. Cell body-which includes the cell nucleus.
2. Dendrites.
3. Axon.

Each neuron has both input and output zones for receiving and sending signals.

The dendrites (from a Greek word meaning tree) which are short branch like fibers extending from the cell body, are the input zones, where information is first received. The role of dendrites is to pick up signals from other neurons. A neuron can have several dendrites.

The axon, which is a single fiber that extends from the cell body provides the exit, or output, pathway for the neural signal. Some axons are quite long and a meter or more. Others are very short and are measured in micro meters. The terminals of one neuron, the gap between the neurons and the dendrites of the next neuron are collectively known as the SYNAPSE.

The nervous system is made up of 3 kinds of neurons that specialize in 3 general functions:

1. Sensory neurons, respond to incoming stimuli (input) such as sounds, sights and touches and transmit information from sense organs (ears, eyes and skin) toward the brain and spinal cord.
2. Inter neurons in the spinal cord and the brain integrate (process) the information coming in on sensory pathways.
3. Motor neurons-relay information (output) away from the brain and spinal cord to the body's action systems. The muscles and glands, which in turn respond as directed.

Neural Transmission/Transmission of Nerve Impulses

When a neuron is stimulated, the nerve impulse that is generated travels down the axon and into the axon terminals, where it causes the release of specialized chemicals. These chemicals travel the small distance accross the synapse to the next neuron. Thus information is conveyed both:

1. Within neurons (*Axonal Conduction*).
2. From one neuron to the next *(Synaptic Transmission)*.

Nervous System

Human body consists many psycho systems. That is Circulatory system, Respiratory system, Digestive system and Nervous system. Each are highly connected. In psychological perspective nervous system is more important.

Brain

Brain is the basic unit of nervous system connected with 10-12 crores neurons. The main duty of these neurons is transporting/ transmitting the data from one part of the body to another. Each neurons have Dendrites, Axon and Cell body. The power of-transmitting-neuron in the unusing time is called *resting potential.*

There is no direct connection between two neurons. There is a gap between first neuron's axon and 2nd neurons dendrite. It is called *synapse*. When a nerve impulse passing via synapse is it energetic or poor. It is decided by a *synapse junction*. Example: The alcohol, drugs, etc. affect the synapse junction and leads to changes in our emotion and behaviour.

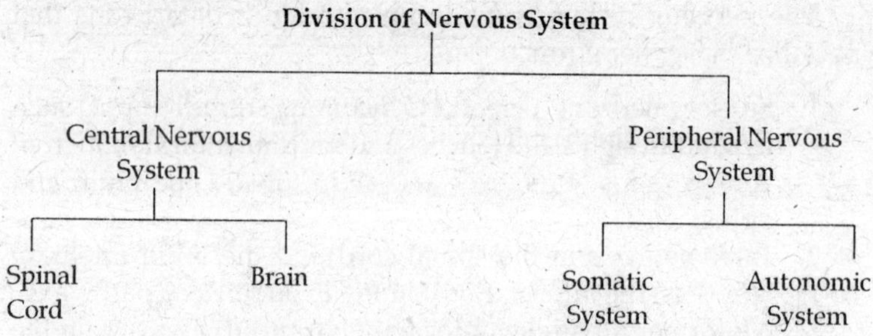

Fig. 2.2: Division of Nervous System.

Central nervous system includes all neurons and all nerves of brain and spinal cord. Somatic system consists brain, spinal cord, senses muscles and outer part of body. Autonomic system consists, the nerves in inner body system like breath, heart beating, digestive system. Spinal cord is a block of neurons passes through back born, this is a way to stimulus to passes up and down to brain. And it also causes Reflex Action.

Brain is divided in to three –

1. Forebrain.
2. Midbrain.
3. Hindbrain.

Forebrain is the most important part. Thinking process, sense experience, speech, learning are the main activities of forebrain. Hindbrain is area of connecting brain and spinal cord – Pons, cerebellum, medulla oblongata are the parts of hindbrain. *Hindbrain* controls, breathing, heart beating, blood pressure. Cerebrum (part of forebrain) divided into two i.e., cerebral hemispheres – the valuable data's collected regarding cerebral hemispheres through *Splitbrain Studies*. Roger Speri (USA, 1950) start this research. He discovered brains left hemisphere using for mathematical/analytical/ reasoning/linguistic capabilities and right hemisphere for spatial activities. But some time, basic sensory motor activities controlled by whole brain.

The Endocrine System

Reuben has been experiencing an unusual problem recently. The amount of food he eats has increased significantly, yet he is hunger all the time, he has even lost weight. An examination of Reuben's work schedule and home life indicates that he has few worries and experiences little stress.

Besides nervous system, which is crucial the activities of sensing, processing and responding, another system plays a major role in shaping and controlling behaviour and mental processes.

The Endocrine system consists of a number of glands that produce chemicals known as hormones. When stimulated the endocrine glands release hormones into blood stream. The important glands are pituitary gland, thyroid gland, adrenal glands and sex glands.

REFERENCES

1. Aggarwal, J.C. (2002). *Essentials of Educational Psychology*, New Delhi: Vikas Publishing House Pvt. Ltd.
2. Berk E. Laura (1997). *Child Development*, Allyn and Bacon, Boston, London.
3. Dandapani, S. (2000). *Advanced Educational Psychology*, New Delhi: Anmol Publications Pvt. Ltd.
4. De Cecco, P. John and Crawford R. William (1988). *The Psychology of Learning and Instruction*, New Delhi: Prentice Hall of India Pvt. Ltd.
5. Dr. Grewal, J.S. (1984). Early Childhood Education, National Psychological Corporation, Agra.
6. Hurlock, Elizabeth B. *Child Development*, New Delhi: McGraw Hill International Book Company.
7. L.S. Vygotsky. *Educational Psychology*.
8. Lyle, E. Bourne, Jr. Nancy Felipe Russo. *Psychology Behaviour in Context*. New York: NW Norton.
9. Madhavan Nair, S. (1998). *Educational Psychology*. Ottapalam: Breeze Publications.
10. Mangal, S.K. (2003). *Advanced Educational Psychology*, Prentice Hall of India Pvt. Ltd., New Delhi.
11. Morrison, George, S. (1997). *Fundamentals of Early Childhood Education*, New Jersey: Prentice Hall, Inc.

12. S.B. Kakkar. *Reading in Educational Psychology.*
13. S.S. Chauhan. *Advanced Educational Psychology.*
14. SCERT, *Psychological Foundations of Early Childhood Education,* Vidyabhavan, Poojappura, Trivandrum, 12.
15. Sivarajan K. *Psychology of Learning and Instruction.*
16. Smith K. Peter, Cowie Helen and Blades Mark (1998). *Understanding Children's Development.* Blackwell Publishers, Oxford.

MODEL QUESTIONS

1. "Cognitive development of an individual is the result of his successful attempt for equilibration." – Explain the statement in terms of the key concept formulated by Piaget.
2. Give a brief description of the biological bases of human behaviour.
3. Sketch the social development of a child from birth to age three.
4. Discus briefly the relative role of nature and nurture in growth and development.
5. What are the developmental tasks of Indian adolescents? How can a teacher help the adolescents to overcome the difficulties of this stage.
6. Suggest one curricular and one co-curricular activity that could help adolescents society specific development needs. Give reasons why you think, these would be helpful for the purpose.

3
Learning

Infants learn to talk and college students learn to pass tests. People of all ages learn to drive cars, count their change and look forward to the smell of a holiday turkey roasting ...... Even animals learn to come when called, to feel excited when their master comes home, to follow a scent.

Learning is a Key Process

Learning is a key process—some would say the key process—in human behaviour; it pervades everything we do and think. It plays a central role in the language. We speak, our customs, our attitudes and beliefs, our goals, our personality traits (both adaptive and mal-adaptive) and even our perceptions.

Early Approaches to Learning

Early theories of learning introduced the idea that human behaviour can be explained by natural laws. In particular, Descartes' (a 17th century philosopher) use of the 'reflex' as a basic unit of behaviour and the concept of 'association' have had lasting influence.

A very different view was held by British philosophers, the associationists such as Thomas Hobbes (1588-1679), Hobbes held that human behaviour is a product of mental acts, which are similar to reflexes in that occur automatically and mechanically.

John Locke (1632-1704) emphasized that virtually all ideas are learned. Locke proposed that humans are born without ideas or knowledge of how to behave. They are blank states, 'tabulae rasae' upon which experience writes it story.

In the 1800's, when psychology ceased to be a branch of philosophy and become a science the ideas of the associationists began to be tested in the laboratory. Psychologists began to investigate how people and animals associate events with one another—how they learn?

THE WORD 'LEARNING'

The English word learning probably comes from an Indo-European root, lies—which meant a 'track' or 'furrow'. Before reaching its present form, it went through many changes: 'Laestan', 'leornian', 'lernen'. At various times in the evolution of our language it might have been understood as following a track, continuing, coming to know, or perhaps even getting into a rut. The verb last, to endure, came from the same root.

NATURE OF LEARNING

Learning occupies a very important place in our life. Most of what we do or do not do is influenced by what we learn and how we learn it. Learning therefore, provides a key to the structure of our personality and behaviour. An individual starts learning immediately after his birth or in a strict sense even earlier in the womb of the mother. Experience, direct or indirect is found to play a dominant role in moulding and shaping the behaviour of the individual from the very beginning. These change in behaviour brought about by experience are commonly known as learning. In this way, the term learning broadly speaking, stands for all those changes and modifications in the behaviour of the individual which he undergoes during his life time.

Definitions

Learning can be defined as any relatively permanent change in behaviour that occurs as a result of practice or experience (c.f. Kimble, 1961, pp. 1-13).

The definition has three important elements:

1. Learning is a change in behaviour for better or worse.
2. It is a change that takes place through practice or experience; change due to growth or maturation are not learning.
3. The change must be relatively permanent; it must last a fairly long time. Exactly how long cannot be specified, but we usually think of learned changes in behaviour.

The term learning covers every modification in behaviour to meet environmental requirements (Gardner Murphy, 1968).

Learning is the acquisition of new behaviour or the strengthening or weakening of old behaviour as the result of experience (Henry P. Smith, 1962).

Any activity can be called learning so far as it develops the individual (in any respect, good or bad) and makes him alter behaviour and experiences different from what they would other ways have been (Woodsworth, 1945).

Learning is the process by which behaviour is originated or changes through practice or training (Kingsley and R. Garry, 1957).

Learning is an episode in which a motivated individual attempts to adopt his behaviour so as to succeed in a situation which he perceives as requiring action to attain a goal (Pressy, Robinson and Horrocks, 1967).

Learning is the acquisition of habits knowledge and attitudes. It involves new way of learning doing things, and it operates in an individual's attempts to overcome obstacles or to adjust to new situations. It represents progressive changes in behaviour.... It enables him to satisfy interests to attain goals (Crow and Crow, 1973).

Hilgard (1958), "Learning is the process by which an activity originates or is changed through reacting to an encountered situation, provided that the characteristics of the changes in activity cannot be explained on the basis of native response, tendencies, maturation or temporary states of the organism (e.g. Fatigue or Drugs, etc).

According to H.J. Klausmeir, "Learning is a process whereby a change in behaviour results from some from of experience, activity, training. Observation, and the like, change in some behaviour which results from such forces as bodily injury, disease, fatigue, or use of drugs is not considered learning." (Herbert J. Klausmeler, Learning and Human Abilities, New York: Harper and Row, 1961, p. 10).

"Learning can be defined as changing one's potential for seeing, feelings, and doing through experiences partly perceptual partly intellectual, partly emotional, and partly motor" (William C. Morse and G. Max Wingo, Psychology and Teaching 2nd ed., Bombay: D.B. Taraporevala Sons and Co. (P) Ltd., 1968, p. 170).

Morris L. Bigge is of the view that "Learning .....is a change in a living individual which is not heralded by his genetic inheritance. It may be a change in insights, behaviour, perception or motivation, or a combination of these" (Morris J. Bigge, Learning Theories for Teachers, Delhi: Universal Book Stall, 1967, p.1).

Winfred F. Hill, "While it is almost impossible to give an exact definition of learning that will be generally acceptable to psychologists, we cannot certain phenomina to which the terms or is not applied (W.F., Learning: A Survey of Psychological Interpretations, London: Methuen and Co. Ltd, 1963, p. 1). "In psychological usage what is learned need not be 'correct' or adaptive (we learn bad habits as well as good), need not be conscious or deliberate... and need not involve any overt act (Attitudes and emotions can be learned as well as knowledge and skills). Reaction as diverse as driving a car, remembering a pleasant vacation, believing in democracy, and disliking one's boss all represent the results of learning."

The above definitions reveal the following facts:

1. Learning is a process and not a product.
2. It involves all those experiences and training of an individual (right from birth) which help him to produce changes in his behaviour.
3. Learning leads to changes in behaviour but this does not necessarily mean that these changes always bring about improvement or positive development. One has equal chance to drift to the negative side of human personality.
4. Instead of change in existing behaviour or acquisition of new behaviour.
5. Learning prepares an individual for any adjustment and adaptation that may be necessary.
6. Learning is purposeful and goal oriented.
7. The scope of learning is too wide to be explained in words. It is a very comprehensive process.
8. Learning is universal and continues.
9. Learning as a process is of different types and involves different methods.
10. Learning does not include changes in behaviour on account of maturation, fatigue, illness, or drugs etc.

FUNCTIONS OF LEARNING

The definitions of learning suggested above contains the various functions leaning serves. As Remmers suggest, learning may be said to function in three important-ways:

1. Change in behaviour in the new situation.
2. Continuation of the changed behaviour
3. Use the changed behaviour in various other situations.

(Remmers, H.H., Ryden, E.R. and Morgan, C.L. Introduction to Educational Psychology, New York: Harper and Bro's, 1954).

CONDITIONS OF LEARNING

Learning is an active process in which the learner interacts in a given situation. Learning vary in their effectiveness. Learning can be made effective by observing some conditions. The following conditions have been found to be important in ensuring good learning:

1. Motivation,
2. Psychological safety,
3. Feed Back, and
4. Practice.

This is especially true in the learning of skills – physical or motor and non-physical skills.

CHARACTERISTICS OF LEARNING

Yoakam and Simpson (Modern Methods and Techniques of Teaching, New York: The MacMillan Company, 1948, pp. 25-29) have stated the following general characteristics of learning.

1. Learning is growth.
2. Learning is adjustment.
3. Learning is organization of experiences.
4. Learning is purposeful.
5. Learning is intelligent and creative.
6. Learning is active.
7. Learning is both individual and social.
8. Learning is a product of the environment.
9. True learning affects the conduct of the learner.

According to W.R. Mc. Caw (W. Ralph Mc Caw, Educational Psychology, New York: Monarch Press, 1964, p. 33) learning has the following nine characteristics:

1. Learning is a continues modification of behaviour. It continues through out life.
2. Learning is pervasive. It reaches into all aspects of human life.
3. Learning involves the whole person, socially, emotionally and intellectually.
4. Learning is often a change in the organization of behaviour.
5. Learning is development. Time is one of its dimensions.
6. Learning is responsive to incentives.
7. Learning is always concerned with goals.
8. Interests and learning are positively related.
9. Learning depends on readiness and motivation.

THE RESULTS OF LEARNING

As we know learning is a process and it leads to certain results. These results or products are basically change in behaviour. Mc Caw (W. Ralph, Mc Caw, Educational Psychology, New York: Monarch Press, 1946, p. 32) has given below a analysis of the products of learning.

1. Simple responses.
2. Muscular habits.
3. Perceptual responses.
4. Attitudes.
5. Emotional responses.
6. Problem solution.
7. Motives.
8. Language.
9. Personality.

ELEMENTS OF LEARNING

Psychologists have analyzed the elements of learning. These elements have been stated by McCaw as given below:

1. Goal.
2. Readiness.
3. Situation.
4. Interpretation.

5. Response/Action.
6. Consequence of the action.
7. Generalization.

IMPORTANT MODES OF LEARNING

Psychologists have studied the important modes of learning. According to them, the important modes of learning are:

1. Observational learning.
2. Trail-and-success learning.
3. Generalization: Concept formation.
4. The project method.
5. Problem Solving: Find Phases of Reflective Thought.
6. Incidental Learning.
7. Primary and Concomitant Learning.

FACTORS INFLUENCING THE CAPACITY FOR LEARNING

The capacity of a person has for learning, at anyone time, is a function of the sense. He/she makes of the experiences of interaction both in the here and now and in events in the past. This includes all experiences of interaction, with individuals and groups, family and friends, and in institutions, for example with teachers. Inevitably some of the interaction in these environment is affected by the wider, social, political, cultural and economic environment. What each of us makes of all these experiences depends partly on the way in which they reflect and confirm our inner world (or intra personal experiences). There is a dynamic relationship between the way we relate interpersonally, and our intra personal experience. The troubles of distributed and disturbing children present themselves in relationships and also in their inner worlds (see Figure 3.1).

Developing understanding of the multifaceted nature of processes involved in influencing the capacity for learning enables and enhances the teachers abilities to work with these processes inorder to improve access to learning. Interaction has a powerful effect upon development.

Conclusion

Learning involves acquisition of new behaviour. It is a kind of change in relation to a pattern of behaviour.

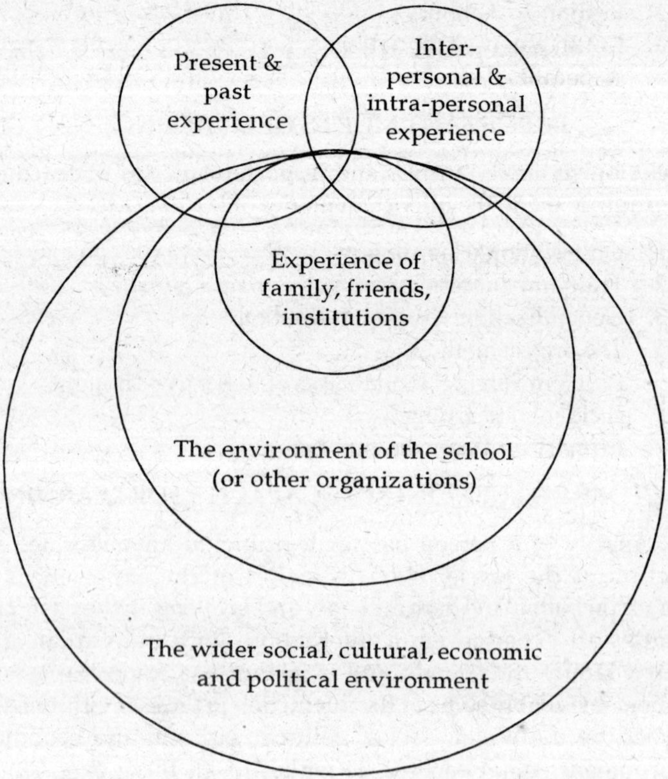

Fig. 3.1: Factors Influencing the Capacity for Learning.

Learning is also dependent upon one's innate intelligence and other capacities. It is on the basis of hereditary endowment that one can learn different types of activities and behaviour patterns.

Learning is related to matur ation. Unless and until there is the needed maturation satisfactory learning is not possible. Then there is the environmental aspect of learning which includes opportunities as well as facilities to learn.

FACTORS INFLUENCING/AFFECTING LEARNING

Introduction

Learning can be defined as any relatively permanent change in behaviour that occurs as a result of practice or experience (cf Kimble, 1961, pp. 1-13).

According to Kingsley and Garry, the factors influencing behaviour in learning situations could be represented in the following questions, the answer to which should yield a clear idea of the variables affecting learning:

1. How the motives are the goals. Capable of satisfying the motives, are determined?
2. What factors influence the variability of responses?
3. Which factors affect the speed of discovery, fixation and retention of the correct response, and what the conditions are, under which they operate?
4. What the conditions or circumstances are under which the learned response is utilized or transferred to new and different situations?

The variables that emerge out of the responses to these questions can be grouped in to three major categories. They are:

1. Those which are related with the individual—*Individual Variables.*
2. Those which are related with the material—*Task Variables.*
3. Those which are related with the method—*Method Variables.*

INDIVIDUAL VARIABLES/ SUBJECT VARIABLES

Age as a Factor in Learning

There is a popular belief that children learn better than adults or old people. The more people grow in age the more they believe that their ability to learn new material is decreasing. The relation between age and learning has been investigated in studies. The result of studies are presented with the help of Figure 3.1. The ability to learn new material increases until about 20 years of age, then remains constant till 30 and declines rapidly after 50. The older children learn more efficiently than younger children. This is because older children possesses advanced maturational level, sharper intelligence and broder experience.

An experiment was conducted to test the retention of items at different intervals of time after viewing a motion picture. The results of this experiment presented in Table 3.1.

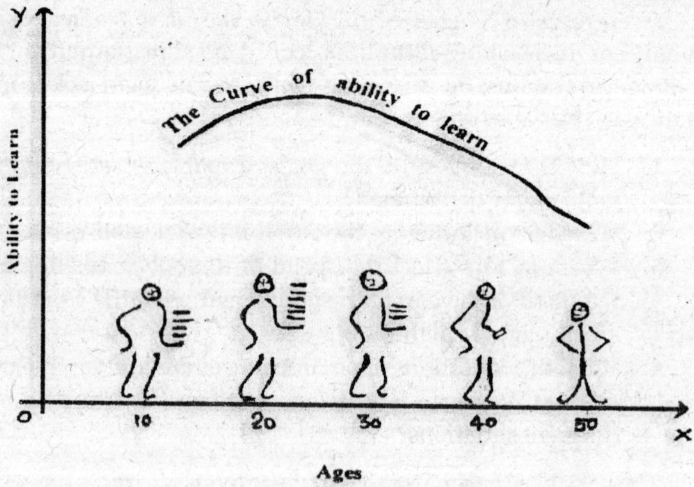

Fig. 3.2: Curve of Ability to Learn.

The performance of older person is found to begin and end at a higher level. However, in comparing school children at different ages with adults in the learning of motor skills, the difference is found due to strength, experience and motivation, and not due to the factor of age. Beyond the early years, practically all differences, specially the higher starting scores can be attributed to great range of experience and to difference in motivation.

Table–3.1
Age as a Factor of Learning

	Number of Items Retained After		
Group	*1 Day*	*6 Weeks*	*12 Weeks*
Adult	88	72	73
15-16 years	81	71	65
11-12 years	66	59	56
8-9 years	52	47	48

It is not correct to regard childhood as the golden age for memorization. Ability to memorize increases upto late teens or early twenties. Difference in speed of learning and retention depends not upon age but on mental age or levels of intelligence. As regards memory the following results have been obtained:

1. There is no decline or rise with increased age upto the age 70 vocabulary, general information and reasoning by analogy.
2. There is some progressive decline in the memory of school subjects, typing, perceptual speed and imagination.
3. There is rapid declare in decline in recall of new material, code learning and role memory.

Variations in methods and motivation may make it possible for children to learn a given task even at an earlier or late age. While determining age grade level of instructional material ease and rapidly should not be the only criteria. We should also look to its usefulness at a certain age. For example, an illiterate adult can learn to read and write rapidly than a child. But a child profits more from earlier instructions in reading and writing than the adult.

Maturation

The learning which an individual is capable of taking up is dependent on the level of his maturation. Maturation is a natural developmental process in which development takes place in the individual. The maturational changes are the result of the unfolding and ripening of internal as well as external organs and are relatively independent of activity, practice or experience. The swimming of tapoles and the flying of birds can be attributed to maturation. But in most of the activities of human being it is different to decide whether these activities result from maturation or learning. The child does not learn to talk until he reaches a stage in maturation. But it is also equally true that he does not learn the language just because he attains that stage. The language he learns, is that which he hears. Therefore, maturation and learning are closely related to each other. Maturation which depends upon heredity endowment provides to raw material for learning and determines the more general patterns and sequences of the individual's behaviour. But without practice, development will not take place through maturation alone.

Sex Difference as a Factor in Learning

There is no significant difference in learning between sexes. Still it is generally observed that boys are superior in motor activities involving the exercise of strong gross muscles where as girls excel in skills requiring delicate co-ordination of smaller muscles and strict attention to details. In regard to verbal learning, girls are superior in word fluency, reasoning and rote memory and boys in spatial and verbal meanings. Studies in vocational aptitude tests have shown that boys obtain superior scores in mechanical aptitude and in science and mathematics whereas girls obtain higher scores in clerical aptitude and language skills.

Sex differences as observed in various fields (Bergen, 1943).

1. There has not been found any sex difference in intelligence.
2. Girls are found higher in aptitudes such as word fluency, perceptual details, memory and fine motor-co-ordination, while boys are found superior in numerical reasoning, spatial ability and grass motor co-ordination.
3. Girls have higher interest in aesthetic, social service, domestic science and literary fields. Boys have higher scientific, mechanical, computational and theoretical interests.
4. Girls have more emotionality, sociability and jealousy. Boys are more aggressive, dominant, self-confidence, ambitions and independent.
5. Girls show better performance in language, speech, art and music. Boys are better in social science, science and mathematics.

Effect of Previous Experience

Now learning depends upon old learning. Learning at the stage helps learning at the subsequent stages. If the child fails to learn writing, reading, arithmetic in the beginning classes, he cannot make any progress in these skills. Thus, the learning is always influenced by the previous experience. Previous learning in a field makes the task familiar and therefore, more approachable. In the absence of previous experience, the individual will be facing a new situation and as such learning will be slow. The successful experience serves as a motivational force to consequent performance, while unsuccessful experience puts a drag on further learning and lowers the level of aspiration.

Influence of Family Background and Socio-Economic Status

Rural and urban environment produce difference in learning ability and achievement. Studies conducted in this field have shown that tasks having verbal content and requiring speed favour urban children. The verbal facility of urban children is because of excessive verbal content in urban culture where people must learn to talk in different styles and about, different subjects. If there is nothing to talk about, then they must talk about weather, and mood.

The difference in learning of rural and urban children is due to the range of stimulation available to them. For example, in cities and big towns these are more libraries, magazines, books, school facilities, museums, T.V. programmes.... Another distinction in learning is found in children belonging to working class and white collar jobs, and lower, middle and upper class. These children differ from the children of other classes in educational achievement as well as on in home life, attitudes, social customs and values, and economic status.

Capacity of the Learner

By capacity we mean a person's potential for learning. Capacity of the individual necessarily controls his performance. It influences the acquisition of any given skill. Intelligence, aptitude, etc., are some of the abilities influencing learning.

Physical Handicaps

All learning depends on integrated physiological functioning. It is generally believed that physical defects tend to retard progress in learning. Defective vision, hearing and speech are some of the defects which affect learning progress.

Motivation

An important factor in learning is motivation. It energizes the organism and gives direction to action by projecting valuable goals. Without motivation no learning is possible.

Effect of Knowledge of Improvement

Studies of knowledge of results, or feedback as it is often called on learning. Knowledge of results acts as a strong incentive to learn. It is found that the group which is provided information about improvement, is able to make satisfactory progress than the group which is deprived of this information. In one study, it was found that there was no improvement without knowledge or results, there was progressive improvement with it, and there was deterioration after its withdrawal.

TASK VARIABLES

The nature of the learning material in different forms such as the length of the material, the difficulty level of the material and its meaningfulness constitute the task variables.

Length of Material

If the length of the learning task exceeds the memory span of the learner, the time taken to learn, will be more. It has been provided that when the length of the word list to be remembered exceeds the memory span, these occurs a noticeable increase in difficulty.

Ebbinghaus found that if the length exceeds, the memory span more time needs to be devoted to learn them. Retention was found higher for the longer lists even though were presented to the subjects the same number of times as the shorter ones. Other studies also found greater percentage of retention for the longer lists with both the recall and learning methods. If the material is learned continuously at one sitting, the time required for memorizing the material increases, but if the distributed method of learning is used then increase in time roughly correspond to the length of the series.

Difficulty Level of Material

Difficulty of the learning material affects the ease with which it is learned. If the material is difficult the rate of learning is slowed down and forgetting becomes more and fast. For learning difficult material the leaner has to spend more energy and time and its creates fatigue which in turn slows down the rate of learning of such material.

Meaningfulness of Material

There is greater ease and facility for memorizing meaningful material as compared with meaningless material. Meaning enables the individual to identify previous experience to which the material to be learnt can be associated. Such associations facilitate effective learning.

Results of experimental studies have clearly indicated that meaningful material can be easily memorized as compared to meaningful material. Being meaningful means that the material conveys some sense and has some associations and previous experience with the learner.

Guilford's experiment on 'the effect of meaningful material on retention' measured number of trials required for complete mastery of the three types of material. The average number of trials required to learn three lists are mentioned below:

1.	Non-sense syllables	20.4 trials
2.	Unrelated words .	8.1 trials
3.	Related words	3.5 trials.

Results of other researches also verify these findings which suggest that higher the meaningfulness, the faster the learning, the lower the meaningfulness, the greater the forgetting. There is little learning without meaning.

No student should be asked to memorize something he cannot understand. All the material for learning should be made meaningful, and this can be done by providing the requisite previous experience.

METHOD VARIABLES

Distributed V/s Massed Practice

Practice makes perfect. But mere practice will not produce any improvement. With practice there must be some kind check or appraisal of achievement so that improvement could be ensured. Practice on any task can be done in two ways. If one has to memorize a poem, he may do it in one sitting and go on reading until it is committed to memory or he may spread the work of practice over a few days. The former is known as massed practice and the latter is distributed practice. Experiments have shown that for better results in normal cases, practice must distributed rather than massed.

Learning over a period of time is more effective than massed learning. Spaced practice is found superior where length or amount of materials to be learned is the main consideration. This is true about verbal learning as well as learning of motor-skills. Massed practice is also considered to be a more economic technique. But massed learning results in quick forgetting.

Spacing of the period will depend upon the learning task, and the age of the leaner. For difficult material the periods should be shorter than easy material. For lengthy materials to be remembered the learning should be spread over several periods.

What should be the length of the rest period in the between two working periods? The results of the experimental studies in this field suggest that the extreme of spacing or massing are disadvantageous. The effective length of the interval should vary within the nature of learning tasks and the length of the practice period.

Whole Vs Part Method

This refers to whether the learner repeats the material as a whole everytime or only a part of it. If the unit for study is meaningful and compact the whole method is better. In cases, where the material is rather long and parts themselves are more closely integrated than the whole, the part method may work well. For the best results, a combination of both the methods is advocated.

In the case the task is very lengthy, then it becomes necessary to break it into functional and meaningful units. The essential advantage of the whole method is that it provides an overview of the total task or skill to be learnt. The whole method is found to be superior if the material is organized into a meaningful unit, and it is closely knit, and if it is not very long. It is also observed that the whole method is effective for learning poems. The poem is better remembered if one recites the total poems, repeatedly than if one learns by heart the first line before going to the second, masters second line before going to the third, and so on. With complex motor, tasks practice with the whole method is preferable.

Recitation During Learning

A study by Gates in 1917 demonstrated that the amount reproduced was much greater for reading with recitation than for reading alone. Recitation was found effective for learning spellings, vocabulary, arithmetic facts and other subjects. It is important to note that recitation after each readings is better than to have the readings and recitations grouped separately. Further, it is necessary to read the material through a few times without recitation, and then reading and reciting alternatively.

Hearing recitation is not as valuable and effective as giving it. Recitation may or may not be oral. It has been experimentally studied that review – test is as effective a method of retention as oral recitation. Test-reviews should be given immediately after learning. They are most effective between 1 to 3 days.

Superiority of recitation is due to the following reasons:

1. Practice of recalling during the course of learning results in active attitude, vigorous effort and concentrated attention.
2. Individual actually practices what he is attempting to learn.

Recitation through within review is a very useful method in education as it has the advantage that it can be used as a group procedure.

Extent of Learning

If we want to ensure better retention and recall, practice must be continued beyond the point of the first errorless reproduction. Experiments have shown that better retention and recall are ensured by over learning. Over learning helps retention even after a long period of time.

Sensory Modality

We learn things using our senses. One may receive impressions better through the ears. Hence a multiple approach should be taken. In other words, learning becomes most efficient when it is done through a combination of sensory experiences. TV attracts people better than radio since it extends message to two scenes – eyes and ears at a time. The use of audio-visual aids in the classroom is justified and recommended on the basis of the proved efficiency of the multi-sensory approach.

Use of Audio-Visual Aids

The use of Audio-Visual materials in the classroom is propagated on the basis of a multi-sensory approach. But the mere use of audio-visual aids does not itself ensure greater learning. An enthusiastic but up planned use of slides, picture-cards, recording and films may produce – more confusion than learning.

Researches in this field have demonstrated that audio-visual devices, such as T.V. and sound films can provide as much learning as a teacher by using a variety of teaching techniques. Films are also found to be more effective when skills or knowledge to be given in a specific manner.

Conclusion

Learning is a process, many factors determine efficient learning. These factors are related to learner, subject-matter and method.

Ability to learn new material increases until 16 years and starts declining round about 70 years. Since in life situations contain far fever elements the performance of older persons begins and ends at a higher level. Beyond early years differences in leaning is generally due to difference in experience and motivation, and not age alone.

Physiological difference in boys and girls does not lead to difference in skills, attitudes and interests. Active initient to learn shown better learning, this has been well-demonstrated.

Early learning determines the progress of future learning. Difference in family background and socio-economic status produce difference in achievement. Feedback in learning has proved very effective, and acts as a strong incentive.

Easy material produces more speedy and efficient learning. A combination of recall and reading is more effective than reading alone. Overlearning is learning beyond the point of the first errorless reproduction. Over learning helps in retention. Learning over a period of time is more effective. Effectiveness of the method depends upon nature of learning material, previous knowledge/experience and attitudes. Audio-Visual aids make multi-sensory-approach.

TRANSFER OF TRAINING/LEARNING

Definition

Transfer of training/learning is defined as the carryover of habits, of thinking feeling or skills from one learning area to subsequent learning, either facilitating the latter or inhibiting it.

Types of Transfer

- *Positive Transfer*: If learning of task A facilitates subsequent learning of task B, C or D, it is called positive transfer. For example, learning of maths helps to solve problems in physics.
- *Negative Transfer:* If learning of task A hinders subsequent learning of task B, C or D, it is called negative transfer. For example, one who is driving Enfield may find difficulty in driving a Hero Honda due to the position of brake lever.
- *Zero Transfer:* Learning of task A neither inhibits nor facilitates learning of task B, C or D, it is called zero transfer. For example, art of cooking neither enhances nor hinders playing football.

- *Bilateral Transfer:* A form of positive transfer: when motor skill learned by one side of the body is easily transferred / learned by the other side of the body. (From right hand to left hand through hemispheral transfers). This is also called 'Cross Education.'

Theories of Transfer of Learning

Theory of Identical Elements (Thorndike, Woodworth)

Identical Elements means, mental process which have the same cell action in the brain as their physical correlates.

This theory states that the transfer from one situation to another is possible to the extent that there are common/ identical elements in the situation.

Here the carryover from one situation to another is roughly proportional to the degree of resemblance in the situation and identical element in the old and new tasks.

Theory of Generalisation (Charles Judd)

This theory lays stress on the generalisation of specific experiences and formulation of some rules/principles, so that they may be transferred from one situation to another.

Judd proved his theory through an example with a control group and experimental group of children. He assigned to both groups the task of shooting at a target submerged in water. Both group done the task equally balanced. Then experimental group alone was taught the principle of refraction and then the 2 group's shooting performance at the submerged target in water was noted. Experimental group which received instruction on refraction showed excellent performance.

On the basis of this experiment Judd concluded that, it is generalisation of the understanding of some relationship, which is usually transferred from the earlier situation to the later one.

Why Transfer of Learning is Included in B.Ed Curriculum?

- Make conscious effort to ensure positive transfer and avoid negative transfer.
- Identify similarities and dissimilarities in materials to learn, develop understanding/ insight and make generalisation.

- Give importance to Rule/Principle and generalisation rather than isolated facts, while teaching.
- Use A.V. Aids.
- Avoid rote memory.
- Use effective method of teaching.
- Besides the above the curriculum should be suitable i.e. Correlation among subject, within subject and between subject and environment.

LEARNING OF CONCEPTS

The concept is the sum total of what you know about the object. It is a mental image that represents all members belonging to the same category in terms of a set of minimum essential attributes being shared by all members belonging to the category. The members may be things, shapes or phenomena. For example, concept of vegetable, house, metals, etc.

Steps in Concept Learning

Multi-sensory experiences (sensation)→ perception (meaningful interpretation of sensory experience) and generalization of perceptual experience.

Sensation + Meaning = Perception
Perception + Abstraction + Generalisation = Conceptualisation

1. Observation of examples and non-examples.
2. Analysis of attributes.
3. Comparison based on attribute.
4. Categorisation.
5. Definition.
6. Identification of one's own examples for the category.

Two Strategies

1. *Concept Formation:* In concept formation the learner or individual forms the concept on his/her own.
2. *Concept Attainment:* Concept attainment is learning a concept under the guidance of the teachers.

It is the process in which children discover the concept which the teacher has in mind.

The knowledge of concepts and concept formation can be used in education in the following ways:

1. Students should be made aware of the similarities and differences between materials.
2. They can be made conscious of names, examples and characteristics.

There are the psychological assumption underlying the following models of teaching.

(*a*) concept attainment model.
(*b*) advance organizer model.
(*c*) cognitive model of teaching.

3. Concepts can impart knowledge of the structure of the material.
4. Constructive and negative aspects can be developed.
5. Students can be taught to evaluate information.
6. The success of teaching depends upon the growth of concepts of the students.
7. Inadequate experience may lead to defective concepts. (Example, blind men conceptualizing an elephant).

LEARNING OF ATTITUDES

'An affective by product of cognitive experience'.

An attitude is a mixture of belief and emotion that pre disposes a person to respond to other people, objects or institutions in a positive or negative way.

"An attitude is a neuro physical state of readiness organised through experience exerting a direct or dynamic influence on the individual responses."

Attitudes summarize past experience and predict or direct future actions. It is an acquired behaviour diverted towards something.

Expressions of attitude in three ways

- Belief component → what person believes about the attitudinal object.
- Emotional component → feelings toward the attitudinal object.
- Action component → here a person reacts.

Attitude Formation

- Direct contact (personal experience).
- Classical conditioning, observational learning.

- Interaction with others.
- The effects of parental value.
- Group membership.
- Mass media.
- Chance or coincidence.

According to Allport, the following are the four processes.

- Accretion of experience (Generalisation).
- Individuation (specification).
- Suggestion (accepting).
- Imitation (modelling).

Attitude Measurement

Attitude can be measured in several ways.

- Open ended interview
- Social distance scale
- Attitude scale
  - → Likert scale
  - → Thurstone scale
  - → Semantic differential (Test to differentiate meaning attached to particular works. Example, 'Amma' – attitude to mother can be judged by analysing their response to the word)

SKILL LEARNING

What is a skill? Proficiency in performance acquired through neuromuscular and skeletal co-ordination and co-ordination of various responses, to the level of automation.

- Physical skills. Example: drawing a map or driving.
- Non-physical skills. Example: reading, writing, etc.
- In the academic learning, many skills are involved.
- The moment a learner picks up a skill, the ease and efficiency of doing a work is improved.

Psychological Principles Involved in Learning Skills

(a) Motivation is essential.
(b) Self-initiation and learners own active practice.

- *(c)* Observation of demonstration by expert.
- *(d)* Spaced learning is always desirable → internal consolidation and co-ordination takes place.
- *(e)* Plateau is a common phenomenon in skill learning–30 minutes practice is ideal.
- *(f)* Over learning is essential to acquire skills.
- *(g)* Speed and accuracy both to be insisted ever since the early practice sessions.
- *(h)* 'Catch them young and teach them young' is the key word for skill learning.
- *(i)* Self-monitoring and reinforcement will facilitate.

LEARNING OF VALUES

Values are described as socially defined desires and goals that are internalized through the process of conditioning, learning and socialization.

In other words, values are moral or professional standards of behaviour or principles.

Examples → artistic values, legal values, scientific vales, etc.

Source of Values →
- Philosophy
- Religion
- Science
- Social customs, culture
- Constitution

'Values are caught rather than taught' emphasises the role of the teacher. He/she should be a model in every respect.

How are Values Acquired by Children?

- Initiation.
- Identification—child identifies himself with an adult and internalize the adult rules.
- Observation.

How are Values to be Taught in the Classroom?

- Include in the books, value oriented actions from the life histories of the great men, discuss the issues.

- Encourage pupils to make choices on their own and to make them choose freely without any fear or hesitation.
- Help pupils discover and examine the alternatives that are available for choosing.
- Help the pupils to weigh the consequences of each alternative and the actions that ensure.
- Encourage pupils to think and understand what they prize and cherish and therefore value.
- Provide the pupils opportunities to demonstrate their choices and discuss the consequences.
- Encourage the pupils to act in accordance with their choices.

List of Values

Democratcy Values

D – Dignity of the individual
E – Equality and Gender values
M – Mutual understanding
O – Open mindedness
C – Co-operation
R – Rational thinking
A – Adult franchise
C – Concern for others
Y – Yearning for living

Universal Values of Secularism

Love, reverence, tolerance, truth, co-operation and mutual understanding.

Moral Values

Honesty, truthfulness, moral stability, good character.

Social Values

Sense of discipline, social conformity, social justice, social sensitiveness and altruism.

REFERENCES

1. A. Charles Catania (1992). *Learning,* 3rd Ed. New Jersey: Prentice Hall, Engle Wood Cliffs, 1.
2. B. Kuppuswami (1994). *Advanced Educational Psychology,* New Delhi: Sterling Publishers (P.) Ltd., 111-14.

3. Biggie, Morris – *Learning Theories for Teachers* (IV Edition).
4. Bower, G.H & Milgard – *Theories of Learning* (1982).
5. Braner – *The Process of Education.*
6. Braner – *Towards a Theory of Education.*
7. Charles Catania (1992). *Learning.* New Jersey: Prentice Hall, Englewood Cliffs, 1.
8. Charles, E. Skinner – *Educational Psychology.*
9. Clifford, T. Morgan, Richard. A. King, John R. Weisz and John Schopler (1993). *Introduction to Psychology,* 7th Ed. New Delhi: Tata McGraw Hill Pub. Co. Ltd., 140.
10. David, A. Lieberman (2000). *Learning Behaviour and Cognition* 3rd Ed. Woods Worth, a Division of Thomon Learning-USA, 328-365.
11. Dr. K. Shivarajan (2000). *Educational Psychology.* Calicut: Calicut University Co-operative Press, 170-183.
12. Dr. K.S. Pillai (1991). *Educational Psychology.* Trivandrum: Kalaniketan, 188-200.
13. Dr. Sitaram Jayaswal (1974). *Advanced Educational Psychology.* Agra: Vinod Putak Mandir, 336-342.
14. Emeralled, V. Dechant and Henry P. Smith (1977). *Psychology in Teaching Reading* 2nd ed. New Jersey: Prentice Hall Inc., 50-52.
15. Hizard and Bower – *Theories of Learning.*
16. Joyce and Weil (1997). *Models of Teaching.* New Delhi: Prentice Hall of India Pvt. Ltd., 110001.
17. K.G. Rastogy (1983). *Educational Psychology.* New Delhi: Rastogi Publications, 161-178.
18. Lester, A. (1983) and Lefton and Lalra Valvatine (1983). *Mastering Psychology,* 2nd ed. USA: Allyn and Bacon Inc., 22.
19. Lester. A. Lefton and Lalra Valvatne (1983). *Mastering Psychology,* 2nd edn. USA: Allyn and Bacon Inc., 22.
20. Paul Greenhalgh (1994). *London:* Routledge, 11-13.
21. Peter, D. Spear, Stephen, D. Penrod and Timothy B. Baker (1998). *Psychology: Perspectives on Behaviour.* New York: John Willey and Sons, 239-289.
22. Rama, S., Anandan, Anil, R. & Nambiar, B. (2005, July). *Psycho-Pedagogy.* Paper presented at the seminar on Psychological Foundations of Education, DAMTEC, Calicut.
23. Robert, S. Feldman (1993). *Understanding Psychology,* 3rd ed. USA: Mc-Graw Hill Inc.
24. S.K. Mangal (2000). *Advanced Education Psychology,* 6th Ed. New Delhi: Prentice Hall of India (P) Ltd., 143-45.
25. Valentine (1951). *The Psychology and its Bearing on Education.* Herne Hill Great Britain.

MODEL QUESTIONS

1. Explain the role of 'readiness' in effective learning. Bring out the role of maturation and environment in readiness.
2. Explain the idea, 'learning for transfer', with the help of an example, examine the scope of this in ordinary classroom situation.
3. Explain the significance of interests in the learning process.
4. Explain the idea 'transfer learning' suggest instructional strategies for its realization.
5. What are the factors influencing learning? Explain.
6. How the meaningfulness of the material make learning easy?
7. Define Transfer of Training.
8. Differentiate positive transfer from negative transfer.
9. Give an example of Cross Education.
10. Explain Woodworth's theory of transfer of learning.
11. Discuss briefly the theory of Identical Elements .
12. In what ways does Transfer of Learning, useful for teachers?
13. Give the meaning of 'concept' and describe the ways of developing concepts.

4

Theories of Learning

BEHAVIOURIST THEORIES

Ivan Petrovich Pavlov

Pavlov's Theory of Classical Conditioning

The Russian psychologist Ivan Petrovich Pavlov was the first to explain the process of conditioning. Conditioning means modification of the natural response. Natural stimulus may be sometimes be substituted by an artificial stimulus. In this way, new connection of artificial stimulus and natural response is created. After performing various experiments Pavlov puts forth a new theory of learning known as theory of classical conditioning or conditioned response theory.

Classical conditioning is a type of learning in which a stimulus acquires the capacity evoke a response that was originally evoked by another stimulus. This type of learning acquired another name that is responded conditioning.

Pavlov's Experiment

While studying the functioning of the digestive system, a Russian psychologists named Ivan Pavlov encountered an unforeseen problem; the dogs in his experiments salivated not only upon actually eating but also when they saw the food, noticed the man who usually brought its, or even heard his footsteps. Pavlov began to study this phenomenon, which he called 'conditioning'. Since the type of conditioning emphasized was a classical one-quite different from the conditioning emphasized by other psychologists at the later stage—it has been re-named classical conditioning.

Pavlov conducted experiments on a dog. He trained a dog to stand harness on a table in a sound proof laboratory. A minor operation was performed on its cheek and its salivary glands were connected to a glass container through a rubber tube. The necessary arrangements were made for the collection and accurate measurements of the saliva that the dog secreted.

An electric bell rang, than the hungry dog made certain movement but did not salivate at the sound of the bell. The food was given and at the sights of the food aroused the response of salivation. Whenever food was given to the dog, the bell rang. The combination of stimuli, bell and food was repeated many times. After a few trials, the dog was given no food but the bell was rung. It was found that even in the absence of food, the ringing of the bell caused salivation in the dog. The dog here learned to salivate at the sound of the bell. This kind of learning was termed learning by conditioning.

During the process of conditioning, the artificial stimulus which is weaker is presented to the individual before or simultaneously with the unconditioned stimulus which is stronger. This is repeated many times and then the stronger stimulus is replaced by the weaker stimulus i.e., the weaker stimulus evokes the response of the stronger.

Pavlov's Classical Conditioning is diagramatized as

Symbols Used

US – Unconditioned Stimulus (Natural Stimulus)
UR – Unconditioned Response (Natural Response)
CS – Conditional Stimulus (Artificial Stimulus)
CR – Conditioned Response (Artificial Response)

Before Conditioning

(US) Food → Salivation (UR)
(CS) Bell → Hearing (UR)

Conditioning Process

(CS) Bell + (US) Food → Salivation (UR)

After Conditioning

(CS) Bell → Salivation (CR)

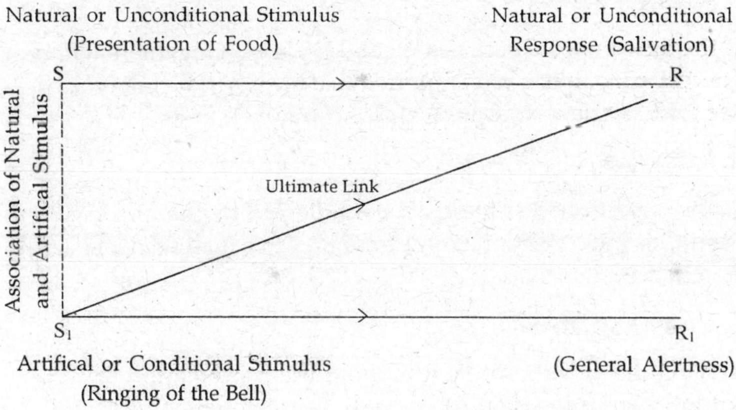

Fig. 4.1: Pavlov's Conditioning Process.

The above experiments thus brings to light four essential elements of the conditioning process. The first element is a natural stimulus, technically known as Unconditioned Stimulus (US) i.e., food. It results in a natural response called the Unconditioned Response (UR). This response constitutes the second elements. The third elements is the artificial stimulus i.e., the ringing of the bell which is technically known as a Conditional Stimulus (CS). It is substituted for the natural stimulus (food). To begin with, the conditioned stimulus does not evoke the desired response i.e., the Conditioned Response (CR). The fourth elements is the chain of the conditioning process. However, as a results of conditioning, one learns to produce behaviour in the form of a conditioned response to a conditioned stimulus.

Factors Affecting Conditioning

There are certain factors which control conditioning.

1. *Motivation*

Inner motive play a very important role in conditioning. In this experiments, hunger was the motivation.

2. *Association*

In this experiments, we can see an association between natural and artificial stimulus which results in salivation, the conditioned response.

3. *Timing of Stimuli*

If the time interval between CS and US is too long, there will be no conditioning. It has been reported that the best time interval is 0.2-2 sec with the new stimulus (artificial stimulus) firsts.

4. *Extinction*

If the conditioned stimulus is not followed by the unconditioned stimulus, the conditioned response may gradually disappear. This is called as *extinction.*

5. *Distracting Stimulus*

During the process of conditioning the combination of weaker-stronger stimulus is repeated, then if a third irrelevant stimulus is also presented, it will inhibits or block the conditioned response.

Significance of Conditioning

The theory of conditioning as advocated by Pavlov, thus considers learning as habit formation and is based on the principle of association and substitution. It is simply a stimulus-response type of learning wherein place of a natural stimulus like food, water, sexual contact etc can evoke a natural response. When both the artificial or natural stimulus (ringing of the bell and the natural stimulus are brought together several times, the dog becomes schooled or conditioned to respond to this situation. A perfect association occurs between the types of stimuli presented together. As a result, after sometime, the natural stimulus can be substituted or replaced by an artificial stimulus and this artificial stimulus is able to evoke the natural response.

Educational Implications

Through conditioning, fear, love or hatred towards the subjects can be created. The child may develop a distaste and hatred if the attitude of the teacher is defective. A sympathetic approach is very effective. A positive attitude can be built-up towards the subjects through conditioning. The use of audio-visual aids can go a long way in conditioning the students in developing desirable habits, interests and attitudes. It is helpful in removing unhealthy attitudes, fears, habits and phobias. Thus, conditioning approach helps the teachers and parents in their tasks.

Principles of Classical Conditioning

The theory of classical conditioning emphasized by Pavlov and Watson gave birth to a number of important concepts and principles in the field of learning such as:

1. *Extinction*

It was noted by Pavlov that if the conditioned stimulus (ringing of the bell) is presented alone a number of without the food, the magnitude of the conditioned response of salivation begins to decrease, and so does the probability of its appearing at all. This process of gradual disappearance of the conditioned response or disconnection of the S-R association is called *extinction.*

2. *Spontaneous Recovery*

It was also discovered by Pavlov that after extinction when a conditioned response is no longer evident, the behaviour often reappears spontaneously but at a reduced intensity. This phenomenon, the re-appearance of an apparently extinguished Conditional Response (CR) after an interval in which pairing of Conditional Stimulus (CS) and Unconditioned Stimulus (US) has not been repeated – is called spontaneous recovery. The process of spontaneous-recovery shows that somehow, the learning is suppressed rather than forgotten. As time passes, the suppression may become so strong. That there would be, ultimately no further possibility of spontaneous recovery.

3. *Stimulus Generalization*

Pavlov's dog provided conditioned response (salivation) not at the sights of the food but to every stimulus like ringing of the bell, appearance of light, sound of the footsteps of the feeds etc., associated with its being fed. Responding to the stimuli in such a generalized way was termed as stimulus generalization with reference to a particular stage of learning behaviour in which an individual once conditioned to respond to a specific stimulus is made to respond in the same way in response to other stimuli of similar nature.

4. *Stimulus Discrimination*

Stimulus discrimination is the opposite of stimulus generalization. Here, in sharp contrast to responding in a usual fashion, the subjects learnt to react differently in different situations. For example, dog may be made to salivate not only at the sights of the green lights and not of the red or any other. In this way, conditioning through mechanisms of stimulus discrimination one be learns to react only to a single specific stimulus out of the multiplicity of stimuli and to distinguish and discriminate one from the others among a variety of stimuli presents in our environments.

Conclusion

The conditioning theory of learning put forward by Pavlov actually involves the conditioning of respondent behaviour through a process of stimulus association to substitution. Here the responses of the learner becomes to conditioned behaving in the same way or responding similarly to similar situations—that he no longer needs the natural stimuli to evoke the related natural response. As a results, the new substituted stimulus behaves like an original stimulus and is able to evoke the desired response.

Thorndike's Trial and Error/Success Theory

Edward Lee Thorndike (1874-1949) was an American Psychologist.

His Experiment with Cat

A deprived cat in a puzzle box with a lever that would enable it to get out if pressed—and a fish visible to it kept out side—random trails, progressive elimination of errors and successive approximation of learned response.

Principles of Learning-based on Thorndike's Experiment

1. Learning involves trial and error.
2. Learning is the result of formation of connection or bonds (S-R).
3. Learning is incremental not insightful.
4. Learning is direct; not cognitive.
5. The S-R connections are established in nervous system.
6. The connection (bond) strength can be increased or decreased.

Laws of Learning-based on Thorndike's Experiment

All laws explain how to strengthen/weaken S-R Bonds:

(a) *Law of Effect*: When a modifiable connection between stimulus and response is made and is followed by satisfying state of affairs, that connections strength is increased. When made and accompanied by an annoying state of affairs, its strength is decreased. It emphasises the role of reward and punishment in education.

Revised Law of Effect: An unpleasant situation/punishment need not necessary decrease the strength of S-R connection.

(b) *Law of Exercise:*

1. *Law of Use:* Other things being equal, the more frequently, a modifiable connection is made between a stimulus and response, that connection strength is increased.
2. *Law of Disuse:* Other things being equal when a modifiable connection not made between stimulus and response over a period of time, that connection strength is decreased.
3. *Revised Law of Exercise:* Mechanical use/disuse does not necessarily lead to effective learning/total forgetting.

(c) *Law of Readiness:*

1. When any conduction unit is ready to conduct for it to do so is satisfying.
2. When any conduction unit is not ready to conduct, for it to conduct is annoying.
3. When any conduction unit is ready to conduct for it not to conduct is annoying.

Satisfaction strengthens the bond, but annoyance weakens.

Supplementary Laws of Learning

1. *Law of Multiple Response*: When an individual faces a problem, he responds in a variety of ways before arriving at correct response.
2. *Law of Attitude*: Individual leans better if he develops a positive attitude.
3. *Law of Analogy*: When an individual faces a problem, the response he makes will resemble to an earlier response in a similar situation.
4. *Law of Pre-potency of Elements*: Learner reacts to the learning situation in a selective manner, due to the influence of past experience.
5. *Law of Associative Shifting*: Any response may be elicited from

the learner, of which he is capable, in association with any situation to which he is sensitive.

Why Trial and Error Theory is Included in B.Ed. Curriculum ?

(*a*) Motivate the child before learning.
(*b*) Make use of the previous knowledge.
(*c*) Arrange task from simple to complex.
(*d*) Strengthen S – R connections of those things to be remembered by regular use/ practice weaken others by disuse or by annoying consequences.
(*e*) Rote memory and mechanical repetition may be resorted judiciously.
(*f*) Punishment should be judiciously used.
(*g*) Provide maximum opportunity to review.
(*h*) Provide rewards, prize and praise.

SKINNER'S OPERANT CONDITIONING

B. F. Skinner (1904-1990) was a Professor of Harward University.

Operant Conditioning/Instrumental Conditioning Theory

It is defined as a process of learning whereby a response is made more frequent/ more probable by reinforcement. He holds the view that behaviour can be shaped by reinforcement, and by chaining reinforcement, complex behaviour also can be shaped.

Skinner's Experiment with Rat and Pigeons

Skinner Box-deprived organism – emitted response – instantly followed by reinforcement – e.g. Pecking a disc and getting a pellet of grain-repetition of the response.

Important Terms

1. *Reinforcement/Reinforcer:* A reinforcer is the stimulus whose presentation or removal increases the probability of a response reoccurring. It is important that reinforcer is contingent upon response i.e., response result in the occurrence of reinforcer. Reinforcement is the process of manipulating the reinforcer.
2. *Positive Reinforcement:* Any pleasant stimulus whose presentation increases the likelihood of a particular behaviour. Example: Prize to a child.

3. *Negative Reinforcement:* Any aversive stimulus, the removal of which increases the likelihood of a particular behaviour. Example: Electric shock.
4. *Punishment:* The presentation of an unpleasant stimuli after an undesirable response.
5. *Omission Training:* Positive reinforcement is withdrawn following an undesirable response. For example, Parents turning off TV following some undesirable behaviour.
6. *Primary Reinforcer:* Reinforcer which directly satisfies physiological needs. For example, food, water.
7. *Secondary Reinforcer:* Reinforcer that satisfies acquired need rather than inborn ones. For example, money is a good secondary reinforcer. It does not satisfy any physical need directly.

Shaping

It refers to the judicious use of selective reinforcement to bring certain desirable changes in the behaviour of the organism. The basic process in shaping is successive approximation to the desired behaviour. Example: Skinner taught a Pigeon to walk in through shaping.

At first Pigeon got its reward for simply turning its head in right direction, then for taking a step in the right direction, then for making the correct turn, and so on until it had learned to do a complete.

It is useful as a technique for introducing desirable modification in the behaviour.

Stimulus Generalisation: Tendency of similar stimuli to elicit same response.

Stimulus Discrimination: Probability for response to occur more often in the presence of one stimulus than others.

Why Skinner's Operant Conditioning is Included in B.Ed. Curriculum?

1. Learning process should be so designed as to create minimum frustration and maximum satisfaction, because behaviour depends on consequence.
2. Useful for behaviour modification.
3. The complex learning task to be presented in simple units with provision for reinforcement after each unit.

4. Motivation, especially extrinsic should be given importance.
5. Reinforcement should be given at proper time.
6. Avoid punishment.
7. Ignore improper behaviour for extinction.
8. Useful for programmed instruction and PSI.

Programmed Instruction (PI)

It is a method of teaching, using teaching machines, a device for serial presentation of 'frames' with smallest teaching units with provision for immediate testing and feedback—self-learning strategy with built in feedback mechanism.

Following steps of shaping is used in PI:

1. Complex task should be reframed into simpler tasks, for presenting.
2. Reinforcement contingent upon performance of each step. (Knowledge of result or feedback is the reinforcement.)
3. Learning proceeds at his own pace. (Self-initiated learning)

Personalised System of Instruction (PSI)

It is also known as Keller Plan. Fred. S. Keller developed it to teach psychology for post-graduate students, dividing the entire portion of the course into small units, each learned by the student, tested by the Proctor before proceeding to next unit.

1. Materials of courses is divided into simple units, each must be mastered before entering to the next.
2. Take their own pace.
3. Being allowed to go to the next unit after mastery of first unit is the reinforcement.

CLARK L. HULL

Introduction

Clark L. Hull (1884-1952) was born in Akron, New York, on May 24, 1884. He was from a poor family and apparently missed a lot of schools as a result of having to work on the family farm. He is reported to have been ill health throughout much of his childhood. He had extremely poor eyesight. His early training before he became a Psychologist was in engineering and something of the engineers outlook is evident from his attempts at constituting an elaborate, formal and precise structure of psychological theory. But after reading James's principles of psychology, Hall switched to psychology and went on to the University of Wisconsin, where he obtained a Ph.D. in 1918. Hulls' early interests included systematic investigations of human and animal aptitudes, of thinking machines (Robots), of hypnosis, and of the effect of tobacco on intellectual functioning. In 1929, he went to Yale, where he became a research professor and generated the monumental system that, in extremely simplified form makes up the rest of this chapter. Following his first major descriptions of this system in principles of behaviour (1943), he rapidly became the most frequently cited psychologist in the United States. A final revision of this book was published first after his death in 1952.

Main Components of Hull's System

Hull's explicity behaviouristic system is marked by all of the behaviourist's concerns for objectivity, precision and rigor. Thus, although he bean by investing postulates—which might sound like a pretty metalistic undertaking—his main concern was to derive specific, testable hypotheses from them. Then he attempted to verify them ion laboratory situations.

True to the behaviouristic approach, Hull looked at a human behaviour in terms of stimuli an responses like Pavlov, Watson, Guthrie and Thorndike, he was convinced that environmentally conditioned responses underlie behaviour. However, he dealt with stimuli and responses in considerably more detail than did most of his contemporaries. For Hull, stimuli consists of all the conditions that affects the organism but that might or might not lead to behaviour; he referred to these antecedent conditions as input variables. Similarly responses are described as output variables. Similarly responses are described as output variables. Several of his postulates are devoted to explaining the nature of input and output variables as well as the relationships that exist between two. A third set of behaviour variables which forms a central part of Hull's system, is referred to as intervening variables.

Important aspects of input and output variables can be observed and measured; in contrast, intervening variables are purely hypothetical. They are inferred from input and output. They are the scientist's best, most educated guesses about what might be happening between the presentation of a stimulus and the occurrence of a response.

Hull's interest in intervening variables is a significant departure from the pre-occupations of the early behaviourists such as Watson and Guthrie, who actively shunned speculation, trying to keep the study of behaviour as objective as possible. For this reason, Hull sometimes described himself as a neo-behaviourist rather than simply as a behaviourist.

Hull was greatly impressed by Pavlov's work on reflexive behaviour and classical conditioning. This Pavlovian influence is reflected in part by the fact that the cornerstone of Hull's system is his belief that all behaviour consists of S-R connections. The central concept in behaviour is that of habit, and a habit is an S-R connection, or a collection of such connections termed a habit-family hierarchy.

Another source of profound influence on Hull was the work of Thorndike, particularly relating to his law of effect. The influence of reward of learning became the main explanatory notion in the final system.

The Four Stage Analysis of Learning Situation

The learning situation for Hull consists of a prediction in four stages. The first stage consisted of the independent variables from which he was predicting, the fourth stage of the dependent variables to which he was predicting, and the second and third stages of intervening variables connecting them. Thus, knowing the values of the independent variables, one could compute the values of the intervening variables at stage two. From these, one could compute in turn the value of the intervening variable at stage three, and from that finally predict the values of the dependent variables.

The independent variables can be manipulated by the experiences and are in the form of stimulation, deprivation, magnitude of reward or number of reinforced training trials. The intervening variables are hypothetical states of the organism and cannot be observed. They are assumed to be directly controlled by the independent variables. Hull identified four intervening variables such as *habit strength* (SHR), *incentive motivation* (K), *drive* (D) and excitatory potential (*Reaction potential*) (SER). The dependent variables are in the form of responses which can be observed and measured. They are related to reaction potential and are usually measured by amplitude or size of the response, the speed of the response and the total number of responses that will occur, after reinforcement is removed and before extinction is completed.

Habit Strength (SH_R)

Habit strength is the most important concept in the theory of need reduction. It implies the strength of the bond connecting a stimulus with response. To point out the nature of this connection habit strength is abbreviated SH_R, the H standing for habit and the S and R subscripts standing for the stimulus an the response which the habit connects. This habit is a permanent connection which can increase but cannot decrease in strength. Hull maintains that for a long-term learning, the formation and strengthening of habits are essential. Each time a response occurs in the presence of a stimulus and this event is quickly followed by reinforcement, the habit strength of this stimulus-response connection increases. This reinforcement also involves a reduction in the strength of achieve stimulus. It may also be noted that the rate at which habit strength builds up with successive reinforced responses follows the well-known 'law of diminishing return' so that each successive reinforced response contributes less to SH_R, than the previous one. Ultimately a point is reached at which additional reinforced responses contribute very little more to habit strength.

Generalized Habit Strength ($S\overline{H}_R$)

In learning S-R is formed and reinforced. The corresponding neural connection is formed. By this the habit is strengthened by repeated S-R connections. This is denoted by habit strength. Each time S – R is formed drive is reduced and habit is strengthened. The habit is again strengthened when a person does released activities. Now the habit strength is called generalized habit strength.

Generalized Reaction Potential ($S\underline{E}_R$)

This is the reaction potential observed when substracting the aggregate inhibitory potential from reaction potential.

$$\text{i.e., } SER - SIR = SER$$

Drive (D)

Drive is a temporary state of the organism, produced by deprivation of something the body needs or by painful stimulation. There are many different specific drive conditions, of which hunger, thirst and pain are the typical examples. Drive is the basis for both primary and secondary reinforcement, it activates habit strength into reaction potential and provides differential stimuli that guide behaviour. There are three functions associated with a drive.

Each drive condition, such as hunger or thirst, produces a characteristic drive stimulus. This stimulus indicates the particular need from which the body is suffering. A rapid reduction in this drive stimulus is reinforcing. As a consequence any response that occurs just before a reduction in achieve stimulus tends to be learned as a response to whatever stimuli are present.

The drives are activating or energizing. All drive conditions combine to make up the total drive level of the organism. This total Drive (D) serves to raise the individuals activity level. This activating effect of D can be seen both in an increased level of general body activity and in the increased vigour with which all learned habits are performed.

Drive plays a discriminative or steering role. It determines the need state of the organism and the subsequent learning, for example, to go to one plate for water when thirty, to another place for food when hugry.

Incentive Motivation (K)

The term incentive motivation refers to the motivating effect of the incentive that is provided for making the response. We all know from experience that people tend to mark harder for a larger reward than for a smaller one. In other words, the level of performance is commonly higher when a larger reward is given after the response occurs. Hall considered the magnitude of the reward as one aspect of reinforcement. The larger the reward, the greater the reduction in drive (need), and hence the greater the increase in habit strength. It was however, noted that this treatment was not satisfactory. Experiment showed that changes in the magnitude of the reward produced very rapid changes in the level of performance. This difference was particularly difficult for Hull to explain when the change was from a larger to a smaller reward. If the reward was made smaller and performance became poorer, this result appeared to imply that the habit strength had become less. Yet habit strength involved a permanent bond, one that became stronger with reinforced practice but never became weaker.

Stimulus Intensity Dynamism (V)

The term stimulus intensity dynamism refers to the fact that a stronger stimulus will evoke a greater response, habit strength remaining equal. It is abbreviated as 'V'. It is another multiplier affecting reaction potential through the multiplications of habit strength, drive and incentive motivation. This in the form of an equation it may be described as

$$SER = SHR \times D \times K \times V$$

Where,
SER = reaction potential
SHR = habit strength
D = Drive
K = incentive motivation
V = Stimulus intensity dynamism

It may be observed that if the value of any of the four intervening variables is zero, the reaction potential automatically becomes zero.

Reactive Inhibition (IR)

In terms of our experience, we know that the presence of adequate habit strength and drive is sometimes not sufficient to ensure an effective response. There are moments when inhibition may prevent or check the appearance of an otherwise readily evoked response. If for example, an organism has been responding for a long period of time in a conditioning experiment, fatigue well-appear. In and of itself fatigue well-generate a form of inhibition which Hull calls reactive inhibition and being overpowered by it, the organism cases to respond. It is abbreviated as IR and is subtracted from the multiplied value of habit strength, drive, incentive motivation and stimulus intensity dynamism of the evoking of stimulus in order to find out the value of the net reaction potential. Thus the equation becomes.

$$SER = SHR \times D \times K \times V - IR$$

Conditioned Inhibition (SIR)

If an arbitrary stimulus is presented at the same time that the response is g radually diminishing due to fatigue, it gives rise to a phenomenon called conditioned inhibition. Here the associated stimulus acquires the strength of inhibiting response. The term conditioned inhibition is abbreviated as SIR. It is noted that both reactive and conditioned inhibition are additive in their effects in diminishing reaction potential. Further, it is important to emphasize that conditioned inhibition does not spontaneously dissipate with time. It is an acquired inhibition and hull believes that time per second has no effect on learned reactions. Only unreinforced repetition of conditioned reactions could cause a dimination or reduction in a response.

Momentary Oscillation (SOR)

According to Hull there is evidence to indicate that variation in inhibition takes place in terms of loss of chance and that inhibitory potentials oscillate from instant to instant. The concept of momentary oscillation is abbreviated as SOR. It refers to the assumption that any given amount of reaction potential is not an exact value but the average of a random distribution of values. Hull referred to two implications of the oscillation principle which are as follows.

It explained the frequently observed phenomenon that stimuli may elicit reactions which have never been conditioned to them. more specifically, such variable reactions occur because the oscillation process results in variations in the intensity of muscular contractions, thus making every co-ordinated act slightly different from every other.

Oscillation implies that behaviour can never be predicted with certainly at any given point in time. However, prediction is nevertheless possible, since oscillation follows the law of chance. As a result prediction can be made in terms of the central tendency of behaviour and of course, this procedure involves collecting data from a large number of observations.

Aggregate Inhibition Potential (SIR)

The tendency that the organism has not to respond is labelled aggregate inhibitory potential SIR. It results in part from the amount of work involved in responding and in part from any habits of not responding that might have been learned by the organism, usually as a function of repeated performance of the responses. According to Hull responses requiring a high expenditure of physical energy are less likely to be engaged in than those that require less work. Also, with continued repetition of a response, inhibitory potential accumulates. Its effect is to lower the net reaction potential until eventually the response no longer occurs. That is if inhibitory potential is equal to or greater than reaction potential, then it follows mathematically that net reaction potential will be zero or negative—in which case no behaviour will occur. Inhibitory potential results from repetition and fatigue dissipates quickly, notes Hull, so that the response might reoccur again very soon.

Reaction Threshold and Response Evocation (SLR)

The term threshold means that intensity value of a stimulus which is just adequate to produce a response. It is also known as 'liminal value'. It is abbreviated as SLR. Other things being equal, if the effective reaction potential is above threshold, then a response will appear. If effective reaction potential is below threshold, no response will appear. In the case of incompatible responses, the response whose reaction potential is greatest will be the response that is evoked.

Reaction Latency (StR)

The term reaction latency is a measure of the response and is abbreviated as StR. It implies that the time taken between the production of a stimulus and the appearance of a response. For example, if the stimulus of a high intensity is presented to a subject, the time taken for the appearance of a response, i.e., reaction latency will be quite less as compared to a stimulus of low intensity.

By way of a final glance at Hull's observable measure of learning, we may formulate these major concepts in the form of the following equation:

SER = SHR × D × V × K – (IR + S I R)- S OR
Where SER = the momentary effective reaction potential
SHR = generalized habit strength
D = drive
V = stimulus intensity dynamism
K = incentive motivation
IR = reactive inhibition
SIR = conditioned inhibition
SOR = oscillation of reaction potential
SER = SHR × D × V × K – SIR – SOR
Where SIR = IR + SIR
Also SER = SER-SIR, SER = SHR × D × V × K – (IR + SIR)\SER = SER – SOR

We may interpret the formula to read as follows:

The effective reaction potential (performance) depends first of all, upon effective habit strength (learning) multiplied by the values of drive (D), stimulus intensity dynamism (V) and incentive motivation (K). Thus, if either effective habit strength or drive or stimulus intensive dynamism or incentive motivation is zero, no response can be evoked. Second, the product of effective habit strength and drive, stimulus intensity dynamism and incentive motivation is diminished by the addition of two antagonistic factors, reactive inhibition and conditioned inhibition. The relationship is such that if either is zero, or very weak in magnitude, then the reaction potential is high. Finally, the influence of the oscillatory potential SOR is subtractive in its effect. As such, it may be stated that as oscillation decreases effective reaction potential increases and vice versa.

Contributions and Educational Implications of Hull's System of Learning

Hull's system of learning acclaimed and remembered for putting forward a most systematic, scientific and mathematical theory of learning. Hull was able to popularize a very innovative and objective behaviouristic approach to learning which was more effective in comparison to the approach of his predecersons. The significant contributions and educational implications of his theory can be briefly summarized as:

1. Hulls theory rejected the trigger-like mechanism of stimuli response advocated by Thorndike and introduced the concept of intervening variables between S and R. The things within the individual definitely act and react with what is received in terms of stimuli from the external environment before emitting of an overt response. Hull provided the amended S – O – R formula in place of the traditional S – R approach. He termed the environmental influences, upon the individual as 'inputs', and his responses as 'outputs', and what goes from the individual as 'processes'. He asserted that 'input' and 'output' can be measured experimentally and, therefore, behaviour in its processes and products can be subjected to experimental verification.
2. Hull's theory attached sufficient importance to the needs,

drives, incentives, reinforcement and adequate motivation for achieving satisfactory results in the process of teaching and learning.

The greater contribution of Hull's theory lies in its emphasis on linking the learning to the needs of the children. He says that it is the need, drive or drive stimuli that energize and individual to act, behave or learn. Therefore, he advocated the need-based goals of education, including need-based curricula and methods of teaching.

Whereas needs start the process of learning, reinforcement and incentives act as catalytic agents for increasing one's effort towards achieving the goals of learning. Therefore, in any education process we must involve sufficient possibilities of proper motivation and reinforcement incentives.

3. Hull's theory tried to extend the concept of reinforcement. Prior to this, reinforcement was considered only in terms of rewards and satisfaction but Hull stated that to escape pain or punishment or to reduce need is also a kind of reward and helps in reinforcement.
4. Hull's theory did great emphasis on the formation of good habits as a means of the learning of desirable behaviour. In practice, Hull reduced the art of learning to mere habit formation and its proper reinforcement. It brought into prominence the role of adequate practice did and strengthening of reinforcement. However, he preferred an increase in the member of trials or reinforcement to an increase in the proper quantum of reinforcement and thus advocated continuous and gradual introduction of small doses of reinforcement rather than one, single heavy dose.
5. Hull's theory brought into focus the fact that different individuals have different capacities. It presented a systematic and mathematical treatment of individual differences. Hull attributed individual differences to the variation of the values of numerical constants varied from species to species, from individual to individual and from one physiological states to the other in the same individual. If a group participates in a learning situation and everything else is kept constant through experimental controls, then the constant should change in a systematic way from

different age groups of the learners. For any group of learners, the constant should not change when identical conditions are introduced. Such views propagated by Hull's theory emphasized the need for planning education according to the individual differences of the learners keeping their respective ages in mind.

6. Hull's theory emphasized the need for proper rest and other measures to reduce the ill effects of fatigue in any act of learning. The principle of work and appropriate rest, may thus be said to have evolved as a result of the experimental findings of this theory.
7. Hull's theory stood against any inhibition-causing obstacle in the path of learning or emitting the desired response. It stressed the prime need of minimizing or removing all types of inhibitions, internal or physiological and external or learned, for achieving good results in the process of teaching and learning or obtaining the desired behaviour in an individual. In a practical classroom situation, therefore, a teacher has to be very careful in the proper distribution of the drill and practice work. So as to avoid unnecessary fatigue and the resulting inhibition. Similarly, the principle of change and variety in terms of subjects, teachers and classroom etc., may be introduced for bringing down the ill-effects of boredome and fatigue.
8. Hulls system of learning advocated the following chain sequence for improved results the teaching-learning process.

   (a) *Drive:* This is something which is needed by the learner inorder to behave or respond.

   (b) *Cue:* There must be something to which the learner must respond.

   (c) *Response:* The learner must be made to respond or do something in order to learn some act.

   (d) *Reward:* The learner's response must be reinforced or rewarded, thus enabling him to learn what he wants to learn.

COGNITIVE THEORIES OF LEARNING (GESTALT SCHOOL OF PSYCHOLOGY)

Formalized learning theory developed in late thirties when proponents of various approaches attempt to build their own theory to explain the problems of learning. A theory of learning cannot be defined to satisfy all interested persons. We can quote the definition of a theory as, a provisional explanatory proposition or set of propositions, concerning some natural phenomena and consisting of symbolic representations of (1) the observed relationships among independent and dependent variables, (2) the mechanisms, or structures presumed to underlie such relationships, or (3) inferred relationships and underlying mechanisms intended to account for observed data in the absence of any direct empirical manifestations of the relationships (Learning Themes edited by Melrin H. Marx).

The Role of Theory

The formulation of a theory plays two important roles: (1) It gives detailed systematized information of an area of knowledge. (2) The second role is

(a) to summarize or to describe.
(b) to explain (mechanisms of behaviour in learning process).

Classification of Theories

All learning theories are classified under two broad categories:

I. S–R Theories.
II. Cognitive Field Theories.

S–R Theories

(a) S–R Theories without reinforcement

(i) Conditioning by Pavlov.
(ii) Watson's Learning Theory.
(iii) Guthrie's Learning Theory.

(b) S–R Theories with reinforcement

(i) E.L. Thorndike's Theory.
(ii) Hull's Theory.
(iii) B.F. Skinner's Theory.

Cognitive Field Theories

(i) Gestalt Theory of Learning.
(ii) Lewin's Field Theory of Learning.
(iii) Tolman's Sign-Gestalt Theory of Learning.

Cognitive Theories of Learning

- Gestalt learning theory or, theory of Insightful learning
- Kurt Lewin's Field theory
- Jean Piaget's Psycho-Genetic Epistemology
- Bruner's Cognitive Assumptions
- Ausubel's Theory of Reception

Fig. 4.2: Cognitive Theories – Diagramatic Representation.

Gestalt Theory of Learning/Theory of Insightful Learning/Insight Theory of Learning

The view propagated by behaviourists in the form of an association between stimuli and responses for understanding learning faced great difficulty in explaining the learning process or behaviour involving higher cognitive abilities. The chance success through trial and error or association through connectionism and conditioning may account for simple acquisition of knowledge, skills, interests, habits and other personality characteristics, but is not sufficient to account for problem-solving, creativity and acquisition of other similar cognitive behaviour including insight (learning that appears to come suddenly).

Dissatisfied with the approach of behaviourists, the cognitive psychologists tried to see learning as a more deliberate and conscious effort of the individual rather than a product of mere habit formation or a stimulus-response machine-like mechanism. According to them,

- In a leaning process, the learner does not merely receive or make responses to the stimuli, but definitely processes, i.e., interacts with and does something about what he receives and his response is determined by that processing.
- Teaching is a process of developing insight or understanding in the learner.
- Learning is the organization of percepts and purposes by the learner.

Gestalt psychology emerged when traditional psychology was under fire in America and Germany. Thorndike and Watson were developing objective methods to study behaviour. At the same time, three German psychologists – Max Wertheimer, Kurt Koffka and

Wolfgang Kohler – being dissatisfied with molecular approach to behaviour, were busy in developing a new approach to behaviour. They,

- Considered man's inner process the proper subject for study.
- Vehemently criticized the behaviouristic view that everything we see or think is put together of tiny pieces like those of a jigsaw puzzle.
- Advocated that we perceive and think of wholes.
- Assumed that our perception of the world is of meaningful wholes and that is different from and more than an accumulation of sensations, images or ideas.
- Rejected the simple stimulus-response (S-R) connections as the explanation of behaviour.
- Introduced the concept of organization between stimulus-response approach developed by Behaviourists.

Thinking along these lines, these group of German psychologists called *Gestaltists* and particularly Wolfgang Kohler originated a learning theory named insightful learning.

'Gestalt' is a German noun for which there is no English equivalent. So the term was carried over into English psychological literature. The nearest English translation of gestalt is 'configuration'/'pattern'/'shape'/'form' or more simply an 'organized whole' in contrast to a collection of parts.

Gestalt psychologists believe that

- We react to pattern of our own perceptions, when we face a problem, depending upon the set of stimulating conditions in the environment.
- We learn, not by associating bits of experiments, but by forming new gestalts, i.e., by seeing new patterns and by organizing them into a meaningful whole in the total situation.
- When we struggle with a problem, the solution may come to us all of a sudden. This quick change in our perception is called 'insight'.
- The process of learning is a 'gestalt' – an 'organized whole'.

In short, the basic idea of the theory is that

"A thing cannot be understood by the study of its constituent parts, but only by the study of it as a totality or whole."

According to Gestalt psychologists, learning occurs neither as a result of trial and error nor as a conditioned response to unnatural or conditioned stimuli. On the other hand, it occurs by insight into the whole situation to be learned. Learning does not carry gradually or step by step or trial after trial but suddenly by an insight into the learning situation as a whole.

In practical terms, Gestalt psychology is primarily concerned with the nature of perception. That is, an individual perceives a thing as a whole. To them, the meaning of sensation or perception is always related to the total situation. According to them, perception always involves a problem of organization. A thing is perceived as a relationship within a field which includes the thing, the viewer and a complex background incorporating the viewer's purposes and previous experience.

Basic Principles of Perceptual Organization

Gestalt psychologists conducted most of their experiments in the field of perception. On the basis of their experimental studies, certain laws of perceptual organization have been developed by them. Some of them are given below:

1. *Principle of Figure-Ground*

Everything we perceive stands against a background. There is a close relationship between figure and ground. We listen a song against the background of music.

2. *Principle of Pragnanz*

This states that our perceptual patterns always tend to be simple, regular and complete with no loose ends. The gaps are closed by the perceiver. It is a goal directed tendency to restore the equilibrium.

3. *Principle of Transposition*

To form new pattern, the perceived items may undergo extensive changes without losing their identity.

4. *Principle of Similarity*

It suggests that similar words, numbers and objects tend to associate in a group and easy to recall than dissimilar ones. We tend to group objects in a perceptual field on the basis of their similarity.

5. *Principle of Proximity or Nearness*

It states that objects which are close in space and time tend to form a Gestalt.

6. *Principle of Simplicity*

It suggests that perception break up the complex things into simple and can assimilate.

7. *Principle of Goal Direction*

It states that reorganization of objects is directed to a goal. The Gestalt's theory of perception has been summarized by Kohler as follows:

Our view will be that instead of reacting to local stimuli by local and mutually independent events, the organism responds to the pattern of stimuli to which it is exposed; and that this answer is a unitary process, a functional whole, which gives in experience, a sensory scene rather than a mosaic (bits of sensation) of local sensation.

8. *The Principle of Closure*

The law states that we tend to close the open edges of a figure to make the stimulus configuration complete. Groupings are usually made in terms of enclosed or completed figures rather than open ones.

Gestalt psychologists tried to interpret learning as a purposive, exploratory and creative enterprise. A learner, while learning, always perceives the situation as a whole and after seeing and evaluating the different relationships, takes the proper decision intelligently. He always responds to the roper relationships rather than to specific stimuli. Gestalt psychology used the term 'insight' to describe this process.

It was Kohler, who used the term 'insight' first of all, to describe the learning of his apes. During the period 1913-1917, he conducted many experiments on Chimpanzees in the Canary Islands and embodied his findings in his book *Mentality of Apes* (1925). These experiments demonstrated learning by insight. The four classical experiments are given below:

Experiment 1: A Chimpanzee named Sultan was confined in a cage—There was a stick in the cage and outside the cage some bananas were put. In the first instance on 'seeing the bananas the Chimpanzee showed restlessness and tried his best to reach the bananas but he could not. All of a sudden, he perceived the stick and established relationship between the stick and the bananas. With the help of the stick, he fished inside the bananas.

Experiment 2: In the second experiment, two stick were used. One was hollow at one end so that the other stick could be thrust into it form a longer stick. The Chimpanzee could only get the bananas with the help of both the sticks fitted in each other. He first tried to get the bananas with the help of one stick but he failed. All of a sudden, he succeeded in fitting both the sticks and could get the bananas.

Experiment 3: In this, the experimental setting was slightly changed. The bananas were hung from the ceiling of the cage and a box was put in the corner of the cage. The Chimpanzee attempted to get the bananas but could not reach to them. He suddenly established relationship between the box and the bananas, put the box under the bananas and climbed on it and got the bananas.

Experimental 4: Slight change was introduced in this experiment, two boxes were kept instead of one. The Chimpanzee had to use both the boxes in order to get the bananas.

In these experiments, Kohler used many different Chimpanzees. Sultan, who was the most intelligent of Kohler's Chimpanzees, could solve all the problems. Other Chimpanzees could solve the problems only when they saw Sultan solving them.

These experienced by Kohler, show that

- the animal must perceive the total situation and relationship among all relevant parts of the problem before insight can occur in solving the problem.
- insight follows a trial and error behaviour on the part of the animal. Once the animal learns to solve a problem by insight, there is every possibility of high degree of transfer to similar problems.
- the main factor in Gestalt Theory of learning is the development of insight. The individual and his environment form a psychological field. This perception of the field and gradual restructuring of it is insight.

Moreover, these experiments demonstrated the role of intelligence and cognitive abilities in higher learning such as problem solving. The apes, somewhat higher animals, did not resort to the blind trial and error mechanism adopted by Thorndike's cat or the simple habit formation as in the case of Pavlov's dog. They reacted intelligently by

(*a*) Identifying the problem
(*b*) Organizing their perceptual field
(*c*) Using 'insight' to reach a solution

Once the situation is perceived as a whole and the perceptual field is properly organized, a problem becomes solvable through flashes of insight.

In human beings, we come across such learning a number of times on different occasions. For example, a student may suddenly discover that in the 9's table, the sum of the digits in the answer is always 9 ($9 \times 5 = 45$, $4 + 5 = 9$). The student's learning of a new meaningful relationship is a result of his insightful learning.

Insightful learning depends upon the following factors:

1. Experience	:	Past experiences help in the insightful solution of problems. A child cannot solve the problems of modern mathematics unless he is well-acquainted with its symbolic language.
2. Intelligence	:	The learner should have basic intelligence. The more intelligent the individual, the greater will his insight be (Sultan-more bright).
3. Learning Situation	:	How insightfully an individual will react, depends, upon the situation in which he has been placed. Some situations are more conducive to insightful solution than others. Insight occurs when the learning situation is so arranged that all the necessary aspects are open to view.
4. Initial Efforts	:	Initial efforts in the form of trial and

(Contd.)

		error do not last long and they open the way for insightful learning.
5. Repetition and Generalization	:	After obtaining an insightful solution of a particular type of problem, the individual tries to implement it in another situation, demanding a similar type of solution. The solution found in one situation helps him to react insightfully in other identical situations.

The Steps Involved in the Insightful Learning:

1. Survey of Problematic Situation-recognizes an obstacle between on the way to the goal.
2. Attitude of concentrated attention to the problematic situation.
3. Analysis of various factors involved in the situation and their relationship.
4. Trial of mode of responses.
5. In case of initial mode of response proves inadequate, trial of some other response.
6. Frequently recurrent attention to the objective or goal and motivation.
7. Restructuring of the perceptual field.
8. Appearance of critical point at which the organism suddenly, directly and definitely performs the required act.
9. Steady repetition of adaptive response.
10. Notable ability to discover and attend to the essential aspect or relation in the problematic situation.

The most general principle of learning is the goal directed tendency or pragnanz to restore the equilibrium. Learning takes place when there is a tension or disequilibrium of forces in the psychological field; the learning process removes the tension.

Insight and Motivation

In cognitive learning theory, motivation and purpose are much the same. The learner's goal is the end result he anticipates and desires. The goal controls the behaviour of the learner. The teacher's most important responsibility is to help the leaner find worthwhile goals which may be clear and realistic. They should recognize and use the prominence of social and achievement motives in school learning. The teacher must know about what is familiar to students and then he must introduce elements of novelty but not for rapidly. Good teacher must pace his presentation to maintain the interest and attention in learning. The teacher's management of conflicting motives may be an important factor in student's success.

General Features of Cognitive Learning Theory

1. Cognitive Learning Theory aims to be a comprehensive theory of learning—deals with all type of learning from the simplest to the most complex.
2. Cognitive theorists have emphasized the importance of subjective experiences of the learner.
3. Cognitive Learning Theory is not a theory basically in terms of what the person knows, but the individual responds in terms of what he perceives or believes and the explanation of this functioning must be sought in terms of the factors and relation which govern such perception.
4. The fundamental interest of cognitive learning theory is an interest in:

   (a) Perceptual or representational processes as the main functional unit in terms of which the psychological functioning proceeds.

   (b) In the background factors and processes that produce these perceptual or representational processes.

Implications of the Theory of Insightful Learning

1. It has made learning purposeful and goal-oriented task–learning does not involve simple reflexive or automatic machine-like responses. The learner has to be motivated by arousing his interest and curiosity for the learning process and he has to be well-acquainted with the specific aims and purposes of the learning.
2. It has given birth to the important maxim. 'from the whole to the parts' in the field of learning. A problem requiring solution should be considered as a whole and after being assessed as a whole, may be tackled for solution on a piecemeal basis. Example: If a person wishes to memorize a

Table–4.1
Gestalt Psychology of Learning—At a Glance

<table>
<tr><td>Meaning and Definition</td><td colspan="2">Configuration based on wholistic perception</td></tr>
<tr><td>Meaning of Perception</td><td colspan="2">Sensation + Interpretation</td></tr>
<tr><td rowspan="3">Factors Influencing Perception</td><td>Peripheral</td><td>Figure ground ratio, proximity, similarity common direction, simplicity, frequency of occurrence, intensity, movement, colour, brightness</td></tr>
<tr><td>Central</td><td>Attention, attitude, past experience sensory capacity, values, motives, expectations</td></tr>
<tr><td>Experiments</td><td>Kohler's experiments, Wertheimer's experiments</td></tr>
<tr><td rowspan="2">Insightful Earning</td><td colspan="2">Infers from experiments</td></tr>
<tr><td>Factors influencing insightful learning</td><td>Experience, intelligence, situation, compact visual pattern—wholistic percept, initial effort, ability to restructure the perceptual field, repetition and generalization</td></tr>
<tr><td>Educational Implications</td><td colspan="2">Purposeful and goal oriented, whole to part, organization, integrated approach and problem solving</td></tr>
</table>

poem, it should be presented to him as a whole and after being read and understood as a whole, it may be broken into parts of stanzas for being effectively memorized.

3. The unity and cohesiveness in the organization of curriculum, scheme of studies, work-plan are the contribution of the theory of insightful learning (as it requires the organization of the perceptual field and learning material as a whole (i.e., in the form of a 'gestalt').
4. The teacher must make an effort to expose relationship that expose a sensible hypothesis or effort. Reviews outlines, analogies and use of simple diagrams serve a great purpose to organize the subordinate ideas.
5. In every type of instruction, we start with meaningful wholes.
6. An attempt is made to focus attention on elements and relationships that determine the correct response.

7. Teacher's guidance must match the students' level of thought or ways of working. If a student has not advanced above the level of concrete thinking, information presented symbolically will not help him. Learning must be graded according to the intellectual development of the learner.
8. Teacher can help the students to find purpose or order in learning (Total perception → relationship → organization → insight → learning).
9. Use of blind, mechanical trial and error should be minimized.
10. The theory has brought motivation in the fore-front of learning so that the teacher should motivate the child by arousing his interest and curiosity.
11. It has made learning an intelligent task requiring mental abilities instead of automatic response to specific stimuli. So the learner must be given opportunities for using his mental abilities.
12. In order that the learner will be able to solve problems by insight, meaningful learning, learning by understanding and reasoning must be encouraged in the school.

FIELD THEORY OF KURT LEWIN

Kurt Lewin's Biography

Born in 1890. He was one of the famous and charismatic psychologist. Now-a-days he viewed as father of social psychology. He emigrated to USA and dead in 1947.

The Concept of Field and Key Concepts

Life Space (Psychological Field)

Total psychological world in which a person lives at a certain time.

Topology

Which deals with the relation of position in a life space.

Vector

Force which influence movement.

Valence

Positive valence and negative valence according to the attraction and repletion of a person by an object.

Cognitive Structure

Perceptual field or environment including the person as known and understand by the person.

Learning Theory of Kurt Lewin

- Learning as change in cognitive structure: Relativistic process by which a learner develops a new insight-cognitive restructuring as a result of differentiation of life spacing.
- Learning involves change in Motivation.
- Learning involve alternation of voluntary control of body musculator.
- Learning involves establishment or alternation of role behaviour interpersonal situation (Social learning).

Educational Implication of Field Theory

- *Reward and Punishment:* Reward helps to move the individual toward the goal and punishment more the individual away from the goal.
- *Success and Failure:* Success experience makes some progress direction towards the goal. Failure reverse the effect.
- Motivation acts as a vector force.
- *Memory:* Worthwhile, unfinished, ego involved tasks remembered better.
- *Components of the Curriculum:* Useful, pleasurable, attractive, taskful, subjects only etc.

JEAN PIAGET'S COGNITIVE LEARNING THEORY

Biographical Out Line

Born in 1896 in Switzerland. He got his Ph.D. at 22 years old. He dead in Geneva, at the age of 84 on 1980. He is a genetic epistemologist. He wrote 40 book and presented around 100 papers on psychology.

Key Concepts

- Scheme-Hypothetical mental structure for representing generic concepts stored in memory.
- Schemata-plural of scheme.
- Cognitive structure.
- Cognitive functioning.

The Process of Learning

- *Assimilation*: Integration of new information with existing internal mental structure.
- *Disequilibrium*: Due to the mismatch between assimilation and accomodation.
- *Accomodation*: The process of adjustment or change of mental structure.
- Equilibrium.
- *Adaptation*: Biological in nature.

Stages of Cognitive Development

- Sensori-motor period (0-2 years)
- Pre-operational period (2-7 years)
  - Pre-conceptual
  - Intuition
- Concrete operational (7-11 years)
- Formal operational (12-15 years)

Educational Implications

- *To the Learner*: The learner as found 'an accord of thought with things'.
- *To Teacher*: Help the child to assimilate the content.
- *Teaching Methodology*: Teachers must emphasis the critical role that experiences with the environment.
- *Learning Style*: Active discovery learning.

JEROME S. BRUNER

Introduction

As one of the most ardent exponents of the cognitive development approach Bruner has contributed much to the technology of information processing leading to the development of the cognitive structure of an individual. He strongly propagated the message of discovery learning and in this attempt coined a very famous phrase- i.e., learning to learn. He believed that the process of learning (through discovery) is more important than the mere material learnt. He also held that "every learner should learn how to learn." In order to realize this message Bruner has suggested certain strategies to teachers.

Bruner's Model of Concept Learning

J.S. Bruner suggested a model of concept attainment and structures in teaching. He proposed that economy in thinking and responding requires that we categorize, phenomenon according to their common attributes.

What is a Concept?

There are five components for earning concept:

1. ***Name***

The term which discriminate the concept from other concepts.

2. ***Exemplars and Non-exemplars/ Examples and Non-Examples***

This exemplars are known as positive examples which have all the attributes of concept.

Non-exemplars are also known as non- examples.

3. ***Attributes***

An attribute is a properly or characteristic of an object which differentiate it from other. Colour, texture, form, size, number of pacts, position and sound are examples of attributes. We categorize objects having common characteristics into one group. For example, we categorize objects having common characteristics such as certain animals having four legs, a tail and a barking voice as dogs. Similarly, we can also categorize more abstract concepts such as enemy or friend etc., for teaching about a concept the teachers must identify such attributes of that concept which differentiate it from others. For example, a dog and cat have four legs and a tail, but cat has a different voice than the dog.

There are essential and non-essential attributes. Essential attributes are most important traits of the concept, which satisfy the concepts completely and the attribute which disqualify that concept without that attribute. The non-essential attributes are also associated with concept but they are not very essential to satisfy it. These non-essential attributes are also known as noisy attributes.

4. ***Attributes Range or Attribute Value***

The range variations of the attributes of concepts (shape, colour, size etc.,) are called attribute value. Bruner used a set of cards, some cards having borders, others without. All the cards have centre figures varying in shape (square, circle or cross in colour (red, green or black) and in number (single, double or triple). Each card thus combines four attributes: figure shape, figure number, figure colour and presence or absence of borders. Each attributes has three values (variations) as listed above.

5. ***Rule***

Rule is the definition or the statement by which we specifying the essential attributes. The difficulty to define a concept will increases according to the increase in number of attributes.

Aspects of Cognitive Development

Jerome S. Bruner emaciates six aspects of cognitive development.

- Cognitive development is characterized by increasing independence of a response from a stimulus.
  Example: Children learn to put off their gratification of desires, and modify their responses.
- Cognitive development is characterized by an internal storage and information processing system that can describe reality quite closely.
  Example: Children learn to use a symbol system to represent. Objects, events or experiences. They learn to predict, extrapolate or hypothesis.
- Cognitive development involves an increasing capacity to express by words or symbols what one has done and what one will do. i.e., it involves self-consciousness.
  Example: Children imbibe social norms and strive for adult recognition.
- Cognitive development depends upon systematic interaction with members of society.
- Cognitive development is quite closely related to language development. Language is the key to intellectual development. Effective communication takes place only through language. The child sees language not merely as a means of representing experiences, but also of transforming experiences.
- Cognitive development is marked by increasing ability to perform concurrent activities and to allocate attention sequentially to various activities.

Stages of Cognitive Development

According to Bruner, formulation of a concept is depends upon the following stages:

1. ***Enactive Stage***

This is the stage in which the child understands his environment only through the medium of actions (bodily actions) – not through words or imageries. Concepts are formed with the help of activities or direct experiences i.e., environment of bodily movements. Example: The infant understands his environment by touching, biting and catching.

2. ***Iconic Stage***

Icon means image. This stage is a great advancement in cognitive level. Here information is gained by imagery, and the child is prisoner of his percept world. Concepts formed with the help of copying of objects, contrived experiences etc.

3. ***Symbolic Stage***

Concepts formed with the help of symbols. In this stage, language, logic and mathematics come to play in increasing proportions (abstract level). This stage is characterized by compatibility and semantically rich statements.

Strategies of Concept Learning

The most important contribution of Bruner to the theory of learning is his study of meaning and nature of concept and their learning. Concepts being the vocabulary of the language of science meaningful internalization of concepts was considered by Bruner as his key to discovery learning and learning to learn.

A strategy is a systematic procedure used to learn a concept. There are two major types of strategies: Analytic and non-analytic. According to Brooks (1978), analytic strategies represent techniques for identifying attributes, prototypes, or rules; non-analytic strategies merely involve memory of particular positive instances of a concept used to determine whether new stimuli are also instances of the concept.

Analytic Strategies

Bruner (1956) conducted an extensive investigation of the strategies used to learn the attributes characteristics of a concept, the prototype of a concept, or the rule defining a concept. They identified four major strategies.

According to Bruner two main thinking strategies are adopted for classification and concept learning. These strategies are selection and reception.

Selection Strategy

In this selection strategy the learner himself makes the classification by forming his own judgements and by testing them, i.e., here the learner is attaining or forming the concept without the assistance of teacher. He himself is finding the attributes and nobody interferes him by looking at examples and non-examples.

Reception Strategy

In the reception strategy positive and negative instances are given by an expert and by studying them in terms of attributes they receive the concept. In this no choice is there for the learner. Clues are given by the teacher, and examples and non-examples are given by the teacher. Then he arrives at the concept. Examples and non-examples are only meant for guidance and not dry explanation.

Concept Attainment Model

The teacher says that I have an idea in my mind. Then she is giving the examples and non-examples. Examples are followed by "Yes" and non-examples followed by "No". In the second step, she tells things, children have to label it by saying "Yes" or "No". In the third step, children gives examples and non-examples and also label it by "Yes" or "No". Selection strategy is divided into four groups. Bruner identified four strategies in concept attainment. They are:

1. Simultaneous scanning strategy.
2. Successive scanning strategy.
3. Conservative-focusing strategy.
4. Focus-gambling strategy.

1. *Simultaneous Scanning*

In this type of strategy, the subject uses each positive instance (each correctly identified card), to deduce which combination of attributes and values are no longer valid. The subject must keep in mind simultaneously all the rejected combinations in order to narrow down the range of subsequent alternatives. In simultaneous scanning the student formulates several hypotheses and then looks for examples. It is very exacting for the individuals must deal with several independent hypotheses and carry them all in his mind. This technique is not very efficient since it places a great deal of strain on the subject's memory.

2. *Successive Scanning*

In this technique the subject makes an overall estimate of each correct characteristic of the concept and tests each one by one. This is called successive scanning since the subject tests individual hypothesis about the correct characteristics one at a time in succession. It reduces the amount of relevant information which must be remembered, but it also reduces the amount of relevant information each encounter may provide.

3. *Conservative Focusing*

In this technique, each attribute is tested by selecting a card that is different from a focus card in only one attribute. This procedure enables the subject to test the impact of that change from the focal stimulus. The subject continues to select stimuli differing in only one attribute from the focal stimulus until the concept is learned. Conservative focusing is a very efficient strategy of learning a concept; it requires only one more trial than the number of dimension. For example, the concept to be attained is 'red circle'. Assume that the subject encounters a positive card with three red circles and two borders. This card becomes the focus card and each variable is examined by selecting additional cards. The selection sequence is given below. A plus sign in the parentheses means that the card is a positive instance of the concept, a minus sign in the parentheses means that the card is negative instance.

Four Cards

- 3 red circles, 2 borders (+) 2 red circles, 2 borders (+) → first decision to eliminate 'three figures' as a relevant variable.
- 3 green circles, 2 borders (–) → second decision; retain red as relevant attribute value.
- 3 green crosses, 2 borders (–) → third decision, retain red circle as relevant attribute value.
- 3 red circles, 1 border (–) → fourth decision; eliminate 'two

borders' as relevant attribute value. Conclusion: The concept is 'red circle'.

This technique is more efficient since the subject uses a correct instance as a point of reference and selects additional cards to test each attribute value individually.

4. *Focus Gambling*

This strategy is similar to conservative focusing in that the first positive instance becomes the focus of the concept and similar to simultaneous scanning in that more than one hypothesis is tested on each trial. This procedure can result in rapid concept learning if the guesses are accurate or positive instance. If the subject encounters a negative instance, he cannot tell which attribute was essential. This strategy is called gambling since the subject takes a chance varying two attributes at a time. Since focus gambling tests hypotheses less systematically than conservative focusing does, more trials may be needed to identify the concept.

Purposes of the Selection Strategies

Selection strategies have three purposes:

- They maximize the opportunity to obtain useful information about the concept.
- They reduce the strain of assimilating and keeping track of information.
- They regulate the amount of risk we take in reaching a solution.

Reception Strategy

The reception strategy are divided into two:

1. *Partist Model:* It is similar to scanning. It is to research or to make enquires. Here the individual is actually search for a concepts. The researcher may form one hypothesis, reject it, then again form another and reject it, till he arrives at a concept. There are two divisions here, first he forms a hypothesis, then attribute analysis is done.
2. *Wholist Model:* It is similar to focusing, and it is also searching for the concepts on the basis of attributes. Here analyzing the attributes and then forming the concept. Thus, here the

importance is to analyzing the attributes, then to form concepts. This is done by taking all attributes.

Importance of Analytic Strategy

It is used

- to identify an attribute when stimuli characteristic of a concept have common, highly salient attributes.
- to identify the rule, when the rules that define a category are salient.
- It is very useful when the positive instances of a concept cannot be easily remembered.

Educational Implications

- *Intellectual Empathy:* Teachers should look at the problems from the child's point of view. Remember that 'children are not miniature adults'.
- *Sense Training:* Teachers should present only concrete objects to children in early stages.
- *Encouragement of Heuristic Methods:* Heurism means method of discovery.
- *Follow a Sequence:* Teachers should proceed from known to unknown, simple to complex and concrete to abstract.
- *Self-regulation:* Teachers should permit children and proceed at their own pace. Don't impose anything irritable on them.
- Administration of intelligence rests to assess the processing ability of children.
- *Error Analysis:* There is no meaning in telling them that the children are wrong what is needed is, an analysis and interpretation of their errors in order to lead them to progress.

DAVID AUSUBAL

Introduction

During the functional stages curriculum is limited and hence discovery learning is desirable and feasible. At the same time, students acquire a number of concepts alongside direct discovery. Thus, they have an expanded enriched cognitive map. This become useful to them to 'understand' and 'assimilate' verbal knowledge meaningfully. David Ausubel believes that teachers should present organized meaningful and complete information at first and then

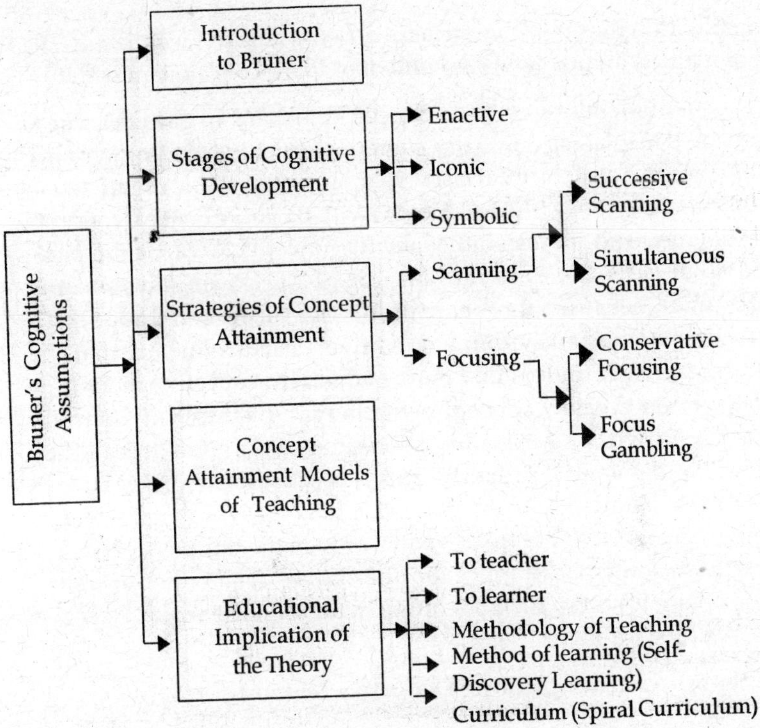

Fig. 4.3: Jerome S. Bruner's Model of Learning.

move to more specific examples. Ausubel calls this approach 'Expository Learning' resulting in meaningful 'Reception Learning'.

Expository Learning begins with a definition of the concepts or principles to be taught, illustrates them and unfold their implications. Lecturing is the perfect examples of expository learning. The lecturer presents the material to be learned in more or less final form gives answers. Present principles, and elaborates the entire content of what is to be learned. Thus Ausubel looked unusual among educational theorists, while verbal learning faced much criticism, Ausubel argued for 'Meaningful verbal learning.'

Ausubel's Theory/Meaningful Reception Learning (Verbal Learning)

The first principle of expository learning is that concepts are meaningful only when the student can visualize them and 'subsume' them within the cognitive structure. Being able to visualize means that it elicits an image in the content of their 'consciousness'.

Ausubel believes that people learn by organizing new information, placing it into the 'cognitive structure' (coding system). The cognitive structure consists of a more or less stable organization of concepts, arranged hierarchically, with the more general concepts at the apex and increasingly specific concepts towards the base. Ausubel calls the general concept of the coding system the subsumer, because all other concepts are subsumed under it. To subsume a concept within a cognitive structure means that the student already understood more general concepts that include or incorporate the new concept being taught. Example: if we try to teach a growth of Australian aboriginals about 'Oaktrees', they would understand it properly. This is because the aborigins live in 'Southern Hemisphere, on a desert, a long was away from water, ships, oceans etc. 'Oak trees' grown only in the temperate parts of Northern hemisphere. Since the aboriginals can neither visualize it nor place it within their cognitive structures, the word 'Oak' has no meaning for them.

Reception Learning follows Deductive Method

Ausubel refers to the presentation of general aspects at the beginning of the lesson followed by specific ones. In other words, meaningful reception learning proceeds from general to specific. This is known as 'Deductive Reasoning', above cited example before trying to define 'Oak', first teach more general concepts of plant, tree and 'decidous tree' all of which subsume 'Oak'. According to Ausubel students can learn a concept only when they are ready to learn it. Student readiness includes current knowledge, stage of cognitive development and pre-dominant mode of intellectual functioning. For example, students who do not know the alphabet, cannot learn to read. In the above example pre-requisite cognitive structure, knowledge and skills must be mastered before the concept 'Oak' can be learned. When students have previous knowledge that would be helpful in understanding the new material, the teacher must help them to see the relevance of the existing structure to the new concepts. Through organizing 'what the aboriginal students already know about plants, we will be able to build a bridge from their current cognitive structures to the concept of 'Oak'.

Three Forms of Advance Organizers

1. Definition of the concept.
2. An analogy comparing new material with some well-known examples.
3. A generalization.

Purpose of Advance Organizers

1. The give students the information they will need to make sense of the upcoming material.
2. They help the students to remember and gather information they already have but which they may be realize, is relevant to the lesson.
3. They high light relationships among ideas that will be presented. Let us consider above purposes of Advance organizer into the title of functions of Advance organizer, as follows.

Functions of Advanced Organizers

1. Advanced Organizers helps the learner to re-arrange the received information into a 'hierarchical order'. And they also helps to reach from general to specific.
2. Advanced organizers are acting as subsumers. 'Subsume' means, to include in a particular category or to codify the object into a particular group. Every knowledge which receives in the mind through the process of 'codification', 'categorization' and through 'integration'.
3. Advanced Organizers are acting as Anchor. It is advanced organizers acting as 'fixers', and they connecting the new information with the old or existing ones.
4. Advanced organizers are acting for the function of Scafolding. Advanced organizers setting the mind to receive the new information, really they pave way for the new knowledge.

The organizers thus acts as a kind of conceptual bridge between new material and old. There are two types of advance organizers:

1. Expository Organizers.
2. Comparative Organizers.

1. *Expository Organizers* provide a broad generalization within which a number of subclasses or species are presented.

Example: Different intelligence test measures different intellectual and cognitive factors.

2. *Comparative Organizers* designed to integrative new concepts with similar concepts found in the cognitive structure. They also help the learners to discriminate with the familiar and new concepts. Two concepts may have similarities as well as differences. Eg.: 5 × 6 can be changed into 6 × 5. Here the multiplia and multipliant can be reversed without changing the product. In division the divisor and the dividend cannot be reversed without affecting the quotient. Hence 8 divided by 8.

Characteristics of Expository Teaching

1. It calls for a great deal of interaction between the teacher and the students.
2. It is deductive.
3. It is essential? rescential? sescential?
4. It makes greater use of examples which may include drawings, diagrams or pictures.

Rote Learning—Contrasted

Ausubel contrasts reception learning with Rote learning or Blind memorization. Whatever is acquired by students without adequate comprehension is easily forgotten. According to Ausubel people acquire knowledge through reception learning in which concepts, principles and ideas are presented to them. The more organized and meaningful the presentation the more thoroughly the person will learn. Simply memorizing the content of the text is not meaningful. Connections must be made with the students existing knowledge. Hence, according to Ausubel Rote memorization is very in effective learning strategy.

Role of Teacher

In expository learning, teachers start lessons with advance organizers or general principles—that will help student to integrate the material into already existing cognitive structure. They present the material to be learned in small steps organized logically and sequenced in ways that are easy to follow and that highlight the similarities or differences between new material and related concepts prepositions. They regularly asks questions in order to answer that each step is thoroughly mastered by the students before moving on to the next one. They end a lesson with an integrative review of the main points and follow up with assignments that require students to re-organize existing cognitive structures to subsume the new material being learned. In short, this teaching model considers the teacher a transmitter of knowledge.

Educational Implications

To use Ausubel's approach, the teacher begins by presenting the major ideas and organization and the students submit ideas and responses throughout the lesson. There is considerable interaction between the students and the teacher. The lessons are presented deductively from the general to the specific and the information is presented in a sequenced step-wise manners. Ausubel's expository approach encourages the case of examples and focuses on relationships such as similarities and differences in information.

Expository teaching seems most appropriate when students have some knowledge of the material and purpose of the lesson is to identify relationships or expand existing knowledge. Because students have to be able to work with relationships, the expository approach is most appropriate for students in upper elementary grades and higher.

Advantages of Expository Teaching

1. Expository teaching is more popular in our school today because it is more efficient and takes less time than discovery learning.
2. When confined with practice it is very successful in teaching concepts and principles.
3. In expository teaching there is considerable interaction between the students and teacher.
4. It offers a good means of helping students retain important information.
5. It promises the students ability to transfer information and skills from one situation to another.

Ausubel's Reception Learning

During the functional stages of curriculum is limited hence, discovery learning is desirable and feasible. At the same time students acquire a number of concepts along with 'direct discovery'. This they have an expanded and enriched cognitive map. This becomes useful to them to understand and assimilate verbal knowledge meaningfully. (Thus Ausubal appears unusual among the educational theorists, supports 'meaningful verbal learning' or 'meaningful reception learning). Verbal learning is not similar with Rote learning. The Rote learning is that in which students acquire things and concepts without adequate comprehension and is easily forgotten, but meaningful reception learning is adequately comprehensive.

Table–4.2
Learning Theory of Ausubal

Learning Theory of Ausubal or Meaningful Reception Learning		
Biographical overview	Born on 1918 in New York, Came to Educational Psychology from the field of medicine.	
Introduction to Ausubal's Theory	Knowledge is hierarchically organized, Ausubal stresses meaningful learning-discovery learning.......	
Key Concepts	Advance Organizer	... is formation that is presented clear learning and that can be used by the learner organize and interpret new incoming information
	Scaffolding	... is something which is taken down when no longer needed.
	Subsumption	... is the process by which new information enters to consciousness and is directed or organized to fit with an already existing larger category.
The process of meaningful Learning	Derivative Subsumption	New concept learned without substantially altering the previous concepts.
	Correlative Subsumption	New concept learned through the alteration or extension of already learned concept
	Super ordinate Learning	New concepts are learned until it was taught you, but related concepts are already there.
	Combinational Learning	A process by which the new idea is derived from another idea that is neither higher nor lower in the hierarchy, but at the same level.
Instructional Implication	The Advance Organizer The Comparative Organizer Progressive Differentiation Integrative Reconciliation	

David Ausubal believes that teachers should present organized, meaningful, and complete information first and then more to more specific examples. Ausubal calls this approach 'Expository teaching' results in 'Meaningful Reception Learning.'

Expository teaching begins with a definition of concepts or principles to be taught, illustrates then and unfold their implication. Lecturing is the perfect example of expository teaching. The lecturer presents the material to be learned in more or less final form, gives answers presents principles and elaborates the entire content of what is to be learned. But content to be presented, meaningfully, systematically, orderly and by connecting the new material with existing old ones – because, learner receives them in a strategic order in his cognitive structure.

Meaningful Reception Learning – Ausubal's Theory

The first principle of expository teaching is that concept are meaningful, only when students can 'visualize' them and 'subsume' them within their 'cognitive structure'. Being able to 'visualize' a concept meant, that it illicit an image in the content of your consciousness. When hearing 'Antartica', the picture of ICY, snowy land must come to the mind.

Ausubal believes that people learn by organizing new information, placing it into the cognitive structure (coding system of Bruner). A cognitive structure consists of a more or less stable organization of concepts, arranged-hierarchically with more general concepts at the apex and increasingly specific concepts towards the base. Ausubal calls general concepts at the apex of cognitive structure as *subsumer* because all other concept are subsumed in it. To subsume is to incorporate a new meaningful material in to existing cognitive structure – The process is called *subsumption* – simply, to subsume a concept within the cognitive structure means that the student already understand more general concepts (subsumers) that includes in the new concept being taught. Example: If you introducing a concept or term 'Eskimo'.

SOCIAL LEARNING THEORY OF ALBERT BANDURA

Vicarious Learning or Modelling Theory or Observational Learning

The Cognitive psychologists who appreciate the role of observation in learning are termed as social psychologists. The theory of learning, propagated by them is known as Social Learning Theory.

Bandura's Social Learning Theory

Albert Bandura is a Canadian psychologist. He completed his master's degree in 1951 and Ph.D in Clinical Psychology the following year. Then he spent one year in Wichita Guidance Centre for his post-doctoral internship. In 1953, he joined the faculty at Stanford University.

Most of Bandura's early publications were in clinical psychology. In 1958, he collaborated with Richard, H. Walters, his first doctoral student, to publish a paper on aggressive delinquents. The following year, the book, 'Adolescent Aggression' (1959) appeared. Another joint publication is "Social Learning and Personality Development", 1963.

Bandura (1986) recognises two major kinds of learning observational and enactive.

(a) Observational Learning

- Observation allows people to learn without performing any behaviour.
- People can learn by observing models being reinforced.
- The care of observational learning is modelling.
- Learning through modelling involves adding and subtracting from the observed behaviour and generalising from one observation to another.
- So modelling involves cognitive processes and is not simply imitation.

Factors Determining Learning from a Model

- The characteristics of the model.
- The characteristics of the observer.
  [People who lack status, skill or power, children, novices etc., are more likely to model than experts]
- The consequences of the behaviour being modelled may have an affect on the observer.

(b) Enactive Learning

Enactive learning allows people to acquire new patterns of complex behaviour through direct experience by thinking about and evaluating the consequences of their behaviours.

Processes Governing Observational Learning

↓

Attention [One must attend to the model]

↓

Representation
[Observation pattern must be symbolically represented in memory]

↓

Behavioural Production [After attending to a model and retaining what they have observed, observer then produce the behaviour]

↓

Motivation [Observational learning is most effective when learners are motivated to perform the modelled behaviour]

- This theory is regarded as a bridge between conditioning and cognitive approaches.
- Studies have shown that aggression is readily learned and released by modelling.
- Television characters can act as powerful models for observational learning.
- Televised violence increases the likelihood of aggression by viewers.
- Yet people learn a lot through mass media.
- Many behavioural patterns are imitated from presents and family members and teachers.

What are the Implications of Social Learning Theory ?

- Beware! Children are keen observers of men and manners.
- They will try to imitate teachers and parents. They should be the role models.
- So try to exhibit good manners in words and deeds.
- Keep in mind—"as is the teacher, so are the pupils.'
- This theory is applicable even in our demonstration classes and micro teaching sessions.
- We should resort to the various devices for controlling media violence.

Albert Bandura and Richard Watters (1963). They advanced the view that what an individual presents is the world at large his personality, is acquired through a continues process of structuring and restructuring of experiences, gathered by means of social learning and situations. Social learning may involve real as well as symbolic models. Example: Children pick up etiquette and attitudes by watching their parents and elders. Viewers initiate traits, and mannerisms from actors and models. An individual thus acquires humorous traits and modes of behaviour from many sources, and all these contributes to develop of his unique personality.

'For see' – The after effects of several aspects without doing, observational learning.

Models

1. Real life models – Parents, teachers, relatives.
2. Symbolic models – Through Radio, TV ...

Four Phases of Observational Learning

1. Attention Phase.
2. Retention Phase.
3. Re-productive Phase.
4. Motivational Phase.

Factors Influence Observational Learning

A. *Stimulus Properties of the Model*

i.e., 1. Models, age, sex, SES.
2. Models, similarity to the subject.

B. *Types of Behaviour Exemplified by the Models*

1. Novel skills.
2. Hostile/aggressive responses.
3. Standards of Self-reward.

C. *Consequence of Models Behaviour*

D. *Motivational Set Given to the Model*

E. *Re-Inforcement* –

1. Direct.
2. Vicarious.
3. Self-administered.

F. *Self-Efficacy*

It is the theory that peoples learned expectations regarding success determining there behaviour. Self-efficacy underlies people's faith is the ability to carry out a behaviour, regardless of how successful they have been in the past.

G. *Reciprocal Interaction*

Reciprocal determinism—The view that the interaction of the environment behaviour and the individual causes people to behave the way that they do.

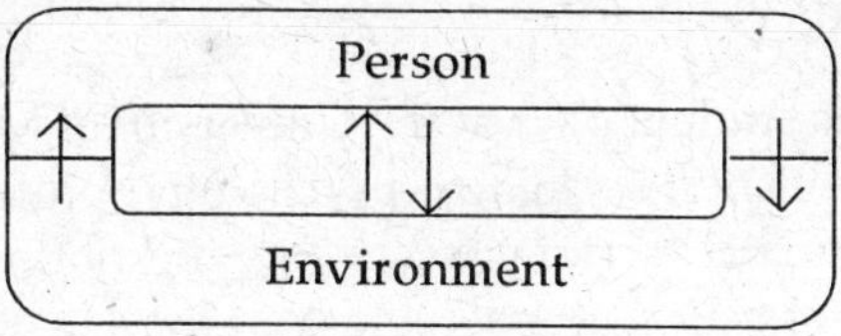

Fig. 4.4: Reciprocal Interaction of Learning.

H. *Environmental Feedback*

1. Performance standard
2. *Self-regulation:* Regarding or punishing one's own behaviour. Reinforce or punish themselves.
3. *Modelling:* The persons whose behaviour he observes and often imitates are known as models and observational learning.

How Does Learning Take Place?

1. Attending to and perceiving the behaviour.
2. Remembering the behaviour.
3. Converting the memory into action.
4. Reinforcement of the limited behaviour.

Criticism

1. There is no consistency in our behaviour.
2. Least importance to what happened inside the personality.
3. No importance to conflicts/Anti-treuelion theory.

Conclusion

Bandura's theory emphasis the power of observational learning. It advocates that most of what we learn is acquired through simply observing and initiating the behaviour of others who are taken as models.

LEVSMENOVICH VYGOTSKY (1896–1934)

The socio-cultural approaches to learning and development were first systematized and applied by Vygostky.

Vygotsky born in the U.S.S.R. in 1896 is responsible for the socio-cultural approaches to learning. He proposed that social interaction profoundly influences cognitive development. Central to Vygotsky's theory is his belief that biological and cultural development do not occur in isolation.

During his student days at the University of Moscow, he read widely in linguistics, sociology, psychology, philosophy and the arts. His systematic work in psychology did not begin until 1924. Ten years later he died of tuberculosis at the age of 38. His works were published after his death in 1934 and suppressed in 1936 and were not known in the west until 1958.

His most famous work is *Thought and Language* published shortly after his death, developed for the first time a theory of language development. Because Vygotsky's focus was on cognitive development, it is interesting to compare his views with those of Bruner and Piaget.

Vygotsky developed the concept of ZPD (Zone of Proximal Development), which he defined as 'the distance between the actual developmental level as determined through independent problem-solving and the level of potential development as determined through problem-solving under the guidance or in collaboration with more capable peers.

Socio–cultural theorists expanding the concept of ZPD, conceptualise leaning as distributed, interactive, contextual and the result of learner's participation in a community of practice. As a result, collaboration learning plays an important role in classrooms. The process of collaborative with another person who is more knowledgeable not only gives the child new information but also confirms those aspects of the issue which the child does understand.

The Major Principles

(a) Children Construct Knowledge

Learners crate their own representations of knowledge.

(b) Learning can Lead Development

- Maturational pre-requests are needed for certain learning.
- Great value to assisting children to use strategies to further their intellectual capacities.
- Zone of Proximal Development [ZPD], i.e., the distance between the child's actual development level and his potential level of development.
- Scaffolding and reciprocal teaching.
- Scaffolding is the hand support to be given by the teacher to the child until the child becomes able to study independently.
- Reciprocal teaching allows for the creation of a dialogue between students and teachers.

(c) Development cannot be Separated from its Social Context

- Similar structure of mind in all human being.
- Two levels of mental functioning – lower and higher.
- For Vygotsky, the social context influences more than just attitudes and beliefs. They have profound influence on how we think, as well as what we think.

(d) Languages Plays a Central Role in Mental Development. Whether there is a Need Here

- Languages as the transmitter of the cultural tools.
- Languages as the medium that carries experience into mind.

(e) Semiotic Mediation

- Learning from outside through psychological tools such as languages systems, counting systems, writing etc.
- Psychological tools to control behaviour.
- According to Vygotsky some of the examples for semiotic means are : Language, various systems of counting, mnemonic techniques, work of art, writing, diagrams, maps and so on.
- Mediation is the key in his approach to understanding how human mental functioning is tired to cultural, institutional and historical settings.

(f) Internalization

- A representational activity that occurs simultaneously in social practice and in the human mind.

- Transformation of communicative language into inner speech and further into verbal thinking.

Why should Teachers Follow Vygotsky's View Points?

If teachers apply the principles put forward by Vygotsky, effective learning takes place which results in better output.

- Provide amble opportunities to the pupil to learn on their own.
- Give scaffolding at the suitable time and lead the child to self-study.
- Provide group learning environments in the classroom.
- Collaborative learning and co-operative learning will enhance effective learning.
- The physical classroom based on Vygotsky's theory, would provide clustered desks or tables and provide space for peer instruction, collaboration and small group instruction.
- Classroom should become a community of learning.

GAGNE'S HIERARCHY OF LEARNING

Introduction

Robert M. Gagne is a prominent educational psychologist, who has developed a behaviouristic eclectic approach to the psychology of learning. His conditions of learning often are employed by methodologists and curriculum specialists to implement the achievement of stated performance objectives their behaviouristic, eclectic methodologies. For Gagne, the purpose of psychology is to observe conditions under which learning occurs and to describe than in the objective terms. Thus his "Conditions of Learning" (1970) are the various sets of observable circumstances that obtain when learning occurs. Here, he distinguishes eight types of learning, beginning with the simple forms and ending with the complex.

The Meaning and Concept of Learning – For Gagne

For Gagne, "Learning is a change in human disposition or capability which can be retained, and which is not simply ascribable to the process of growth" the major taste objective of one's learning is to bring the required change in his way of disposition or the capability of performing one task or the other. The result or impact of learning thus may be subjected to proper measurement. Since these can be properly observed and inferred by observing the differences in performance of the learner before and after learning. These changes in behaviour or ability and potential of the learner are somewhat enduring, as the learner is capable of utilizing and benefiting through the out comes of such learning. Gagne's pivotal idea on learning is that the learning of any new capability requires the prior learning of the subordinate capabilities that are involved, in the new capability.

Gagne's Hierarchical Structure of Learning

Learning has been classified into various categories. Gagne maintained that all learning are not alike and, consequently he divided human learning into eight types. He gave them a hierarchical order based on their internal connections since one type of learning provides a pre-requisite for next higher order learning. The classification is as follows:

1. Signal Learning.
2. Stimulus-Response (SR) Learning.
3. Chain Learning.
4. Verbal associate learning.
5. Multiple discrimination.
6. Learning of concepts.
7. Learning of principles.
8. Problem-solving.

1. *Signal Learning*

Signal learning is the classical conditioned response of Pavlov and Watson. It is stimulus substitution of such a nature that the organism learns to make a generalized response to a signal or stimulus. In classical conditioning, unconditioned stimulus and conditioned stimulus are paired together to produce natural stimulus. The theory of conditioning considers learning as habit formation and is based on the principle of association and substitution.

2. *Stimulus-Response Learning: Operant Conditioning (Learning Type-2)*

S-R learning is the instrumental condition of Thorndike. It is a process of response modification or change within which the learner acquires a precise response to a discriminated stimulus. Thus learning is really a matter of discrimination of correct and incorrect stimulation, of that set of stimuli which produces reward (reinforcement) and that set of stimuli which does not. It is true to say that the response becomes progressively differentiated. For Gagne the organism's discrimination of stimuli is more important than its response being reinforced. Instrumental conditioning is more flexible than classical conditioning because the response that may be conditioned are not confined to natural or innate response but to a variety of response. B.F. Skinner conducted series of experiments on animals and prepared ground for the use of the principles in human learning.

3. Chaining/Chain Learning/Motor Chaining

By chaining is meant the connection of a set of individual Ss→R's in a sequence. Behaviouristic chaining may be either motor or verbal. There are sequences that are made-up of motor responses like that of tuning on T.V. set or washing machine. There are sequences which are entire verbal as greeting:

(a) *Verbal Chaining:* It is a matter of connecting together in a sequences two or more previously learned Ss→R's. Our language is filled with such chains of verbal sequences as horse and buggy. Daddy and mummy are the examples of verbal chaining. In these examples first member of the sequence seems firmly tied to the second.

(b) *Motor Chaining:* The example of motor chaining can be given by a simple task of driving. The task of driving a motor consists of several learned chains of motor activities. Guthrie in 1935 described a case of motor chaining.

A college girl developed the habit of dropping her coat on the floor. Mother asked the girl to get out of the room and hang up the coat in the peg. The girl enters house.. keeps coat on, approach closet-hung up the coat on the peg.

Another example of motor chaining is unlocking a door by a child who has not leaned the sequence of unlocking operations. The following stimulus-response conditions from the process of unlocking a door are given:

1. Key in hand,
2. Facing the lock,
3. Checking the key is right side up,
4. Inserting it in to the lock until the stop is reached,
5. Turns it until another stop is reached, and

6. Pushes the door open. It should be remembered that a chain cannot be established unless the individual is capable or performing the individual links.

4. *Verbal Association/Verbal Chaining*

It is true that man is capable of a tremendous variety of performances with the use of his legs, arms and hands. It is also even more true that his vocalizations show an enormous versatility in social situations. Simplest verbal chain is illustrated in the activity of naming.

A child is shown an object as doll. The next times if he sees the particular object he will be able to say that it is a 'doll'.

There are two chains involved in this:

(i) Observing response Ss-R connection that connects the appearances of the object and distinguishes it form other objects.

(ii) The Second is the Ss-R connection that stimulates the child himself to say "doll".

S - - - - - - - - > R		S - - - - - - - - > R	
Object	**Observing**	**Doll**	**Doll**

Paired Associate Learning

In the learning, learning tasks are presented in such a way that they may be learned on account of their association. The name of a village 'Krishnapuri' is remembered on account of its association with the name of Lord Krishna. Much of the verbal or motor learning may thus be learnt or remembered on account of the technique of paired or multiple syllabus like the following:

Table–4.3
Paired Associate Learning

Paired Words	*Paired Non-Sense Syllables*
Dog-animal	PN-PF
Parrot- bird	NLD-JPS
Cat-Milk	RJBP-RN

When one learns a foreign language, it is not uncommon to acquire a large number of translation responses, in the manner of give-donner or buy-achetor. The traditional prototype for such learning is the pair associate. Sometimes used in non-sense syllables as Riv-GEX. The following are essential conditions for learning verbal associates:

1. According to Gross (1936), the learning of syllables or words is markedly affected by previous discrimination learning of both the first and second member.
2. Efficient learning of a two-element verbal association requires the use of an interviewing link having the function of mediation or coding.

   Give ————> donate ————> donner

3. It is difficult to separate the phenomena of learning single associates from those of multiple associates.

Each link of the chain to be acquired must have been previously learned as an Ss-R. It means that a stimulus must have been discriminated. It should be readily pronunceable.

Mediating connections between each verbal unit and the next must have been previously learned:

1. Verbal units must be presented in the proper sequence:
   (a) Whole chain at a time.
   (b) One after the other.
2. The learner must actively make the response required by the chain.
3. Cues may be used to learn verbal chains.
4. Individual span of memory determines the length of chain that can be learned all at once 7 + 2 is limit of verbal chain. Progressive part method is most efficient. There is no limit to verbal chain. People have learned complete book verbatim.
5. There must be provision for confirmation of correct responses in the learning situation.
6. Multiple Discrimination/Type-5 discrimination.

What is Discrimination?

In the development of discrimination, we take one aspect of the environment and reinforce selectively some response to it. When the behaviour shows a specificity of response to one given stimulus to the exclusion of others, we may say that a discrimination has taken place.

From the very beginning, the infant acquires simple discrimination and differentiation among the objects in his environment. He learns the difference between a feeding bottle and a simple bottle. In learning to walk and to walk, he differentiates more and more specific movements out of a mass of random activity. Discrimination involves higher mental processes. It is the basis upon which we learn to think and solve problems.

Generalization

Watson conditioned fear response in Albert by introducing level sound. It was found that without further training fear spread to white rabbit, and other white objects. This spread of fear response, we call stimulus generalization. When after initial conditioning to some stimulus, other similar stimuli can also operate in calling out the same response, the process is called stimulus generalization. Child learns the worked "daddy" in the presence of a given stimulus. He emits the same word to other stimuli i.e., other men, old or young. It takes further conditioning to narrow down the response 'daddy' to one specific stimulus. Out of this process of generalization, fire discrimination take place.

Differentiation and Discrimination

In discrimination, the emphasis is placed on the stimulus side but in differentiation, the emphasis is placed on the response side. In discrimination, through selective reinforcement, we eliminate the responses to other stimuli. In differentiation, through selective reinforcement of one of a number of related responses, we develop a very specific type of response in the presence of some stimuli. The two processes of operate simultaneously in our personality development.

6. *Concept Learning*

A concept in the form of a mental image denotes a generalized idea about a thing, person or phenomenon. For example, our concept of a tree is a mental image that brings to our mind similarities or common properties of all different trees we know. We will call a thing a tree when it has some specific characteristics of the image of which we already acquired in our mind on account of our previous experience, perception or rich imagination. The formation of such on account of such previous experience, training or cognitive process, is called concept learning. Such type of concept learning proves very significant in recognizing, naming and identifying things. Thus what we do, say, understand, reason, and judge is to a great extent controlled by the quality of our concept learning.

We form concept by finding properties which a class of objects shares in common. We learn generalization within classes and discrimination between classes. For example, we generalize within the dogs class of objects to include those of various shapes, size, colour, but we discriminate them from the class of objects like horse, tree, house, etc.

7. *Learning of Principles*

Learning of principles depends on learning of concept formation and other forms of learning. Principles show regular relationship among two or more concepts. There are a large number of principles that every individual masters in order to function properly in the environment. Principles of grammar, science and mathematics are learned to work more efficiently. Most of the classroom learning contribute to the development of principles.

8. *Problem-Solving*

Problem-solving comes at the highest stage in the hierarchy of learning process. It depends on learning of rules. Such a type of learning requires the use of the cognitive abilities such as reasoning, thinking, power of observation, generalization, information ability to infer and draw conclusion, trying out novel ways and experimentally etc. Based on the ground of earlier experience, effect of coaching, training, formal or informal learning and acquisition of knowledge, habits, attitude, interest and learning get an individual motivated to reach an unknown target or unfolding the mystery of an unsolved problem. How he can accomplish such taste is the function of problem-solving. This type of learning has essentially caused human beings to contribute significantly to the progress of an improvement of society.

Gagne's Revised/Reduced Hierarchy of Learning

Later in the year 1975, Gagne reduced the steps of his hierarchy from eight to six.

1. *Chining:* All the first-four steps in his early hierarchy of learning come under this chaining. That is chaining the response meaning fully and systematically by connecting more and more S–R Bonds. Behaviour arranged is a systematic way.
2. *Multiple Discrimination:* Helps individual to discriminate and differentiate between various, similar and also to give different response to different and similar stimuli. Mental process of comparing of attributes take place.
3. *Concrete Concept:* The concept are formed from concrete things by seeing and observing only the observable things. Ability to form concepts from concrete objects.
4. *Defined Concept:* The individual develops the ability to define concepts in his own words. At this stage he must be able to define concepts in his own words without the presence of the object. He must also be able to define the concepts of abstract things.
5. *Rule Learning/Principle Learning:* If the individual is able to chain more than one abstract concept and form a rule, than it is principle learning. That is here the individual begins to link the different concepts.
6. *Higher Order Principle (Problem-Solving):* Applying the previously learned principle in solving the problems.

Gagne's Systematic Perhaps Strategy or Mastery Learning

Teacher should begin the class from the end or final goal and should proceed back towards the beginning. Gagne says that after introducing the concept the teacher should start testing the previous knowledge. For example, to teach the topic 'Density' the teacher should verify whether the students have concept about mass and volume at the principle learning level. If he does not posses that he is required to look for previous knowledge at lower level of the hierarchy. The teacher should continue this process. He should begin the class from the point where he gets a positive answer.

Suggestions of Gagne to Facilitate Mastery Learning

The mastery learning basically involves three tracks; the main line track, the enrichment line track and the alternative or corrective line track. The instruction begin with establishing an objective and presenting students. If the students is to be in the main line track, the pre-assessment will have to establish that the student has to satisfied the pre-requisite or entry behaviour skills and the students is not familiar with the skills or objectives of the unit of instruction. In mastery learning the student engage in enrichment through one of two channels. The first channel issued when the pre-assessment shows the student already can exhibit mastery of objective one. Hence, the student can move on to additional objective in the unit engage in depth studies or engage in peer-tutoring.

The second channel is the enrichment track is formed after the primary instruction and successful completion of the formative evaluation. At this point the student is on the main line but as presented earlier, if appropriate materials are available and time permits the student could engage in some enrichment activity prior to taking a summative evaluation or proceeding a following objective:

For the effectiveness of mastery learning Gagne's made certain suggestion for teachers. They are:

1. Well-defined objectives.
2. Availability of pre-requisite necessary for learning as particular aspects.
3. Keen attention in the educational process resulting from strong motivation.
4. Re-inforcement resulting from the feeing of success.
5. Immediate knowledge of results obtained from feeling of success.

He gave more importance for the second condition availability of pre-requisite necessary for learning as a particular aspect. According to Gagne testing the previous knowledge in the pre-requisite for mastery learning.

The key concept used by Gagne are thinking (linking) and pre-requisite (previous knowledge).

Conclusion

In Gagne's hierarchy of learning Gagne points out that each step is important and each follows the one proceeding it. He also believes that there may be higher or more than these learning type. Schramuma has rightly observed "most learning is hierarchical, one step must be taken before another which can successfully be accomplished and all the simply type of learning are subsumed under the more complex forms."

REFERENCES

1. Atkilson and Hilgard – *Introduction to Psychology.*
2. Ausubel, D. P. and Fitzgerald, D.(1962). Organizer, general background, and antecedent learning variables in sequential verbal learning, *Journal of Educational Psychology.*
3. Ausubel, D.P. (1962). A Subsumption Theory of Meaningful Verbal Learning & Retention. *The Journal of General Psychology.*
4. Berk – *Development Psychology.*
5. Berkely Calif and Mc Cutchan (1977). *Learning and Instruction.*
6. Brainerd, C. (1978). *Piaget's Theory of Intelligence.* Englewood Cliffs, NJ:
7. Chauhan, S.S. (2002). *Advanced Educational Psychology.* New Delhi: Vikas Publishing House (P.) Ltd.
8. Crow, L.D.T. Crow Alice (1964). *Human Development and Learning.*
9. De Cecco., P. John & Crowford William, R. (1988). *The Psychology of Learning and Instruction-Educational Psychology* (2nd Ed), New Delhi: Prentice Hall Ltd.
10. Dennis Coon (1998) – *Introduction to Psychology – Exploration and Application.* Brooks/Cole Publishing Company ; ITP.
11. Driscoll, Mercy P (1994). *Psychology of Learning for Instruction – Needham, Ma:* Allgn & Bacon.
12. Feist and Leist (2002) – *Theories of Personality* – Mc Grawhill – Higher Education.
13. Fernald/Fernald (2001). *Introduction to Psychology* (V Edition).
14. Flavell, J.H. (1963). *The Developmental Psychology of Jean Piaget,* New York.
15. Gagne, R.M. (1970). *The Conditions of Learning* (II Edition), New York 1970.
16. Gari, R. – *The Psychology of Learning.*
17. Good, Thomas L. and Brophy, Jere E.(1990). *Educational Psychology. A Realistic Approach,* New York: Longman.
18. Hansfather, Samuel, J. (1996). *Vygotsky and Schooling: Creating a School Concept for Learning.*
19. Hilgard, R. (1956). *Theories of Learning.*
20. Ivie, Stanley D.(1998). Ausubel's Learning Theory. An Approach to Teaching Higher Order Thinking Skills. *High School Journal.*
21. James, W. Kalat (1993). *Biological Psychology,* V Edn. Books & Cole.
22. Joyce Bruce, Weil Marcha & Showers Beverly (1992). *Models of Teaching.* New Delhi: Prentice Hall of India (P) Ltd.
23. L. Bodge Fernald and Peter S Fernald (2004). *Introduction to Psychology.* AITBS Publishers and Distributors.

24. Lewin, K. (1935). *A Dynamic Theory of Personality*, New York.
25. Lewin, K. (1936). *Principles of Topological Psychology.*
26. Lewin, K. (1948). *Resolving Social Conflicts: Selected Papers on Group Dynamics*. Gertrude W.
27. Lewin, K. (1951). *Field Theory in Social Science; Selected Theoretical Papers.* D. Cartwright (ed). New York.
28. Mangal, S.S. (2000). *Educational Psychology*. Ludhiana: Prakash Brothers.
29. Miller, P.H. (1999). *Theories of Developmental Psychology* U.S.A – W.H.Freeman and Company.
30. Munn, N.L. *et. al* (1967). *Introduction to Psychology*, New Delhi: Oxford & IBH Publishing Co. (P). Ltd.
31. Pervin Lawrance, A. (1984). *Personality*. New York: Wiley.
32. Piaget, J. (1929). *The Child's Conception of the World*, New York.
33. Piaget, J. (1932). *The Moral Judgement of the Child*, New York.
34. Piaget, J. (1969). *The Mechanisms of Perception*, London.
35. Piaget, J. (1970). *The Science of Education and The Psychology of the Child.*
36. Piaget, J. & Inhelder, B. (1969). *The Psychology of the Child*, New York.
37. Piaget, J. & Inhelder, B. (1973). *Memory and Intelligence.*
38. Prof. Dandapani – *'A Test Book on Advanced Educational Psychology'*.
39. Rama, S., Anandan, Anil, R. & Nambiar, B. (2005, July). *Psycho-Pedagogy*. Paper presented at the seminar on Psychological Foundations of Education, DAMTEC, Calicut.
40. Rober, A. Baron – *Psychology* (V Edition).
41. Robert, S. Feldman – *Understanding Psychology* (IV Edition).
42. Robert A. Baron (2001) – *Psychology, Pearson* – Education.
43. Robert. F. Biehler – *Psychology.*
44. Southwell, E.A. and Merbaum, M. (1964). *Personality, Readings in Theory and Research*, Wadsworth Publishing House.
45. Thope, J. and L.P. Schmuller (1958). *Personality: An Inter Disciplinary Approach*. D. Van Nostrand Co.
46. Vygotsky, L.S. (1978). *Mind and Society. The Development of Higher Psychological Process*. Cambridge; Harward University Press.
47. Wertsch, James. V. Sohmer, Richard (1995). *Vygotsky on Learning and Development*. Human Development.
48. Willam S. Sahakian – *Theory of Learning.*

MODEL QUESTIONS

1. Explain the concept of ZPD.
2. Enumerate the learning outcomes according to Gagne.
3. List the instructional events and corresponding cognitive process in Gagne's theory.
4. Illustrate Gagne's hierarchy of Learning.
5. Explain Gagne's hierarchy of Learning with an example. How this

hierarchy is useful for student teachers?
6. Which are the important principles put forward by Vygotsky?
7. What are the implications of Vygotskian view point?
8. Give a brief explanation to scaffolding and reciprocal teaching.
9. Define Classical Conditioning.
10. What is the educational implication of experimental neurosis?
11. Distinguish between stimulus generalisation and stimulus discrimination.
12. How extinction differ from spontaneous recovery in classical conditioning?
13. Describe briefly the relevance of classical conditioning in education?
14. Explain Parlov's experiment with classroom implications.
15. Comment on revised Law of Effect.
16. Define Law of Readiness.
17. How Law of Exercise is useful for teachers?
18. Explain the principles of learning based on Thorndike's experiment.
19. Describe briefly the supplementary laws of learning.
20. Explain Thorndike's theory of learning with special emphasis on classroom implications.
21. Define Operant Conditioning.
22. Distinguish punishment from Negative reinforcement.
23. Differentiate between punishment and omission training.
24. Discuss how Operant Conditioning is useful for PSI.
25. Explain shaping with an example.
26. Suggest an instructional programme based on operant conditioning theory of B.F. Skinner and explain it.
27. Explain Instrumental Conditioning theory of B.F. Skinner with special emphasis on classroom implication.
28. What according to Bandura are the characteristics of human beings?
29. Differentiate between Observational learning and Enactive learning.
30. Explain the various steps in the vicarious learning process.
31. List-out the educational implications of social learning theory.

5
Remembering and Forgetting

MEMORY

Memory is an active system that receives, stores, organises, alters and recovers information.

How Does Memory Work?

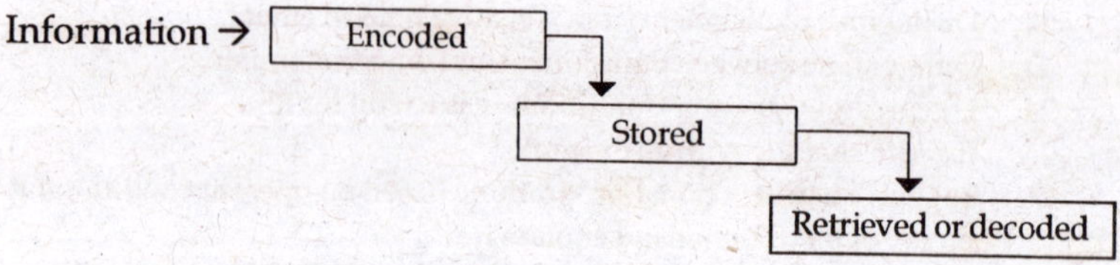

- Encode – to represent information in some form in the memory system.
- Store – to keep in the system.
- Decode – take out from the storage (Retrieve).
- According to Woodworth the four main aspects involved in memory are learning, retention, recall and recognition.
  - Learning – the acquisition of new experience.
  - Retention – The process of preserving the material learnt.
  - Recall – The revival of memorised thing.
  - Recognition – the awareness of the experience by which we identify the material retained and recalling.

The Three Stages of Memory

I. ***Stage***

Sensory Register: Holds an exact copy of what is seen or heard for a few seconds or less.

II. *Stage*

Short-Term Memory (STM): Acts as a temporary store house for small amounts of information.

III. *Stage*

Long-Term Memory(LTM): Acts as a permanent store house for meaningful information.

- *Procedural Memory*: Memory for motor movements and skills. Example: how to ride a bicycle, to cook etc.
- *Semantic Memory*: Memory for meaning without reference to the time and place of learning.
- *Episodic Memory*: Memory for specific experiences.

FORGETTING

It is the inability to recollect previously learned aspects. Hermann Ebbinghaus (1885) developed lists of nonsense syllables and memorized them. Later he tested his memory. Ebbinghaus wanted to be sure he would not be swayed by prior learning, so he memorised non-sense syllables. These are meaningless three – letter words such as GEX, CEF and WOL.

By waiting various lengths of time before testing himself, Ebbinghaus plotted a curve of forgetting. This graph shows the amount of information remembered after varying lengths of time. This is an averaged curve of his research.

Notice that forgetting is rapid immediately after learning and is then followed by a slow decline Curve shows that less than 30 per cent is remembered after two days have passed.

Implication

Before winding up the class, an immediate revision is needed. This should be followed by periodical revisions.

Theories of Forgetting

The Trace Decay Theory

- Forget with the lapse of time.
- Learning results in neurological changes, leaving certain memory traces or engrams in the brain. Through disuse these

memory traces get weaker and finally fade away (Thorndike's law of exercise is associated with this).

The Interference Theory

- It is the inhibiting effect of interpolated learning
- Two types of interference – *(a)* Retroactive inhibition and *(b)* Proactive inhibition.
- In retroactive inhibition, information currently being learned interferes with information already present in memory – Inability to recall past.
- In proactive inhibition old learning or experiences retained in our memory works forward to disrupt the memory of what we learn afterwards – Inhibit the recall of present.

Educational Implications

1. Ensure degree of thoroughness of learning.
2. Dissimilar tasks should be introduced in the time-table.
3. Highlight distinctly, the difference in almost similar tasks.

The Repression Theory (Motivated Forgetting)

- It is a mental function which cushions the mind against the impact of painful experiences.
- Through repression, painful, threatening or embarrassing memories are held out of consciousness by forces within one's personality.
- It is a form of avoidance.
- It is a psycho-analytical theory.

Educational Implications

Learning should be a pleasurable experience to the pupils

Major Causes of Forgetting

Learner Factors

1. Physical health
2. Interest & motivation
3. Emotional aspects
4. Mental conflict
5. Intoxication
6. Lack of maturation

Failure to encode

Learning Factors

1. Methods of learning
2. Interference
3. Lack of learning
4. Time of learning
5. Absence of cues

Nature of the Content

1. Complexity of the task.
2. Lack of organisation of the content.
3. Meaninglessness of the content.

Measures to Check Forgetting (Improving Memory)

1. Knowledge of results – This helps one to identify ideas that need extra practice.
2. Recitation
3. Rehearsal
4. Selection – Practice very selective marking in texts and use marginal notes to further summarize ideas.
5. Organisation – Reordering make learning more effective.
6. Whole versus part learning.
7. Serial position – Try to break long lists of information into short sub-lists, and make the middle sub-lists the shortest of all.
8. Cues – (Stimuli that aid retrieval).
9. Over learning.
10. Spaced practice – try alternating short study sessions with brief rest periods.
11. Sleep – sleeping after study reduces interference.
12. Review – Review is like an icing on the study cake.
13. Mnemonics – Memory magic.

A mnemonics is any kind of memory system or aid. Mnemonic strategies increase recall tenfold.

The Basic Principles of Mnemonics

1. Use mental pictures.
2. Make things meaningful.
3. Make information familiar.
4. Form bizarre, unusual or exaggerated mental associations –
   - The more outrageous and exaggerated the association, the more likely you are to remember.
   - Bizarre images mainly help to improve immediate memory.

Mnemonics can be Used to Remember Things in Order – 3 Techniques

1. Form a chain
   - Connect the first item to the second, then second to the third and so on.
2. Take a mental walk
   - Associate topics with the images we see around (Method of loci).

3. Use a system
   - The first letters or syllables of words or ideas can be formed into another word that will serve as a reminder of order e.g., *Vibgyor.*
   - If your are trying to remember how many days there are in a month. We get the answer by reciting, 'thirty days.

(People can extend their memory through the use of mnemonics. Mnemonics only supplement the memory tips given earlier. They are most effective for short-term memory. If pupils employ the principles of mnemonics, they can retain more.)

Conclusion

People who have good memories excel at organizing information and making it meaningful. The above mentioned aspects tell one, how to combine organization and meaning into a powerful method or improving memory.

REFERENCES

1. Benjamin, B. Lahey (1998). *Psychology—An Introduction.* McGraw Hill.
2. Dennis Coon (1998). *Introduction to Psychology: Exploration and Application.* Brooks/Cole Publishing Company; ITP.
3. Joyee and Weil (1997). *Models of Teaching.* Prentice Hall of India Pvt. Ltd.
4. Rama, S., Anandan, Anil, R. & Nambiar, B. (2005, July). *Psycho-pedagogy.* Paper presented at the Seminar on Psychological Foundations of Education, DAMTEC, Calicut.
5. Robert. S. Feldman (2002). *Understanding Psychology.* Tata McGraw Hill Publishing Company Ltd.

MODEL QUESTIONS

1. Explain the curves of forgetting.
2. What are the implications of Ebbinghan's experiment?
3. Which are the two types of interference?
4. What are the educational implications of the interference theory?
5. List out the major causes of forgetting.
6. Explain the basic principles of mnemonics.
7. What is memory?
8. How does memory work?
9. Which are the three stages of memory?
10. Explain the different types of memory.

6

Learner's Personality

In educational world the term 'personality' has a wide significance. Education is considered with an all-round development of the personality of a child, therefore, it is quite essential for a pupil teacher to know about the term personality.

Meaning of Personality

The term personality has been derived from the Latin world 'persona' that was associated with Greek theatre in ancient times, persona was meant a mask which the Greek actors commonly used. Psychologically speaking personality is all that a person is. It is the totality of one's behaviour towards oneself and others as well. It includes everything about the person, his physical, emotional, social, mental and spiritual wake-up. It is all that a person has about him.

Definition

G.W. Allport; "Personality is a dynamic organization with in the individual of those psycho-physical systems that determine his unique adjustment to his environment."

Personality and Its Popular Meanings

According to A. Jones personality consists of thc following:

1. The way you look.
2. The way you dress.
3. The way you talk.
4. The way you act.
5. The skill with which you do things.
6. The way you maintain your health.

Some General Characteristics of Personality

1. It is continues.
2. It is a product of heredity and environment.
3. It is a product inner aspects and outer ones.
4. It is unique.
5. It has two functions-overt and convert.
6. It is dynamic.
7. It has certain conscious and certain unconscious motivation.
8. It functions as a whole.
9. It is the end product of learning.

Nature of Personality

1. Each person is first an individual by inheritance and then acquires a personality by growing in a social world.
2. Personality is one's total integrated behaviour and not just one or more aspects of behaviour.
3. The word 'personality' stands for a concept which is determined by a person's social stimulus value.
4. Personality is not something static like colour or height, but the totality or unity or an individuals action.
5. Personality does not merely unfold; a person uses his capacities to make adaptations in the social world.
6. Personality is a social concept.
7. Personality is a dynamic concept.
8. Personality is all that a person.
9. As personality is the end-product of one's heredity and environment, which is different can individual; it is something unique and distinct.

Distinguishing Features and Characteristics of Personality

1. Personality is something unique and specific.
2. Personality exhibits self-consciousness as one of its main characteristics.
3. Personality is not just a collection of many traits or characteristics.
4. The personality of an individual remains stable to a large extent, it cannot be said to be static, it is dynamic and continuously in the process of change and modification.
5. Personality is sometimes subjected to disorganization and disintegration.

6. Learning and acquisition of experiences contribute towards growth and development of personality.
7. The personality can be described and measured.
8. Personality may be further distinguished from temperament. Which can be termed a system of emotional disposition.
9. Personality should also be viewed differently from the ego or the individual self.
10. Every person's personality include a distinguishing feature.

Factors Determining Personality

The factors affecting personality can be divided into two classes.

1. Biological and
2. Social.

The biological factors affecting the development of personality are of three types.

1. Ductless Glands: Pancreas, Thyroid, Adrenal, Pituitary glands and Gonads.
2. Physique.
3. Body Chemistry.

Some other general factors are:

1. Genetic factors.
2. Environmental factors.
3. Personal Response.

Social Determinants

1. Influence of home on personality.
2. Influence of school on personality.
3. Influence of society on personality.
4. Parental Attitude.
5. Size of family and birth order.

Theories of Personality

1. *Type of Theory* : Ernest Kretschemer, Dr. William, H. Sheldon, E. Spranger, Carl, J. Jung, Sigmond Freud.
2. *Trait Theories*: G.W. Allport, R.B. Cattel, H.J. Eysenck, J.B. Guilford.
3. *Psycho-Analytic Theories*: Sigmond Freud, Jung, Otto Rank

(1884-1949), Erich Fromm (1900), Karen Horney, Harry Stack Sullivan (1892-1949) and Erikson Alfred Adler (1870-1937).

4. *Phenomenological theories*: Abraham Maslow, Henry, A. Murray, Karl Rogers, George Kelly, Kurt Lewin.
5. *Learning Theory of Personality*: Dollard, Millar.
6. *Social Behavioural Theory*: Albert Bandura, Walters (Observational Learning Theory).
7. J.B. Rotter's Expectancy – reinforcement model.

Methods of Assessing Personality

- Subjective Methods
- Objective Methods
- Projective Methods

Subjective Methods

- Auto Biography
- Observation
- Case History
- Interview
- Inventory

Objective Method

- Questionnaire
- Rating Scale
- Socio-metry

Projective Method

- Rorschach Test
- T.A.T.
- C.A.T.
- Picture Drawing
- Story Telling
- Sentence Completion
- Word Associ-ation

Difficulties in the Measurement of Personality

Measurement of personality depends upon the factors mentioned below:

1. The nature of the thing we want to measure.
2. Nature of the instruments with the help of which we have to measure it.
3. Nature of the person who is going to measure.

An impressive personality is often taken to be synonymous with good appearance, healthy physique, pleasing manners, a good character, a pleasant temperament etc. Although personality includes all these aspects of one's self, it is far beyond each or even the sum of all these attributes. It may be defined as a complex blend of a constantly evolving and changing pattern of a persons unique behaviour, emerged as a result of his interaction with his environment, directed towards some specific ends in view.

TYPE AND TRAIT THEORIES OF PERSONALITY

The search for understanding the meaning and nature of personality would be incomplete if we do not discuss some important theories of personality. These theories in one way or another, try to describe the basic structure and underlying entities or constructs involves in personality along with the processes by which these entities interact. The theories of personality in general can be classified in the following broad categories:

- Theories adopting the type approach – Hippocrates, Kretschmer, Sheldon and Jung.
- Trait Approach – Allport, Cattel.
- Trait-cum-type approach – H.J. Eysenck.
- Psycho-analytical approach – Freud, Adler, Jung Horney, Erickson.
- Humanistic Approach – Carl Rogers, Maslow.
- Learning approach – Dolland, Miller, Bandura, Walter.

Type Approach

Hippocrates Classification: The human body consists of the four types of homousius or fluids – The predominance of one of these four types of fluids in one's body gives him unique characteristics leading to a particular personality.

Table-6.1
Hippocrates Classification of Personality

Dominance of Fluid Type in the Body	*Personality Type*	*Temperamental Characteristics*
Blood	Sanguine	Light hearted, optimistic, happy hopeful and accomoding.
Yellow Bile	Choleric	Irritable angry but passionate and strong with active imagination.
Phelgm (Mucus)	Phlegmatic	Cold, calm, slow, sluggish and indifferent.
Black Bile	Melan cholic	Bad tempered, dejected, sad depressed, pessimistic, deplorable and self-involved.

Kretschmer's Classification

Table–6.2
Kretschmer's Classification of Personality

Personality Types	*Personality Characteristics*
Pykmic (having fat bodies)	Sociable, Jolly, easy going and good natured.
Athletic (Balanced Body)	Energetic, Optimistic and Adjustable.
Leptosomatic (lean and thin)	Unsociable, reserved, shy, sensitive and pessimistic.

Sheldon's Classification

Table–6.3
Sheldon's Classification of Personality

Personality Types	*Somatic Description*	*Personality Characteristics*
Endomorphic	Person having highly developed viscera but weak somatic structure (like Kretschmer's Athletic type)	Easy going, sociable and affentionate.
Mesomorphic	Balanced development of viscera and somatic structure (like Kretschmer's Athletic type)	Craving for on muscular activity, self-assertive, loves risk and adventure.
Ectomorphic	Weak somatic structure as well as undeveloped viscera (like Kretschmer's Leptosomatic)	Pessimistic, unsociable and reserved.

Cattel's Theory (1973)

1. *Common Traits*—General population, honesty, aggression, co-operative.
2. *Unique Traits*—Temperamental traits, emotional reactions.
3. *Surface Traits*—Manifestations of behaviour—curiosity dependability, factfulness.
4. *Source Traits*—Underlying structures or sources that determine behaviour such as dominance, submission, emotionality etc.

The most recent advanced theory of personality based on the trait approach has been developed by Cattel (1973) a British born American researcher. He was defined a trait as a structure of personality interred from behaviour in different situations and described four types of traits above mentioned. The theory propagated by Cattel attributes certain specific dimensions to personality so that the human behaviour related to a particular situation, can be predicted. Cattel has adopted factor analysis as a technique for this work. Let us see how this is done.

1. Made a complete list of all human behaviours.
2. Assertain how they are related. He identified 35 specific groups and call them *Surface traits*.
3. Eliminated those which were overlapping. The removal of such over lapping gave his the desired basic dimensions which he called *Source traits*.
4. After obtaining the source traits he tried to use them to predict behaviour employing what is called the specification question.

$$\text{Response} = S_1T_1 + S_2T_2 + S_3T_3 + \ldots\ldots S_nT_n$$

The response of an individual is thus predicted from the degree to which he exhibits each source Trait (T) modified by the importance of the trait for that response(s).

Suppose e.g., that Academic Performance (AP) is predictable from two source traits namely Intelligence (I) and the Reading habits (R), then

$$AP = S_1I + S_2R$$

Now also suppose that Intelligence (I) is more importance for this behaviour than Reading habits (R) in the ratio of 5:3; this may be expressed as:

$$AP = 0.51 + 0.3R$$

Thus in order to predict the Academic Performance (AP) of an individual we need to know his scores on intelligence and reading habits.

The 16 basic or source trait dimensions were named as *factors*. These factors as the building block of personality, i.e., the characteristics in terms of which one's personality can be described and measured.

TYPE-CUM-TRAIT APPROACH – H.J. EYSENCK

This approach tries to synthesize the type and trait approaches H.J. Hysenck a German-born British psychologist, went a step further in the adopting factor analysis technique by extracting second order factors and grouping traits into definite personality types.

Table–6.4
Cattel's Theory—Traits and Factors

Symbols	*Traits*		*Name of the Factors*
A	Reserved (detached, critical, aloof, stiff)	v/s	Outgoing (warmhearted, easy going, participating)
B	Less intelligent (concrete thinking)	v/s	More intelligent (abstract thinking, bright)
C	Affected by feelings (emotionally less stable, easily up set, changeable)	v/s	Emotionally stable (mature, faces, reality, calm)
E	Submissive (mild, easily led, docile, accomodating)	v/s	Dominant (aggressive, stubborn, competitive)
F	Serious (sober, taciturn)	v/s	Happy-go-Lucky (enthusiastic)
G	Expedient (disregards rules)	v/s	Conscientious (persistent, moralistic, staid)
H	Timid (shy, fears, threat, sensitive)	v/s	Venturesome (uninhibited, socially bold).
I	Tough-minded (self-reliant, realistic)	v/s	Tender-hearted (sensitive, clinging, over protected)
L	Trusting (accepting conditions)	v/s	Suspicious (hard to fool)
M	Practical (down-to-earth concerns)	v/s	Imaginative (bohemian, absentminded)
N	Forthright (unpretentious, genuine but socially clumsy)	v/s	Shrewd (socially aware, astute)
O	Self-assured (secure, placid, complacent)	v/s	Apprehensive (self-critical, insecure, worrying, troubled).
Q_1	Conservative (respecting traditional ideas)	v/s	Experimenting (liberal, free-thinking)
Q_2	Group-dependent (a "joiner" and sound follower)	v/s	Self-sufficient (resourceful, prefers own decisions).
Q_3	Uncontrolled (careless of social social rules, follows own urges)	v/s	Controlled (socially precise, exercising will power, compulsive)
Q_4	Relaxed (tranquil, unfrustrated, composed)	v/s	Tense (frustrated, driven, overwrought)

How individual behaviour is organized and acquires the shape of a definite type is revealed by the following illustration:

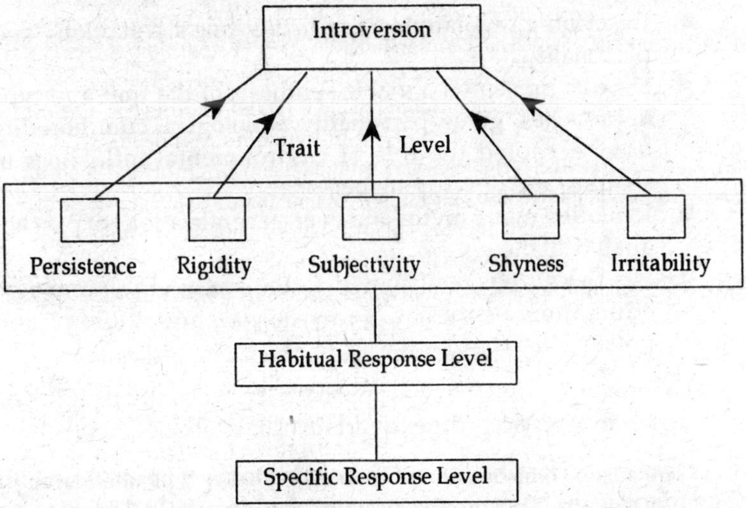

Fig. 6.1: Organization of Individual Behaviour – H.J. Eysenck.

According to Eysenck, there are four levels of behaviour organization:

1. At the lowest level are the specific responses e.g., Blushing.
2. Habitual responses from the second level and comprise similar responses of an individual, to similar situations e.g., inability to easily strike friendships.
3. Organizations of habitual acts into traits.
   Behaviour acts which have similarities are said to belong to one groups and are called traits e.g., give birth to a group of traits called 'shyness'.
4. Organization of these traits in to a general type.

A type is defined as a group of correlated traits. Traits which are similar in nature give birth to a definite type just as the above figure, and traits like pessistance, rigidity, shyness etc., have been grouped in to a type termed as *introversion*.

The three basic dimensions (defined as clusters or groups of correlated traits) derived by Eysenck through his work are:

1. Introversion-Extroversion

2. Neuroticism – (emotional instability-emotional stability).
3. Psychoticism, introvest, extrovest, neurotic, psychotic.

The Contributions of Eysenck's Theory

- Describing, explaining, predicting one's behaviour and personality.
- He was presented a viable synthesis of the trait and type approaches, given personality a biological cum heredity base, accepted the role of environmental influences in shaping and developing personality.
- Exploded many myths and over-generalizations of psycho-analytical theory.
- His theory has contributed to the study of criminology, education, aesthetics, genetics, psychopathology and political ideology.

Theories adopting the type approach try to classify people into categories or types according to certain characteristics.

Hippocrates classified people according to the type of humour or fluid found in the body. *Kretschmer* described specific biological types based on body structures. Sheldon also identified three distinct types based on the relationship between a person's body physique and behaviour. Jung also adopted the type approach in classifying people in terms of introversion and extroversion.

Theories based on the trait approach try to describe people in terms of their unique pattern of traits. They define traits as relatively permanent and relatively consistant general behaviour patterns which an individual exhibits in different situations. Notable among these theories are the personality theories of Allport and Cattel.

Eysenck's theory of personality is based on a trait cum type approach towards personality and starting with the traits it yielded definite personality type.

PSYCHO-ANALYSIS – FREUD'S SYSTEM OF PSYCHOLOGY

Sigmund Freud (1856-1939)

For many, Freud is the best known figure in psychology. His theory of personality focuses on three major concepts: id, ego and superego. Freud believed that psychological problems result from early life experiences. His psycho-analytic approach to therapy is still used today, mainly by psychiatrists.

The psycho-analytic approach to personality was first created and advocated by Sigmond Freud by viewing people as being engaged in a constant struggle to fame with their biological urges. He was a viennese physician. He propagated analysis of the psyche or mind by coining many new terms and used psycho-analysis as a method for understanding behaviour and for treating mental illness. His school of thought is known as the school of psycho-analysis and the approach it adopted for understanding human behaviour and personality is known as the psycho-analytical approach.

Freud's Psycho-analytic Theory of Personality

Freud's theory of personality is built on the premise that mind is topographical and dynamic; there are provinces or divisions which are always moving and interrelated. The human mind has three main divisions namely –

1. Conscious.
2. Sub-conscious.
3. Unconscious.

These three levels of the human mind are continuously in a state of clash and compromise to give birth to one or the other type of behavioural characteristics resulting in a specific type of personality.

The Concept of Conscious, Sub-conscious and Unconscious Mind

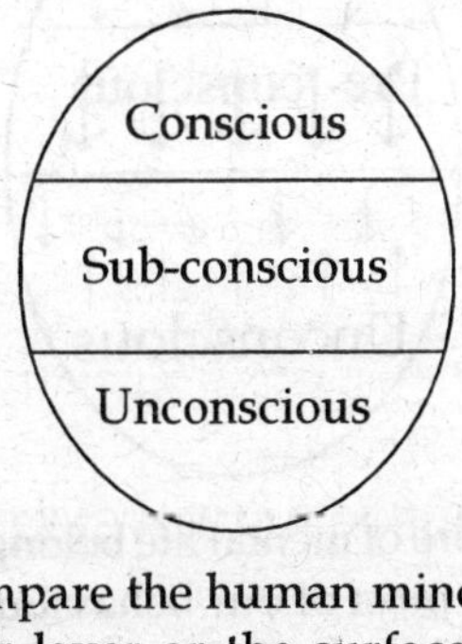

If we were to compare the human mind to an ocean, pond or river, then the upper layer or the surface would represent the conscious mind, the main bed would be identified with the sub-conscious/pre-conscious, and the bottom would form the unconscious.

The *conscious mind* lies just above the surface of the water like the tip of an ice-berg and occupies only 1/10th of our total psyche or mental life. The ideas, thoughts and images that we are aware of at any moment of our mental life are said to life within this upper layer.

Just beneath the conscious mind/layer lies the *sub-conscious mind.* This middle portion of our mind stores all types of information just beneath the surface of awareness dormant or untapped which can be easily brought to the level of consciousness of a moment's notice whenever required. Thus in the middle bed or layer of the human mind there lie all experiences or knowledge which have been gained or learned by an individual through various types of experiences or training.

Below the sub-conscious mind lies the *unconscious,* the most important part of our mind. It is related to the vast part of our mental life which is hidden and usually in accessible to the conscious. It contains all the repressed wishes desires, feelings, drives and motives, many of which relate to sex and aggression. All these repressed and forbidden desires and ideas are not destined to lie permanently in the unconscious. They usually strive and agitate to come up to the sub-conscious or the conscious layers of the mind, sometimes in disguised forms, in dreams and reveries.

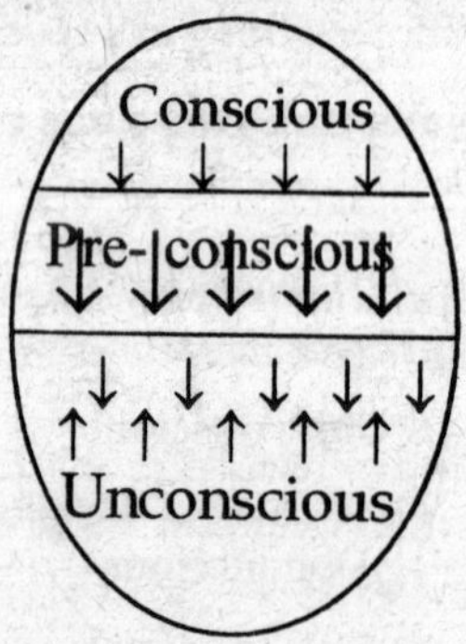

This hidden pressure of mental life belonging to the unconscious is thus responsible for most of our behaviour and in fact, as Freud asserts what we do and how we behave is always determined by the forces residing in our conscious and not by the choices of the conscious mind. Not to speak of normal behaviour the causes and forms of abnormal behaviour and mental illness, are also decided by what is hidden in the unconscious and, therefore, the task of the psychotherapist consists of a search for the relevant in the unconscious and bringing it up in to the conscious.

The Concept of Id, Ego and Super Ego

Freud also believes that the anatomy of our personality is built around the three unified and inter-relating systems, namely Id, Ego and Super Ego.

Structure of the human mind compared to an ice-berg (in the figure the blank area represents the conscious, the doted area indicates the subconscious and the dark area shows the unconscious).

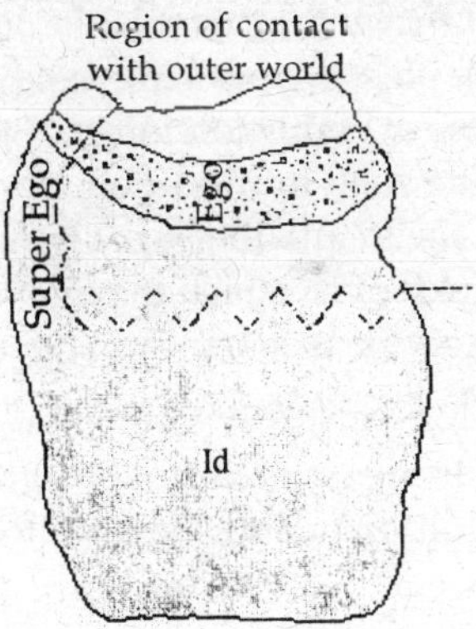

Fig. 6.2: Froeud's Concept of Id, Ego and Super Ego.

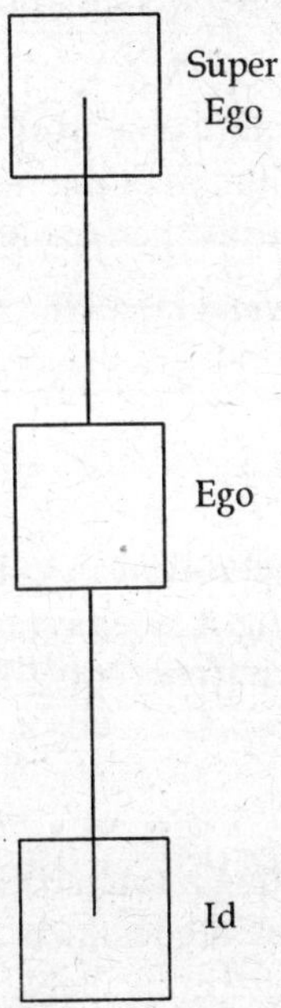

Relative Position of Id, Ego and Super Ego

The *Id* is the raw, savage and immoral basic stuff of man's personality that is hidden in the deep layers of his conscious mind; it consists of such ambitions, desires, tendencies and appetites as are guided by the pleasure seeking principle. It has no values, knows no laws, follows no rules, does not recognize right or wrong as considers only the satisfaction of its needs and appetites to be paramount.

Obviously, the Id cannot be allowed to dominate and so a second system, *The Ego*, functions as a policeman, to check the unlawful activities of the Id. It is the executive unit with the power of veto. It follows the principle of reality and acts with intelligence to control, select and decide what appetites have to be satisfied and in which way they may be satisfied.

Super Ego: It is the ethical or moral arm of the personality. It is idealistic and does not care realities. Perfection rather than pleasure is its goal. It is a decision-making entity which decides what is good or bad to the social norms and therefore acceptable or otherwise.

Freud put forward a dynamic concept of personality by conceptualizing the continues conflict among the Id, Ego and Super Ego. While the Id operating on the pleasure principle, continuously presses for the immediate discharge of bodily tension, the Super Ego concerned with morality prohibits such gratification. Thus a war like situation is created between the Id and the Super Ego with the Ego attempting to mediate. The extent to which the Ego is able to discharge its responsibilities decides the personality make-up of the individual.

1. Individuals who have a strong or powerful Ego are said to have a strong or balanced personality because the Ego is capable of maintaining a balance between the Super Ego and the Id.
2. In case an individual possesses a weak ego, he is bound to have a maladjusted personality. Here two situations may arise.

In one situation, the Super Ego may be more powerful than the Ego, and so does not permit desirable fulfillment of the repressed wishes and impulses which results in a neurotic personality.

It, on the other hand, the Id is more powerful than the Ego, the individual may indulge in unlawful or immoral activities leading to the formation of the deliquent personality.

Psycho-Dynamics – Behavioural Process

How does the psyche system develop and operate in an individual for shaping his personality and determining his behaviour? The question can be answered through the following concepts – Life and Death Instincts – and views expressed by Freud.

Life and Death Instincts

Freud believed in the role of instinct in driving human behaviour. He postulated two main instincts namely the life instincts and the death instinct, as the source of all the psyche energy available in man.

One's life instinct is engaged in the service of one's life and its main aims are survival and the propagation of the species. It is manifested through sex and love. Freud gave the name 'Libido' to the driving force of the life instinct and made it synonymous with the sex urge and sexuality of human beings. The Libido believes in the pleasure principle. The sex urge or sex motive may be regarded as the dynamic force and centre of all human behaviour at all ages. All physical pleasure aroused from any of the organs in the body and through any functions, as advocated by Freud, is ultimately sexual in nature.

Death Instinct relates to the impulse for destruction. It is manifested through acts of aggression, cruelty and even of suicide. Freud held that when one's life instinct is not allowed to function or to govern one's behaviour, the death instinct comes in to the picture for operating behaviour. For example, when one not permitted to seek sexual gratification or derive pleasure, one is bound to lose one's balance, suffer frustration which may consequently lead to the destruction of one's self or of others.

Infantile Sexuality and Psycho-Sexual Development

According to Freud, sex is the life urge or fundamental motive in life. All physical pleasures arising from any of the organs or any of the functions are ultimately sexual in nature. Sexuality is not the characteristic only of the adults. Children from the very beginning have sexual desires also. This, he termed as 'infantile sexuality'. A child passes through the following different stages with respect to his psycho-sexual development.

Stages of Development of Personality

1.	The oral stage	–	0-1 year	Pre-Genital
2.	The anal stage	–	2-3 years	
3.	The phallic stage	–	4-5 years	
4.	The latency stage	–	6-12 years	Post-Genital
5.	The genital stage	–	13 + years	
6.	The adulthood			

1. *The Oral Stage:* The mouth represents the first sex organ for providing pleasure to the child. The beginning is made with the pleasure received from the mother's nipple or the bottle. Thereafter, the child derives pleasure by putting anything, candy, a stick, his own thumb etc., into his mouth.
2. *The Anal Stage:* At this stage, the interest of the child shifts from the mouth erogenous zone to the organs of elimination,

i.e., the anus or the urethra. He derives pleasure by holding back or letting go of the body's waste material through the anus or the urethra. This stage generally ranges from two to three years.

3. *The Phallic Stage:* This phase starts from the stage of four years with the shifting of the child's interest from the eliminating organs to the genitals. At this stage, children came to note the biological differences between the sexes and derive pleasure by playing with and manipulating the genital organs. This stage, according to Freud, may give rise to a number of complexes like deprivation and *Electra* complexes in girls and *Oedipus* complexes in boys. *The deprivation complex* is the result of the feeling generated in the minds of little girls that they have been deprived of the male organ by their mothers.

   Castration complex is generated in boys through their fear of being deprived of the male organs. Certainly as a result of threat received from elders that the organ would be cut-off if they did not give-up the habit of playing with it.

   About the *Oedipus and Electra* phases, Freud, says that they are the result of the sexual attraction or pleasure that children experience in the company of the parent of the same sex frustrates the desire, expresses his or her resentment and is not friendly to the boy or girl. The child may develop *Oedipus* or *Electra* complex by loving the opposite sex parent more and rather hating the like sex parent.
4. *The Latency Stage:* This period starts from six years in the case of girls and seven to eight years in the case of boys and extends upto the onset of puberty. At this stage, boys and girls prefer to be in the company of their own sex and even neglect or hate members of the opposite sex.
5. *The Genital Stage:* Puberty is the starting point of the genital stage. The adolescent boy and girl now feels a strange feeling of strong sensation in the genitals and attraction towards the members of the opposite sex. At this stage, they may feel pleasure by self-stimulation of the genitals, may fall in love with their ownself by taking interest in beautifying and adorning their bodies and may be drawn quite close to members of the opposite sex even to the extent of indulging in sexual inter course.

The Flow of Libido—Anxiety, Conflicts and Disintegration of Personality

Libido, the life maintaining energy which aims at seeking pleasure through sex gratification, may work as the determinant of one's personality make-up. In case the flow of this energy in terms of the satisfaction of the sexual urge is normal and satisfactory, the behviour remains satisfactory and normal. But in the case the flow is repressed, blocked or damned up, it ends not only in free floting anxiety but also gives birth to severe conflicts leading to mental illness and abnormal behaviour.

Psycho-Analysis as a Therapy

Psycho-analysis as a method (of studying behaviour) and a therapy (treating mental illness or abnormal behaviour) is said to involve steps like,

1. Establishing rapport with the subject.
2. Analysis of the behaviour of the subject to uncover the underlying causes of the abnormality by adopting technique like free association, dream analysis, and analysis of daily psychopathology.
3. Synthesis for restructuring and restoring the lost balance of the psyche.
4. Breaking the rappot in order to enable the patient to face the realities of life without the support of the analyst.

Criticism of Freud's System of Psycho-Analysis

Freud's system of psycho-analysis has been criticized mainly on the following grounds:

1. It treats mankind to be selfish, pleasure seeking and animal-like rather than social and humane.
2. It often overgeneralizes on the basis of a single study.
3. It over emphases the role of sex in human life.
4. It attaches too much importance to the role of the unconscious as a determinant of behaviour.
5. It exaggerates the role of early childhood experiences for setting out the course of one's life.

Contribution to Education

1. It has given a good method for the study of Behaviour.

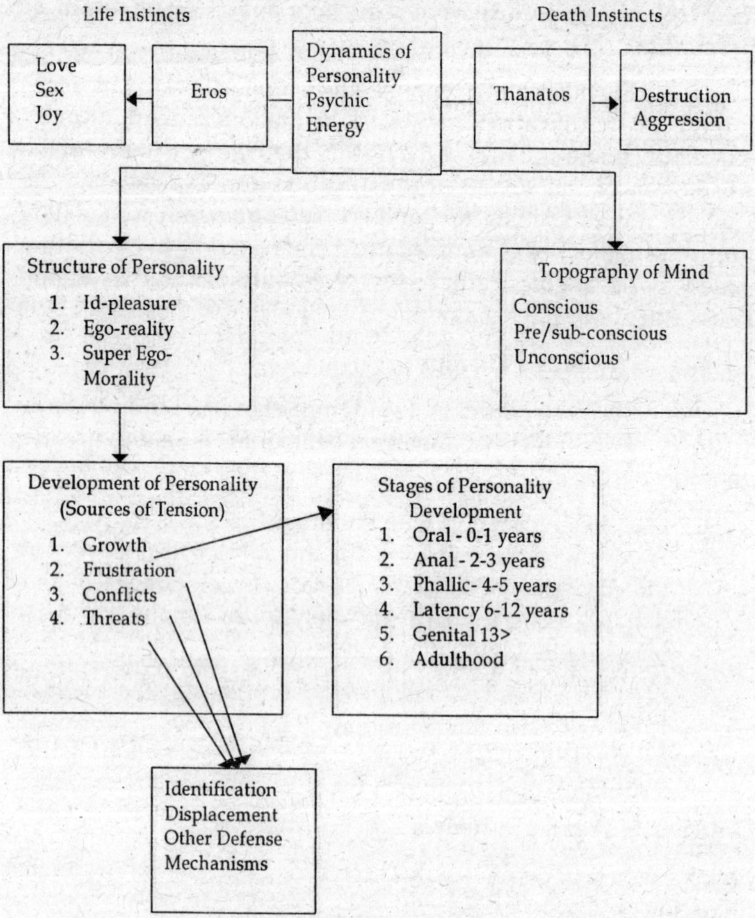

Fig. 6.3: Diagramatic Representation of Freud's Psycho-Analytic Theory.

2. It has provided a good therapy for treatment of mental illness and abnormal behaviour.
3. It has highlighted the importance of good education and a healthy environment in the early years by emphasizing the role of childhood experiences.
4. Freud's concept of the unconscious has helped in understanding the cause of mal-adaptive behaviour.
5. His emphasis on the role of sex in one's life has brought out the necessity of providing sex education to children.

6. Freud's system of psycho-analysis has called for he provision of proper extra curricular activities and suitable hobbies etc. In the school programmes for the release of repressed or blocked libidinal energy and pent up feelings.

Conclusion

Psycho-analysis-Freud's system of psychology represents a fine blend of theory and practice for the understanding and shaping of human behaviour. The psycho-analytic theory put forward by Freud provides the theoretical framework for understanding human behaviour. This theory put forward altogether different views quite contrary to structuralism, functionalism, behaviouralism or gestaltatism to explain human behaviour. For the first time, this system presented a beautiful blend of theory and practice. On the theoretical side it presented a theory to understand and explain the human psyche and on the practical side it provided a method known as psycho-analysis for study of human behaviour, and also as a therapy for treating the mentally ill.

ANALYTICAL PSYCHOLOGY – CARL G. JUNG'S SYSTEM OF PSYCHOLOGY

Jung is best known for his theories about the *collective unconscious*, accumulated awareness of the experience of past generations and civilizations.

Carl Gustav Jung (1875-1961), Physician by profession, was born in the Swiss village of Kesswell in 1875. He came in close contact with Freud and became his staunch supporter and follower to the extent that Freud declared him as 'Crown Prince' and beloved son. However, in the years that followed, very serious ideological differences (mainly on account of Freud's over emphasis on sex) developed between the two such an extent that Jung established a separate school of thought called *Analytical Psychology* for experimenting with and propagating his ideas.

Structure of the Psyche or Mind

Jung, like Freud, accepted the existence of the unconscious besides the conscious in the structure of one's psyche. However, he differed a great deal in his concept of the unconscious. According to Jung, one's mind consists of the following parts:

Conscious Mind

The upper layer of one's mind consists of the memories, thoughts and feelings that result from one's consciousness. It is in fact the seat of one's ego and conscious behaviour. It is only a fraction of the human mind. Below it lies one's vast unconscious divided into two parts. The personal unconscious and the collective unconscious.

Personal Unconscious

The layer of mind concerning the personal unconscious lies beneath but in very close contact with the conscious. It is highly individualistic and personal in nature. It contains are repressed desires, ideas, feelings, fears, guilt's, anxieties, forgotten incidents, dreams, fantasies and other private experiences which might occur in the life time of an individual.

Collective Unconscious

Beneath the layer of the personal unconscious lies the collective unconscious. This is neither personal nor private but is universal to all individuals. According to Jung, the modes of thinking, feeling and doing as held by one's ancestors being transferred from generation to generation become part and parcel of one's conscious. The individual who inherit such vast stores of ancestral characteristics or racial memory, then are conditioned to perceive the world in the same way as the previous generation did. One's collective unconscious thus contains the experiences of the whole race gathered over millions of ancestral years specifically in the form of universal ideas or images called *archetypes*. Since the entire human race has the same origin and common ancestral history, these archetypes or images held and contained in our unconscious are the same. That is why these are called the racial or collective unconscious.

Archetypes

Archetypes are the roots and bases of the collective unconscious. They represent the eternally inherited ideas and forms which are common to every generation and culture since the dawn of mankind. They may either be handed down with the evolving brain in the form of inherited neural patterns or may be acquired direct and indirect experiences. They are available in abundance in old myths and fairy tales and folklore in religions and cultural traditions in enduring literature and art. A variety of archetypes exists, like the *mother archetype*, the *father archetype*, the *hero* and the *persona*, the *anima* and the *animus* and the *shadow* and the *self*.

I. *Primary Roots Archetypes*

The Mother Archetype: It is an eternal idea or image which is inherited from generation to generation and is common and universal to all cultures and races. The images of the 'mother' always appears to be pious, warm, loving, protective and nourishing.

The Father Archetype: In contrast to mother archetype, the father archetype reflects strength, authority, and power. In all cultures where the earth plants, and rivers are equated with the mother image, the sun, sky, oceans, lightning and thunder, are associated with the father image.

The Hero Archetype: This is well-known to us through our concept of a person who is an ideal, and often unselfish, figure in every respect. Similarly in every culture or race we find many other eternal ideas which are quite universal and identical like the image of God, birth and death, demon and devil, saints and wise men and the existence of some energy force moving this world.

II. *Secondary Roots Archetypes*

Persona: This signifies the mask we wear to face society irrespective of our real personality. It represents a role or part played by us like the role of father of son, of wife, or mother, of servant or master, of coward or courageous person chose to meet a particular social situation. One has to wear different masks at different times to cope with the existing social situation. Not learning to play these roles-developing personal or excessive identification with one role (over emphasis on the persona), according to Jung, may lead to personality problems.

III. *Tertiary Roots Archetypes*

Anima and Animus: Anima, associated with the female characteristics and animus with the image of maleress. Jung declared that every male has a female in him and every female a male in her, meaning thereby that characteristics of both anima and animus lie within every individual. The presence of both male and female characteristics in the individual may be due to the plain fact of their living together from times immemorial.

The Shadow: This signifies the archetype that resembles the concept of Freud's Id. Consequently, it may represent all that is bad or mean in man. In the words of Jung; "It personifies everything that the subject refuses to acknowledge about himself." Symbolically, we can refer to it as the devil or satan in man who does not care for morality or social norms. Jung clarifies, the shadow should not be considered as merely an enemy or the worst side of the one's personality, it is has a positive side also in one's creative expression.

The Self: The self as archetype was highly emphasized by Jung. The concept of self is a universal idea that can be found in all primitive philosophies and religion. In Hinduism, we know it as '*atma*', well-known for its individuality, the integrating force of one's personality and component of the universal cosmos, '*Brahm*'. Self in Jung's system carries a wide connotion. It works as,

(a) An archetype—one of the most important bases of the collective unconscious.

(b) An integrating force for all the components of one's psyche, i.e., conscious and unconscious, male and female, good and bad.

(c) A centre of one's personality and the originator as well as balancing force of one's behaviour.

In his topology of the mind, Jung does not deny that the conscious mind is operative in the outside world but he lays greater emphasis on the inner world and the deep-rooted unconscious. However, his unconscious, whether personal or collective, is quite different from that of Freud in the following manner:

1. It is not merely the dumping ground of the suppressed ideas and desires of the conscious.
2. It is not evolved out of the conscious. On the contrary, the conscious has been evolved out of the unconscious. Consciousness cannot create itself- It arises from unknown depths of the unconscious.
3. It consists, not only of the unconscious of one's personal nature but also of the collective and racial nature.

On the lines of Charles Darwin, Jung (1971) put forward the idea of evolutionary growth of the human mind.

The psyche is not of today. its ancestry goes back many millions of years. Individual consciousness is only the flowers and fruit of the season, sprung from the perennial rhizome (Stem and root system) beneath the earth.

Thus, the picture of the human psyche may be composed of various archetypes as the roots (resting in the deep interior), stemming out into the personal unconscious and blossoming out in the open as the conscious.

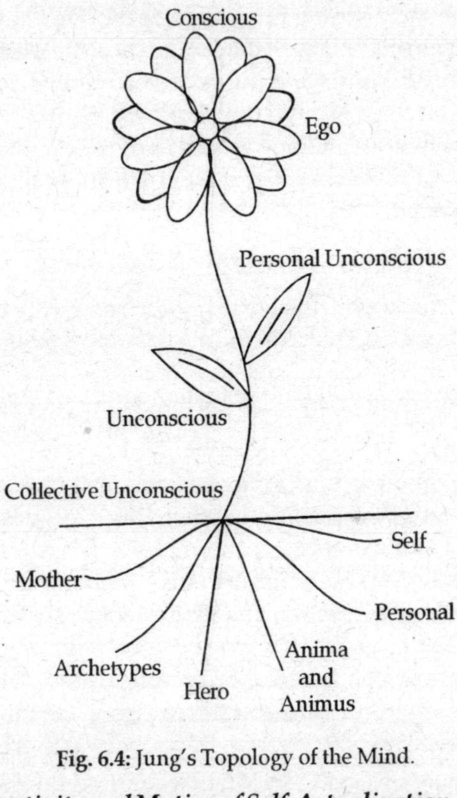

Fig. 6.4: Jung's Topology of the Mind.

Religion, Creativity and Motive of Self-Actualization

For explaining how and why we behave in a particular way, while Freud laid down the idea of the sex urge or the sex motive and Adler, the motive of power seeking or striving for supremacy, Jung advocated the motive of *self-actualization.* According to him, man is not merely a biological entity or social animal seeking gratification for him sex urge or power motive but being a developed and distinctive creation of the Almighty he always aims for some higher goals in his life. Jung believes that *altruism* is as innate in man as egoism. Religion is the need of human beings and morality is deep-seated in their collective unconscious. Therefore, man has a great need for the spontaneous religious forms of expression. Similarly, there is an innate creative spark in every individual the basis of which also lies in the unconscious depths of his mind. These inner creative aspects of one's mind also need some forms of expression. In this way, one has a strong inner urge or motive to express one's talents or abilities or to make self actualization the ultimate goal of one's life. For this purpose, one wants to climb higher and higher on the ladder of continues growth development by getting maximum opportunities for self-expression as well as the development of one's self and wishing for the union of the self (*atma*) with the universal self (*cosmos* or *brahm*).

The Concept of Libido and Personality Development

Jung equated 'Libido' with the life urge or life energy responsible for every type of human activity including of course, sex gratification, i.e., the narrower and limited meaning' conveyed through Freud's Libido. In fact, for Jung Libido was not the channel of self-expression but life itself.

Libido, the life energy, as Jung observes, may flow both ways—inward or outward. The persons in whom life energy flows inward are termed as *introverts*. These persons seek the manifestation of their life through inner activities by going inward and digging up things from within themselves. The philosophers, scientists, writers and similar other persons, who prefer to be busy with their own thoughts and are not bothered about physical stimulation and the realities of their environment fall in this category. On the other hand, persons in whom the life energy flows outward are termed as *extroverts*, such people seek the manifestation of their life through activities related with the outer world. They are successful at adjusting to the realities of their environment, are socially active and more interested in leaving a good impression on others. Politicians, social workers, lawyers, insurance agents, salesman, etc, fall in this category.

Later on Jung extended his two-fold classification of definite personality types to eight personality types (Illustrated as in Table 6.5).

Table–6.5
Jung's Description of Personality Types

Introverted Thinking Type	*Extroverted Thinking Type* E
← THINKING →	
Characteristics	*Characteristics*
(i) More theoretical detached and aloof	(i) Realistic and practical
(ii) Afraid of external realities	(ii) Supports theory with facts
(iii) Tactless and cold	(iii) Propagates his views with insistence and vehemence
(iv) Absorbed in his own intellectual pursuit	
I *Introvert Intuitive Type*	*Extrovert Intuitive Type* E
Characteristics	*Characteristics* (Intuition)
(i) More subjective and more concerned with probabilities than actualities	(i) More outwardly, optimistic and change-seeker
(ii) Moody, unstable, and temperamental	(ii) Attracted by future possibilities of gain and can take risk or gamble
(iii) Behave like the theoretical scientists and prophets	(iii) Quite set in intuitive judgment of the future course of activities
(iv) Quite unstable in their friendship or loyalty	
I *Introvert Sensational Type*	*Extrovert Sensational Type* E
Characteristics (Sensation)	*Characteristics*
(i) Possesses refined tastes and interests but quite choosy and fussy about the things he likes	(i) Good eaters accepting anything eatable at any moment
(ii) Lean and thin as he does not eat well	(ii) Easily bored and demand constant emotional sensation
(iii) Dissatisfied, broody and rather sad in the general appearance	(iii) Carefree, friendly and talkative
(iv) Better in writing than speaking and interested in books and magazines	(iv) No patience for abstract or theoretical ideas

(Contd.)

I *Introvert Feeling Type*	*Extrovert Feeling Type* E
← FEELING →	
Characteristics	*Characteristics*
(i) Day dreamer	*(i)* More social
(ii) Strong feelings, likes and dislikes	*(ii)* Objective in his outlook and admires things of others
(iii) Does not express his feelings to others and goes on suffering internally	*(iii)* Helpful nature and feels for the suffering of others
(iv) May feel strongly but does not resort to any step	*(iv)* Expresses his feelings externally instead of suffering internally

Dreams

In Jung's opinion one's dreams are not merely a means of artificial wish fulfillment. They work as a true companion to one's conscious mind for solving one's day-to-day difficulties and may be utilized in planning wisely in anticipation of one's future.

According Jung, the individual may have two types of dreams springing from the personal unconscious and the collective unconscious. Whereas dreams from the personal unconscious can be interpreted objectively, the dreams from the collective or racial unconscious are to be interpreted subjectively since they usually deal with the dreamer's own attributes and tendencies.

Neuroses

Neurosis, according to him represents regression ongoing back, as a result of a serious obstacle in the flow of the Libido or imbalances created in the mind through disharmony between one's conscious and unconscious. For the genesis of the causes the present is more important than the past. It represents one's lack of ability to cope with one's environment. One's confidence in oneself is restored one can be reset in one's striving for self-actualization.

Jung's Psychotherapy

The therapy suggested by Jung is centred round the key concept of making the patient first understand what is wrong with his self and then to help him in integrating his self. The technique of controlled association (in contrast to the method of free association used by Freud) is used for analyzing the problem behaviour. The patient is then helped to obtain an insight into his problem and afterwards attempts are made to help him to re-establish the harmony of his self with his environment i.e., to seek an independent solution of his problem.

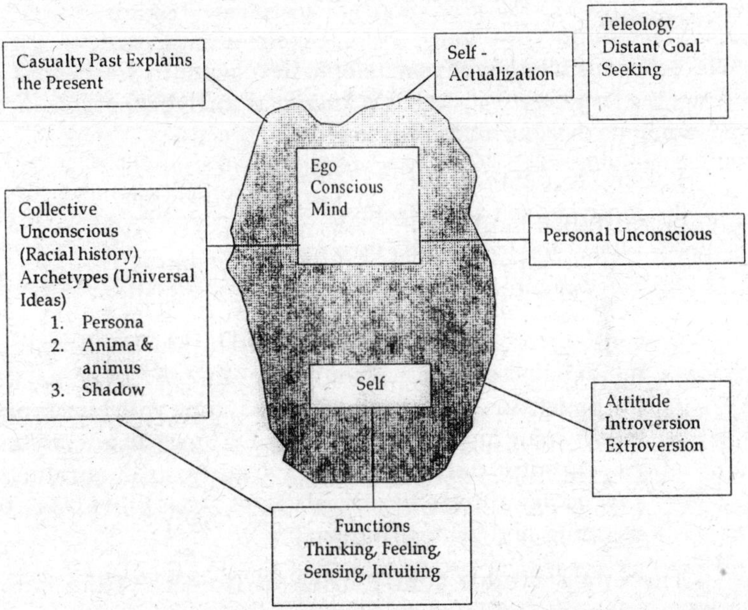

Fig. 6.5: Diagrammatic Representation of Jung's Analytical Psychology.

Contribution of Jung's System to Education

Jung's system contributed significantly to education by emphasizing the need to:

1. plan and design the education of children for maximum actualization of their potentialities.
2. set the goal of education as higher than self-actualization-the integration of the self with the greater self i.e., the cosmos or 'brahm'.
3. realize the need and importance of religious or moral education for integration and welfare of the individual's self;
4. ensure that the process of education does not remove one from one's cultural roots or racial characteristics.

5. developing one's individuality in complete harmony with the development of others in society or mankind as a whole.
6. take care of education and development of the children with their introvert and extrovert nature in view and guarding against their becoming extreme introvert or extreme extrovert.

Conclusion

The school of thought of psychology, developed by Carl Gunstav Jung, the famous psychologist is known as analytical psychology. The major concepts of this system are:

1. structure of the psyche.
2. motive of self-actualization.
3. Libido and personality development.
4. dreams and neurosis etc. Jung's system advocates self-actualization as the ultimate aim of human life and consequently, the therapy suggested by him for the cure of mental illness is centred sound the key concept of making the patient first understand what is wrong with his self and then helping him in integrating it. Jung's system of analytical psychology definitely carries many philosophical, psychological and educational values. It has provided more meaning and value to human life.

The other notable contribution of Jung's system is the categorization of people in to definite personality types based on the outward or inward flow of their libido, i.e., life energy. His emphasis on the moral social and cultural values as against the animal nature stressed by Freud, and the need of the realization of creative aspects inherent in man and integration of his self have essentially been quite helpful in the field of education.

GORDON, W. ALLPORT – TRAIT APPROACH TO PERSONALITY/ THEORY OF DISPOSITION

Trait Approach

In the trait approach the personality is viewec' in terms of various traits. In our day-to-day conversation he ascribe traits to our friends and near one's as being honest, shy, aggressive, lazy, dull, dependent etc. Traits may be defined as relatively permanent and relatively consistent general behaviour patterns that an individual exhibits in most situations. These patterns are said to be the basic units of one's personality that can be discovered through observing one's behaviour in a variety of situations.

Gordon W. Allport (1897-1967), he rejecting the type approaches. Allport; "Traits are the basic units of personality. Each of us develops a unique set of such organized tendencies termed as *traits* in the course of our continues and gradual development." All part distinguished 3 types of traits namely,

1. Cardinal traits.
2. Central traits.
3. Secondary traits.

1. *Cardinal traits* are the primary trait's so dominant in one's personal disposition that they colour virtually every aspect of one's behaviour and attributes. These traits, it found in an individual, are limited in number to just one or two. For example, if a person has *humorousness* as a cardinal trait, he will bring a sense of humour in almost all situations irrespective of it's actual demands. In fact, such cardinal traits although very few in number over rule other traits and thus drift the whole personality of the individual along with them.
2. *Central traits* represent those few characteristics tendencies which can be ordinarily used to describe a person, e.g., honesty, kindness, submissiveness etc. Allport; "For knowing an individual's personality, we need to know only time to ten such central traits."
3. *Secondary traits* are not as dominant as the cardinal or central traits. They appear in only a relatively small range of situations and are not considered strong enough to be regarded as integral parts of one's personality.

Allport's theory of personality is known not only for its emphasis on traits but also for its stress on concepts like functional autonomy, individualized approach in the study of personality, and he discontinues nature of the development of personality, etc.

The concept of *functional autonomy* suggests that function or means which once served a purpose may attain autonomy at a later stage.

Regarding the method of investigation into behaviour, Allport was not interested in looking at large groups of people and identifying general principles of behaviour, (a normative survey or dimensional approach to study personality) but rather in adopting an individual approach known as the idiographic approach. Such an approach demands the study of every individual separately and consequently through his methods of study and findings. Allport always emphasized the uniqueness of the individual having unique traits and unique aspects of personality functioning.

Allport also emphasized another important concept of the discrete and discontinues nature of the development of personality. In his book; "pattern and growth in personality", he mentioned three stages in the growth and development of personality namely,

- the childhood,
- adolescence, and
- adulthood personalities.

Personality is not a continuation from childhood to adulthood rather it is a discrete and discontinues development. The past cannot decide the function of the present. Allport; "The adolescent's or adults functioning is not constrained by his or her past."

Criticism

1. The theory does not give clear and specific consideration to a study of the pattern of growth and development from conception till the end of life as done by the other theories.
2. His belief and assertion that personality is not a continuum between childhood and adulthood holds no ground as one's present cannot be delinked from one's part or future.
3. Pervin (1984) observe that the division-cardinal, central, secondary – is some what confusing.

CARL RANSOM ROGERS

- Humanistic View of Personality.
- Self Theory (1947).

Carl R. Rogers, American psychologist propounded the self-theory based on his idea of *client-centred therapy*. He stresses the importance of an individual's self in determining the process of his growth, development and appropriate adjustment to his environment.

Structure of Personality

Rogers considers that two basic systems are operating in the personal reality (phenomenological field) of an individual—the organism and the self.

Phenomenological Field – A world of subjective experience, the personal and separate reality of each individual.

1. *The Organism:* It represents the totality of one's experience both conscious and unconscious, is an entire frame of reference.
2. *The Self:* It is the accepted conscious part of experience. In other words, self is the concept developed by an person about himself i.e., self-concept. The self as a system of one's phenomenological field can perhaps best understood in terms our concept of 'I', 'me', or 'myself'.

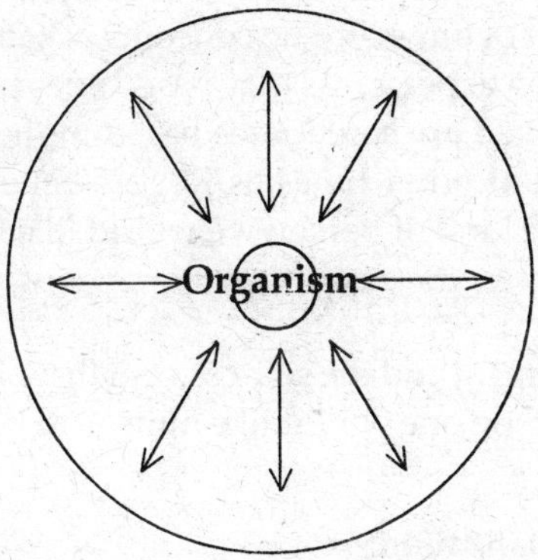

Phenomenological Field.

Phenomenological Field/Phenomenology

- Experiences Available Potentially, Called Symbolized Experiences
  - Symbolized Experience in Life Reality
  - Experiences Interpreted our Own Way
- Experience in the Unconscious Level Called Unsymbolized Experience

Symbolized experience means all the psychological experience gained by the organism which are potentially available.

The Self (Self-Concept)

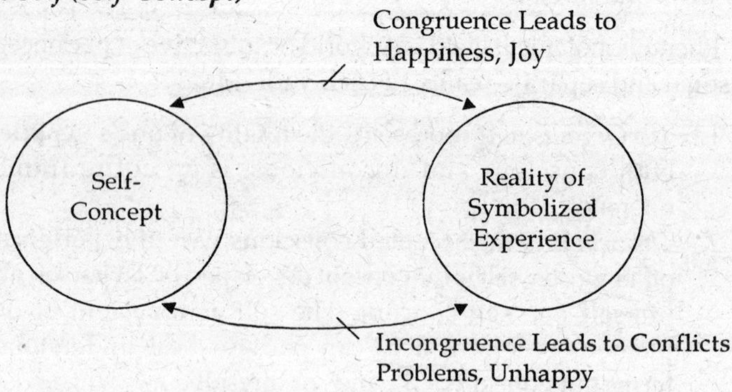

Our inner world interacts with our total range of experience to form the concept of our self. The concepts of self thus develop may differ from person to person as they based ones personal experience. The concepts of self are sometimes based more on personal needs than reality and at other times as Rogers believe, we develop an ideal self, i.e., the kind of person we would like to be.

Ideal Self

Besides the organism and the self-concept there is the ideal self, that is the kind of person one would like himself to be as three themes of rogers:

1. Self-actualization.
2. Self-maintenance.
3. Self-enhancement.

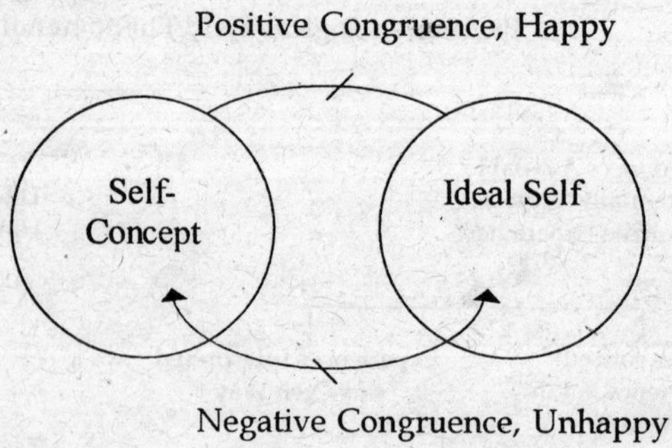

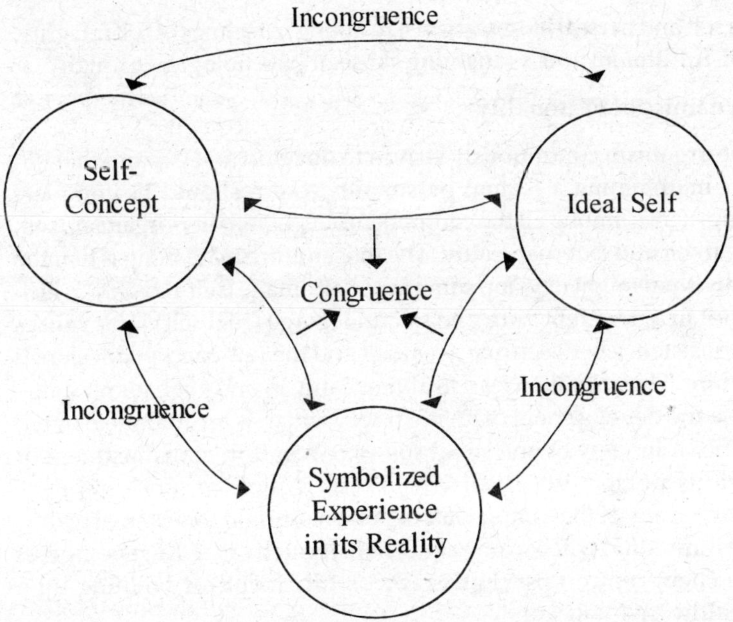

Fig. 6.6: Rogers Concept of Ideal Self.

If a person fulfil self-actualization, he is a fully functioning individual. Unconditioned positive reward is essential for self-actualization.

Roger advocates continuity of growth in terms of a continues evolution of the concept of 'self'. Ones a concept 'self' is formed the individual strives to maintain by regulating his behaviour.

The most unfortunate results in the development of personality occur in cases where an individual develops some false-image. It consistency between one's actual image and false image, may, then lead to abnormality in one's behaviour.

An individuals adjustment, happiness, growth and development all depend upon the union and harmony between the image of his self and the organism. He emphasis that a person normally possesses considerable capacity for growth and the realization of his individual potential and thus tries to advance continuously toward the development of his self to lead to harmony between the concept of his self and his real life experience resulting in feelings of self integrity, self-fulfillment and a satisfying sense of psychological growth.

Dynamics of Personality

The organism continuously strives to develop and expand the self. For maintaining a formal personality, there should be complete congruence among all the components of personality-organism, self, ideal self and external reality. The most unfortunate thing is that the individual might develop some false self-image (self-concept) which is not in agreement with one's actual image (real self). This causes inconsistency between one's real self and the self-concept developed by him. This may then lead to abnormality in one's behaviour. Likewise the development of an ideal self, which is an attainable or too difficult in view of one's real self may result in maladjustment or serious personality disorders. Thus, if incongruence happens between any of the components of personality and the external reality, the individual will become abnormal. In such cases, Rogers suggest the client-centred psychotherapy as treatment for building up a 'healthy' self-concept.

Non-Directive Counselling/Therapy

The development runs into trouble when the self tails for some reason to incorporate, and learns to live with its own new thoughts, feelings or behaviour. The goal of a therapist, in such cases lies in bringing the individual in a united way, from what he or she is not, to what he/she really is.

Pre-Requisites

1. Minimum Willingness.
2. Ability to communicate each other.
3. Readiness and opportunity to receive communication.

Role of Teachers

1. Always try to make congruences in children.
2. Give equal importance is desire of self-esteem.

Rogers v/s Maslow

1. Under maslow's system , self-actualization is possible only after more basic needs have been met by the individual. Rogers feeds that a person has the potential for self-

actualization from the beginning of his life and is working towards it.

2. Self-actualization in Maslow is system means reaching an apex of achievement in a selected area of life. He is more connected with goals that satisfy specific needs. In Rogers system, a person is self-actualized if he feels satisfied by producing satisfactory results in his life and has high self-concept.

Conditions of Self-Actualization

1. The person must respect and have faith in himself, his abilities to achieve his goal.
2. The person must be respected and loved by others.
3. The choices available to the individual must be clearly perceived.
4. The choices must be clearly symbolized.

ALFRED ADLER'S SYSTEM OF INDIVIDUAL PSYCHOLOGY

Alfred Adler (1870-1937)

Adler disagreed with many of Freud's basic beliefs, especially the idea that sexual impulses are the source of personality development. Adler maintained that we are driven by the need to compensate for feelings of inferiority and to strive for superiority in our lives.

Born in Vienna 1870, Alfred Adler began his career as an opthalmologist. He joined Freud's school of psycho-analysis in 1902 and became one of his prize pupils. He broke away from Freud mainly over the latter's overemphasis on sex and founded a new school of psychology. His system is called *Individual Psychology* because it lays emphasis on the individuality of human beings in terms of their unique characteristics at the time of birth, the availability of an exclusive environment for growth and development and adoption of a specific style of life to achieve power and attain perfection.

What the System Tells

Adler, in his system for explaining behaviour, replaced the life instinct or sex motive advocated by Freud with the motive to seek power or attain superiority and perfection. According to him, for the satisfaction of the power motive, one follows one's own path in one's own way and thus develops a unique style of life, depending upon the order of birth, early life experiences and the requirements of the creative self. Success or failure in the satisfaction of the power motive by adopting his own style turns a person in to an adjusted or a maladjusted personality. The individual then further learns the ways of striving and making adjustments and this is how, according to Adler's system, one behaves and leads one's life.

Major Concepts of Individual Psychology

Power Motive and Striving for Superiority and Perfection

How and why one behaves in a particular fashion may be explained in terms of one's striving for the satisfaction of one's urge to dominate, to gain superiority and to achieve perfection in one field or other. This urge to dominate or to strive for superiority or perfection, as adler says, is innate. It is part of one's life and in fact may be termed as life itself.

Why, one may ask, did Adler select the power motive as the only motive to explain human bnehaviour? The genesis of this may be traced to the experiences to which a child is exposed in his early childhood.

1. Every child is born as a helpless mass, entirely dependent upon grown ups for the satisfaction of his needs. Consequently, he may have a burning desire to seek power, to dominate and to attain superiority in order to overcome and compensate for his feelings of inadequacy and inferiority.
2. He may be brought up in such a way that he may develop attitudes for ruling and dominating over others and as a manifestation of his trait, he may crave for superiority and the desire to surpass others.
3. He may be the victim of negligence or develop some inferiority feelings. The urge to strive for superiority helps him over come his feeling of inferiority and in adequacy.

Style of Life

If one wants to live, are has to strive to or establish superiority in one way or the other and consequently one has to adopt one's own style of life. This style of one's life has been the key point of Adler's System of Individual Psychology. One is known and judged by one's life style. According to Adler, all human beings have the same-goal-that of gaining superiority over others but may adopt different ways and means to fulfill their power motive, strive for superiority and reach the goal of perfection. The manner in which they strive and the ways and means they adopt collectively constitute the style of life. Accordingly, one person may try to become superior through developing as a political leader; and other may strive to become a renewed auther, writer, artist, scientist or wrestler.

One's style of life thus depends on the areas of fields in which one chooses the strive for superiority. The whole of one's time schedule, habits of work, personal and social contacts, comprising one's style of life then, will naturally be tailored to the ways and means one chooses for striving towards superiority and perfection.

Adler has mentioned four types of life styles for the development of personality, namely— *(a)* the ruling type, *(b)* the go-getting type, *(c)* the escaping type and *(d)* the struggling type.

What makes them develop these distinct styles of life may be influenced by the following factors:

1. *The Order of Birth*

According to Adler, the order, place and position of the child in the family when he is born is to a great extent responsible for fashioning his style of life.

2. *The Type of Children*

Adler has pointed out that different types of children pick up different styles of life for their personality development. For example, the pampered child may adopt a life-style to get his wishes accepted and for him to be treated as a prince. On the other hand, the unwanted or neglected child may either turn into a timid, shy and insecure person or become a drunkard and criminal.

3. *Fictional Finalism*

The style of one's life also depends upon the mechanism of fictional finalism which means that men live by many purely fictional ideas which do not necessarily conform to reality. We can cite examples such as the following: "stars or lines on our palm decide our future or destiny." "Female child is a curse to the family", "Women are made to be governed or ruled by men", and so on. The belief in such fictional ideas is sure to affect the philosophy and style of one's life.

4. *Compensation for Inferiority*

In many cases, one's style of life is fashioned in relation to some compensatory behaviour for a particular kind of inferiority. For example, the life style of Demosthenes who became the world's greatest orator was the outcome of the compensation for the inferiority he suffered on account of his stuttering as a child. Similarly, the conquering style of Napoleon was fashioned as a compensation for the feeling of inferiority he suffered because of his small physical stature.

5. *The Creative Self*

The creative power of the individual is responsible, to a great extent for determining and shaping his style of life. According to Adler, it is the creative self which gives meaning to life by creating goals as well as suggesting means to achieve the goal. This creative self grows and develops in an individual out of his heredity endowments and environmental experiences. He tends to solve problems and act according to the dictates of his creative self. His style of life is, therefore, said to be fashioned in accordance with the development of his creative self.

6. *Social Interest*

Man is social creature and his style of life is also determined through the varying social interests he shows is maintaining social relationships, extending co-operation, sympathy and kindness and thus in a wider sense helping society to attain the goal of perfection. Striving for superiority in this case, becomes a socialized rather than a selfish need and the life style gets fashioned through one's innate social interests.

How the System of Individual Psychology Operates

Persuaded and motivated to seek power or superiority (on account of seeking compensation, reinforcement or satisfaction of one's creative self), one is forced to adopt the relevant life style suited to one's environmental situation. One continues to struggle for achieving one's goals through the ways and means provided by one's life style. While striving, however, one has to maintain a proper balance between one's needs and efforts. In case one succeeds in making such an adjustment, one remains normal, otherwise one may drift towards maladaptive behaviour.

Merits and Contributions to Education

1. Emphasizing the need of paying due respect to the phenomenal self of the child and providing the means for self-expression and self-actualization.
2. Giving conscious behaviour and deliberate effort a major share in striving towards the realization of life's goals.
3. Giving impetus to 'child centred education' and 'individualized instruction'.
4. Emphasizing the importance of the first-four or five years of life in the shaping of personality and for this purpose devoting due attention to the rearing as well as education of children during this period, taking care to ensure that they do not imbibe inferiority or guilt feelings.
5. Giving due recognision to various social agencies and social activities for shaping the behaviour and personality of children.
6. Providing due importance to the identification and nurturing of creativity.
7. Stressing the need for prevention, early diagnosis and timely treatment of behavioural problems of children and realizing the need of a guidance clinic in the school.

Let's concluding the system of psychology propagated by Adler a prize discipline of Freud, is known as Individual Psychology. The operation of this system revolves around the two key concepts-power motive and style of life.

REFERENCES

1. Adler, A. (1921). *The Neurotic Constitution*. London: Kegan Paul.
2. Adler, A. (1928). *Understanding Human Nature*. London: Allen and Unwin.
3. Adler, A. (1930). *The Education of Children*. New York: Greeberg.
4. Adler, A. (1937). *What life Should Mean You*. New York: Grossett and Dunlop.
5. Adler, A. (1968). *The Practice and Theory of Individual Psychology*. New Jersey: Little Field Adams.
6. Adler, A., Hall, C.S. *et al.* (1978). *Theories of Personality*. 3rd ed. New York: Wiley.

7. Barrone, F. David and Michel Hersen *et. al.*, (1998). *Advanced Personality*. New York: Plenum Press.
8. Borrone, F. David and Michel Herson (1998). *Advanced Personality*. New York: Plenum Press.
9. Chauhan, S.S. (2000). *Advanced Educational Psychology*. New Delhi: Vikas Publishing House.
10. Chauhan, S.S. (2002). *Advanced Educational Psychology*. New Delhi: Vikas Publishing House (P) Ltd.
11. Chauhan, S.S. (2003). *Advanced Educational Psychology*. New Delhi: Vikas Publishing House (P) Ltd.
12. Fredeubeirgh Fraz, A. (1971). *The Psychology of Personality and Adjustment*. California: Cunnings Publishing Co.
13. Freud, S. (1986). *The Essentials of Psycho Analysis*. England: Penguin Books.
14. Guilford, J.P. (1959). *Personality*. Mc Graw Hill.
15. Hall, C.S. (1978). *Theories of Personality*, 3rd ed., New York: John Wiley.
16. Kakkar, S.B. (1995). *Educational Psychology*. New Delhi: Prentice Hall of India (P) Ltd.
17. Mangal, S.K. (2000). *Advanced Educational Psychology*. New Delhi: Prentice Hall of India (P) Ltd.
18. Minsky, R. (1996). *Psycho Analysis and Gender*. New York: Routledge.
19. Morgan, C.T. *et al.* (1994). *Introduction to Psychology*. New Delhi: Tata McGraw Hill Publishing Company Ltd.
20. Munn, N.L. *et al.* (1967). *Introduction to Psychology*. New Delhi: Oxford and IBH Publishing Company (P) Ltd.
21. Previn, Lawrence, A. (1984). *Personality*. New York: Wiley.
22. Ross, T.A. (1921). *Introduction to Analytical Psychotherapy*. London: Arnold.
23. Sharma, R.N. (1992). *Advanced Educational Psychology*. New Delhi: Surjeet Publications.
24. Sharma, R.N. (1999). *Advanced Educational Psychology*. New Delhi: Surjeet Publications.
25. Stagner (1974). *Psychology of Personality*. New York: McGraw Hill.
26. Thope J. and L.P. Schmuller (1958). *Personality: an Interdisciplinary Approach*. D. Van Nostrand Company.
27. Worth, R.S.W. (1965). *Contemporary Schools of Psychology (rev. ed)*. London: Methuen.

MODEL QUESTIONS

1. What are the factors determining personality of an individual?
2. What are the difficulties of measuring personality?
3. Define personality according to Allport and analyze the various aspects implied in this definition. State briefly the techniques of assessing personality. Explain anyone of them in detail.

4. Explain the psycho-analytic concept of psychic structure.
5. Examine the classroom implications of Freud's ideas about the 'dynamics' of personality development.
6. Describe the humanistic approach to personality development, with special reference to the views of Carl Rogers.
7. Briefly describe the dynamics of personality development as viewed by Freud.

7
Individual Differences

INTELLIGENCE

The term "intelligence" is vague and ambiguous in its meaning. Psychologists have been interpreting the term in different ways and are in disagreement on the meaning of the term intelligence. In psychological literature, intelligence has been treated as a construct, no one knowns what intelligence is? Due to the vagueness, in recent years concept of intelligence has become less acceptable and more exposed to criticism by Psychologist but no two psychologists agree on a single definition of the term.

The Concept of Intelligence

Intelligence is often confused with learning, thinking, problem solving, concept formation, attainment and achievement. It is none of these but affects them all in a positive way, i.e., it improves performance.

Ryle argues that intelligence is a 'dispositional word' and not an attribute. It is preferable to say that a person may be disposed to behave or perform intelligently rather than boldly state he is intelligent.

There are two extremes between which 'intelligence' has been conceptualized the open view and narrow operational view. The open view is related with the popular or common sense concept whereas the operational view allows for a scientific precision and loss of some of the rich and polymorphous aspect.

What Intelligence is Not?

1. *Not Knowledge:* Intelligence is not knowledge, though it is related to it. The amount of knowledge, one can acquire is limited by ones intelligence.
2. *No Talent:* Intelligence is not same as talent. Talent involves two things: *(a)* Native capacity and *(b)* Practiced skills, intelligence is native capacity.
3. *Not Memory:* Intelligence is not memory even. It has been observed that sometime personas with low intelligence have very good memory.
4. *Not Skill:* Intelligence is different from skill. Skill is acquired through practice and can be perfected by more practice. But intelligence cannot be enhanced by practice.

Definitions of Intelligence

Miles described the concept of intelligence as polymorphous and open in view of the fact that the number of activities legitimately characterized as indicators of intelligence are available. Thus, intelligence is an example of a multidefinable concept.

Freeman's Classification

(i) Adjustment or Adaptation Ability to the Environment

The individual is thought intelligent in proportion of his ability to adjust to new situation and problems of life.

Stern: "Intelligence is a general capacity of an individual consciously to adjust his thinking to new environment. It is general mental adaptability to new problems and conditions of life."

J. Piaget: "Adaptation to physical and social environment."

Peterson: "It is mechanical means for adjustment and control."

Burt: "It is the power of readjustment to relatively novel situation by organizing new psycho-physical co-ordination."

Printer: The ability of the individual to adopt himself adequately to relatively new situations of life.

(ii) Ability to Learn

This category of definitions emphasize the importance of an individual's ability to learn. Learning ability is an index of one's intelligence.

Buckingham: "Intelligence is the learning ability."

Woodrow: It is the capacity to acquire."

Calvin: "It is the ability to learn."

Wagonon: "Intelligence is the capacity to learn and adjust to relatively new and changing conditions."

(iii) Ability to Abstract Thinking

This category lay more emphasis on the effective use of concepts and symbol in dealing with situations, especially, presenting a problem to be solved through he use of verbal and numerical symbols.

L.M. Terman: "An individual is intelligent in proportion as he is able to carry on abstract thinking."

E.L. Thorndike: Intelligence may be define as "The power of good responses from the point of view of truth or fact."

Ausubel: "A general level of cognitive functioning, as reflected in the ability to understand ideas and to realize abstract symbols in the solution of intellectual problems."

Munn: "Intelligence is the feasibility or versality to use of symbolic processes."

Vernon's Classification

(i) Biological Approach

This category of definitions emphasizes the adaptive nature of human beings. Intelligence accordingly to this approach, is the capacity to adapt relatively in new situations of life. But this concept is not of great use from practical point of view in the study of individual differences within a culture.

(ii) Psychological Approach

This category of definitions are psychological. Few of the definitions contained a clear commitment about the relative effects of hereditary and environmental influences in the development of intelligence.

(iii) Operational Approach

Operational definitions are important to understand the concept of intelligence in clear and definite terms. Instead of defining the word by itself, it is defined by giving the conditions for the truth of a sentence in which the term occurs. Such definitions are called *operational.*

Operational Definitions

D. W. Wechsler: "Intelligence is the aggregate or global capacity of the individual to act purposefully, to think rationally and to deal effectively with his environment."

G.D. Stoddard: "The ability to undertake activities that are difficult, complex and abstract and which are adaptive to a goal, and are done quickly and which have social value and which lead to the creation of something new and different."

Hein: "Intelligence activity consisting in grasping the essentials in a situation and responding approximately to them."

Well: "Intelligence is the property of recombining our behaviour pattern as to act later in novel situations."

Chief Characteristics and Generalization about Intelligence

Inherited Intelligence

Intelligence cannot be increased or decreased. The amount of intelligence that a person possesses is inherited and fixed. The amount though fixed does not reveal itself as the start of life with growth of the child, the amount inherited by a child also grows. The general belief is that the growth of intelligence stops and it reaches its limit at the age of sixteen or seventeen. It is true that a man of forty knows more that he was a boy of sixteen. But this does not mean that the amount of intelligence possessed by him has increased. This may be due to his experience. As regards his intelligence, his position remains the same.

Intelligence and Influence of Environmental Factors

It is certain justifiable to assume that love, affection, concern and generosity judiciously bestowed on growing children, have very desirable effects. Poor environments retard development of intelligence.

The growth of intelligence of certain children may be checked due to certain unfavourable circumstances and when these are removed, intelligence begins to grow and functions normally.

Intelligence, Adjustment and Inventions

An intelligent person has the ability to adjust himself to the changing circumstances with ease, efficiency and speed. He has the capacity to assimilate ideas very quickly and clearly. He can cope the new situations very high intelligence.

The unintelligent or the dullard fail to think of new situations. They are always guided by others. They lack originality.

Distribution of Intelligence

The majority of the school children, says about 60 per cent are found in the I.Q. range 90-110 and are referred to as 'Normal' or 'Average'.

Intelligence and Sex Differences

Generally speaking, the research studies show that the average scores of the sexes are strikingly similar.

Intelligence and Race Differences

Every racial and cultural group contains some gifted children. Franz Boas States, "If we were to select the most intelligent, imaginative, energetic and emotionally stable third of mankind, all races would be represented."

Non-Definable Nature of Intelligence

Some argue, "We measure electricity without being able to define its precise nature. But we can put electricity to use and measure it so we can use and measure intelligence.

Individual Differences in Intelligence

Wide individual differences exit among individual with regard to intelligence. Truly speaking, no two individuals, even identical twins or individuals natured in identical environments, are enclosed with equal mental energy. The assessment of intelligence by various tests has given reason enough to believe that not only does intelligence vary from individual to individual but it also tends to vary in the same undivided from age to age and situation to situation.

Intelligence and Changes in Age

As child grows in age so does the intelligence as shown by intelligence tests. The age at which mental growth ceases, varies from individual to individual. It tends to stabilize after the age of 10 and is fully stabilized during adolescence. The idea that intelligence continues to grow throughout life is not strictly true, since intelligence is basically a function of neurons and neuralgia, its development or deterioration goes had in hand with the development or deterioration of the nervous system. However, in the majority of cases, the growth of a persons intelligence reaches its maximum sometime between the age of 16 to 20 years after which the vertical growth of intelligence almost ceases. Horizontal growth, that is achievement, the realization of the intelligence in terms of accumulation of knowledge and acquisition of skills etc. Many continue throughout an individual's life.

Types of Intelligence

E.L. Thorndike has classified intelligence into three categories which are as follow:

(a) Concrete intelligence.
(b) Abstract intelligence.
(c) Social intelligence.

(a) Concrete Intelligence

Concrete intelligence means intelligence in relation to concrete materials. It is the ability of an individual to comprehend actual situations and react to them adequately. The concrete intelligence is evident from various activities of daily life. This kind of intelligence is measured by performance tests and picture tests in which the individual has to manipulate concrete materials.

(b) Abstract Intelligence

It is ability to respond to words, numbers and letters etc. All tests of intelligence which require manipulation of symbols are tests of abstract intelligence. It is required in the ordinary academic subjects in schools, such as reading, writing and history and so on. The highest level of abstract intelligence is manifested in the thought of philosophers and in the use of mathematical formula.

(c) Social Intelligence

Social intelligence means ability of an individual to react to social situations of daily life. Social intelligence would not include of the feelings or emotions aroused in us by other people, but it is our ability to understand others and to react in such a way towards them that the ends desired should be attained. High social intelligence is possessed by those who are able to handle people well. Adequate adjustment in social situations is the index of social intelligence.

Description of Intelligence

In describing intelligence we deal with

1. Attributes i.e., certain properties or characteristics.
2. Kinds i.e., intelligence manifested in different situations.

1. Attributes: There are 4 attributes or aspects of intelligence viz. *(a)* Level, *(b)* Range, *(c)* Area and *(d)* Speed.

(a) Level

This refers to the degree of difficulty of a task to be solved. If we think of all tasks as varying in difficulty from easy to hard and if they are arranged on a ladder or scale of difficulty, then the height that we can attain on this ladder is the level or altitude.

(b) Range or Width

Refers to number of tasks at any given degree of difficulty that we can solve. The number of tasks which an individual can solve at a given degree will represent the range of intelligence for that intelligence at that level.

(c) Area

It means the total number of situations at each level of to which the individual is able to respond. So it is summation of all the ranges at each level of intelligence possessed by an intelligence.

The levels of intellects of rural and urban children may be the same but, the area of the former will be less than that of the latter.

(b) Speed

Is the rapidity with which we can respond to situation. Speed shows a positive correlation with levels.

INTELLIGENCE QUOTIENT (IQ)

Intelligence assessed through the various intelligence tests is expressed in terms of Intelligence Quotient or IQ. This term was first coined by the German Psychologist. William Stern (1914). According to him a convenient method of ascertaining the level of intelligence is by calculating IQ or Intelligence Quotient. IQ is calculated by dividing the Mental Age (MA) by Chronological Age (CA) and then multiple's it by 100 to remove decimal points. The formula for calculation of IQ was expressed as

$$IQ = \frac{\text{Mental Age}}{\text{Chronological Age}} \times 100$$

Where mental age and chronological age corresponds to that of the individual whose intelligence is being tested.

The Origins of IQ

The emergence of mental testing in the present form is hardly seventy years old. Historical development of intelligence testing can be classified in to three distinctive periods as (1) Pre-Binets period, (2) Binet period, and (3) Post-Binet period. The major weakness of Pre-Binet period was that psychologists failed to identify the nature of intelligence. Binet's most important contribution to the development of intelligence tests was the simple insight that, since he was dealing with young children, he could use their age as an independent criterion of intellectual competence. By giving their tests of samples of normal children of various ages, Binet and Simon found out which set of tests should be solved by the majority of 4 years old, 6 years old, 8 years old etc. The further requirement was that relatively few 4 years old, but essentially all 8 years old should be able to solve 6 years old tests and similarly for the tests for other age groups. The tests were used to assign a child a 'mental age' a child who passed on the principle of the normal distribution of intelligence at the majority of children at a particular age are of normal intelligence and that they have a mental level approximating that age, which could be termed as their mental age. If some child excels in the performance of certain task compared the performance of the majority of the children of his age, he was said to be of higher mental age.

Concept of Mental Age

With the revised scale, Binet introduced the concept of mental age. Mental age means that a given child's score on a test is like test. If for instance, the performance of an eight years old on certain adequately determined tasks is equal to that of the majority of ten years old than he has a Mental Age (MA) of ten years, whereas another child of eight years showing performance equal to the that of the majority of six years old, on the same tasks would be said to possess a mental age of six years. Mental age gives us a measure of the level of intellectual achievement. Mental age increases year by year up to the age of 16 to 18 years of age, when it reaches its maximum.

The Constancy of IQ

Intelligence goes on growing up to the age of 16 to 20 years, but the IQ for most individuals, remains constant. The IQ provides a ratio for determining how bright an individual is as compared to others of his age. Actually, it is an index which is independent not only the particular score which an individual makes on a particular scale but also of the particular age at which he happens to make it. It is thus a measure, which acquaints us with the brightness or intellectual possibilities of an individual more or less permanently.

It is true not only an individual grows in intelligence but the whole group also grow at the same rate. Thus, the intelligence quotient as measure of defining relative brightness or intellectual possibilities of an individual remains practically constant. Under ordinary circumstances an individual's IQ is supposed to remain constant throughout life or at least throughout the age limits covered by the scale. This property of the IQ is referred to by psychologists as the constancy of IQ.

It is true not only an individual grows in intelligence but the whole group (other individuals of his group) also grow at the same rate. Thus, the intelligence quotient, as measure of defining relative brightness or intellectual possibilities of an individual remains practically constant. Under ordinary circumstances an individual's IQ is supposed to remain constant throughout life or at least throughout the age limits covered by the scale. This property of the IQ is referred to by psychologists as the constancy of IQ.

The Intelligence Quotient (IQ) is one of the most common expressions used in mental testing which has been picked up and passed by all. The constancy of IQ is an important concept which must be used with caution. Some conclusions have been drawn by Psychologists which are listed as follows.

1. A given IQ indicates the same relative ability at different ages.

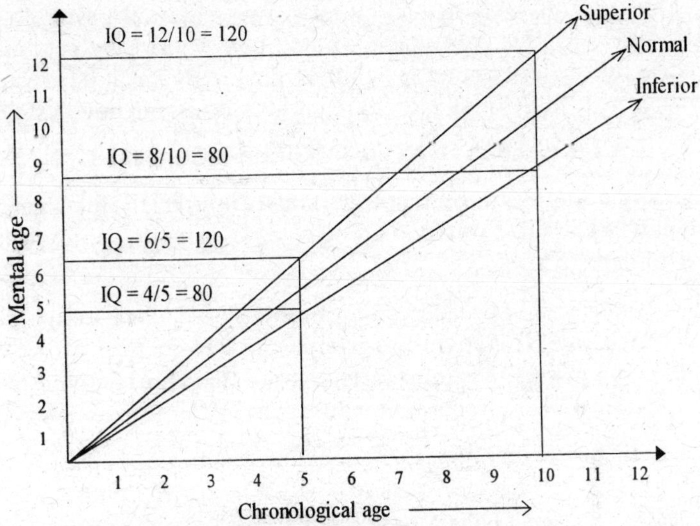

Fig. 7.1: IQ- Graphical Representation.

2. A subject's IQ score, ignoring errors of measurements remains the same from one age to all other unless there is a change in ability level.
3. A given change in IQ indicates same amount of change in relative standing regardless of the ability level of the subject.

Classification of IQ by Terman

Table-7.1
Classification of IQ by Terman

IQ	*Classification*
140 and above	Genius
120-139	Very superior
110-119	Superior
90-109	Average
80-89	Dull
70-79	Boarder line
Below 70	Feeble minded
50-69	Morons
25-49	Imbeciles
Below 25	Idiots

Latest trends and developments in educational psychology didn't accept the relevance of IQ. Lev Vygotsky's social constructivism, Jean Piaget's cognitive constructivism and Howard Gardner's Multiple Intelligence are highly discussing now-a-days.

CLASSIFICATION OF INTELLIENCE TESTS

As far as the administrative point of view is concerned the intelligence tests can be classified into two broad categories namely individual tests and group tests.

1. *Individual Tests:* This tests are administered to one individual at a time. This cover age group from 2-18 years.
2. *Group Tests*: A group tests are one that can be given to a number of subjects at the same time by single examiner.

The history of emergence of group tests can be traced back to 1st World War when the USA was compelled to join the war. A great necessity was felt to construct and device such measure of intelligence testing that can be given to a large number of prospective soldiers and officers for their classification for various jobs, consistent with their mental ability. The Army asked the American Psychologists to develop tests for classifying recruits. The Army Alpha and Army Beta were developed in a short period. These group tests proved remarkably successful in screening recruits.

Another way of classifying is based on the form of the tests. Accordingly, there are two types of tests.

A. *Verbal or Language Tests:* These tests make use of language. Here instructions are given in words. Individuals are required to use language as well as paper and pencil for giving their responses. These tests content is loaded with verbal materials. These may include varieties of items listed below:

   1. *Vocabulary Tests:* In these, the subject is required to give the meanings of words or phrases.
   2. *Memory Tests:* These are designed to test the subject's immediate and long-term memory and include recall and recognition of items.
   3. *Comprehension Tests:* By means of these, the subject is tested for the ability to grasp, understand and react to a given situation.

4. *Information Tests:* The subject is tested on his knowledge about the things around him by means of these tests.
5. *Reasoning Tests:* In these tests, the subject is asked to provide answers, which demonstrate his ability to reason logically, analytically, synthetically, inductively or deductively.
6. *Association Tests:* Through these tests, the subject is tested for his ability to point out the similarities or dissimilarities between two or more concepts or objects.

B. *Non-Verbal or Non-Language Tests:* These tests involve activities in which the sue of language is not necessary except for giving direction. Performance tests are a typical of such tests. The main features of these are:

1. The contents of the tests are in the form of material objects.
2. The tester through oral instructions or conveys what is required of the subject by pantomime and sign.
3. The subject's response are assess in terms of how he reacts or what he does rather than what he says or writes.

Generally, these are individual tests.

Classification of Intelligence Tests

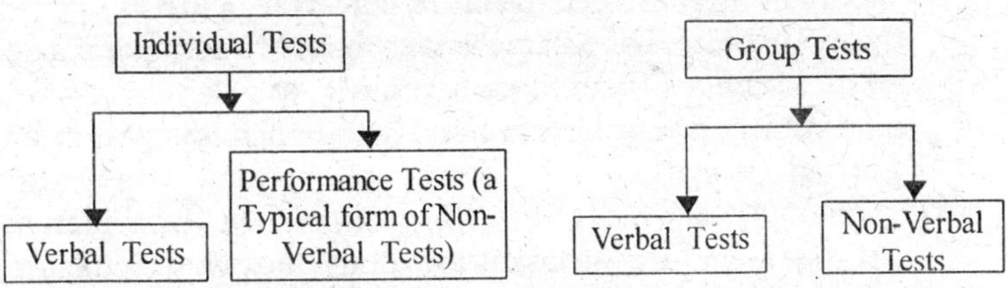

Individual Verbal Tests

Tests involving the use of language, which are administrated to one individual at a time, belong to this category. The Stanford Binet Scale, which is the revised form of scale, is an example. It is revised form of original Binet Simon tests. Alfred Binet, the father of the intelligence tests construction movement, along with Theordore Simon prepared a test as early as in 1905, consisting of 30 items graded for different levels. The first American revision of this test was published in 1931 by Terman at Stanford University and in 1937 another revision was carried out with the help of Maud M.

Meril. This as well as the 1960's revision is known as the Standard Binet Scale and is widely used as an individual intelligence test.

The test in this scale is graded in to age levels, extending from age 2-22 years. The task to be performed by the subject in these tests range from simple manipulation to abstract reasoning.

Individual Performance Tests

As stated earlier, the complete non-verbal or non-language tests of intelligence for testing one individual at a time came under this category. In these tests, the contents and responses are in the form of performance and language is not used and includes items that require responses in terms of motor activities. Generally the activities, on which the performance of an individual is tested are of the following types:

1. *Block Building or Cube Construction:* The subject is asked to make a structure or design by means of blocks or cubes supplied to him. Example, Koh's block design test, Alexander's pass along test.
2. *To Fit Blocks in Holes:* Test material of this type provides numerous blocks and a board on which there are holes, which correspond to these blocks. The subject has to fit the blocks in their corresponding holes on the board.
3. *Tracing a Maze:* The test material consist of a series of mazes of increasing difficulty, each printed on a separate sheet. The subject is required to trace with pencil, the path from entrance to exit.
4. *Picture Arrangement or Picture Completion:* In a picture arrangement test, the task is to arrange the given pictures in series, whereas in a picture completion test the subject is required to complete the picture with the help of given pieces cut out of each picture.

These tests highlight one or the other type of performance. A group of performance tests organized into a scale or battery is used in preference to just one or two tests to obtain a comprehensive idea of a person's mental ability. Some of the better known scales are as follows:

The Pinter-Patternson Scale

A popular scale in U.S.A., this was designed in 1917 mainly for the use of deaf and linguistically backward children. It is a comprehensive scale, which include 15 sub-tests. The performance on the scale is timed and marks area given for performance. These are added up and compared with established norms given in the manual to interpret the subject's general intelligence.

Arthur's Point Scale

Grace Arthur has developed this scale by adopting a point scale than the median mental age for the method of scoring.

Alexander's Battery of Performance Tests: W.P. Alexander designed this scale in Edinburg University. It consists of three tests – passes along, block design and cube construction.

The Group Verbal Intelligence Tests

The tests, which necessitate the use of language and are applied to a group of individuals at a time, come under this category. Some of the earlier tests belong to this category are:

1. Army Alpha Test (developed during World War I).
2. Army General Classification Test (developed during World Ward II).

Group Non-Verbal Intelligence Test

These test do not necessitate the use of language and are applicable to a group of individuals at a time.

The difference between performance tests (used for an individual) and non-verbal test (used for a group) is one of degree as far as their non-verbal nature is concerned. The individual performance tests require the manipulation by the subject, of concrete objects or materials, supplied in the test. Responses are purely motor in character and seldom require the use of paper and pencil by the testee (except in a case like the maze test etc) whereas the test material in the non-verbal tests used for group testing, is provided in booklets and requires the use of a pencil by the testee.

The test material contains pictures, diagrams, and geometrical figures etc., printed in a booklet. The subject is required to fill in some empty spaces, to draw some simple figures, to point-out similarities etc. In this way, all though the subject uses paper and pencil he does not need to know words as numerical figures. The examiner usually through demonstration to make the least possible use of language explains what the subject is required to do clearly.

Some examples of such tests are Army Beta Test, Chicago Non-Verbal Test, and Raven's Progressive Matrices test.

Comparison between Individual Tests and Group Tests

Table–7.2
Comparison between Individual and Group Tests

	Individual Tests	*Group Tests*
1.	It is administered to an individual at a time	It is administered to group at a time
2.	It is costly in terms of administration and time	It is less costly in terms of administration and time
3.	A trained tester is required to administer it	No trained person is required to administer it
4.	There is face to face interaction between the individual and the tester	There is no such face to face interaction
5.	Individual test is more reliable. Guidance can be provided to the individual on the basis of its results	Group tests may be influenced by several factors
6.	It is useful for small children	It is suitable of older children and adults
7.	The tester can motivate the individual by means of praise and encouragement and he can adopt to the needs of the individual child	It is not possible to do so
8.	There is very little scope for cheating	Cheating on a large scale is possible
9.	There is no competition in individual testing	Speed and reading ability may influence the test scores
10.	No special formalities are observed in individual testing	Several formalities are observed in administering
11.	Instructions can be met clear before testing.	A few members of the group may not clearly understand the instructions.

Intelligence Testing in India

I. Verbal Individual Tests

1. *Dr. C.H. Rice's Hindustani Tests:* Dr. C.H. Rice of the Former Christian College, Lahore was one of the first start this work in India in 1921. It is an adopted scale of Binet scale in Urudu. The Bombay-Karnataka Revision tests.
2. *Dr. V.V. Kammath* revised Binet's Scale to suite Indian

conditions and administered intelligence tests to 1074 children and adolescence of all age from 2-20 of both sexes. The locality selected for the experiment was the town of Dharwar. The children selected were fairly representative of the general population of Indian children.

3. The State *Manovigyan Shala* of Uttarpradesh has made a Hindi version of Stanford Binet test. This test is divided into several age groups and named as *Budhi Pareeksha Anooshilan*. Another common verbal intelligence test used in India is *Samanya Budhi Pareeksha*. It has been prepared by State Bureau of Educational and Vocational Guidance, Gwalior.
4. Stanford Hindustani Revision by Patna Training College, Patna.
5. Allahabad Intelligence test for 11+ years (in Hindi) by Dr. *Sohan Lal*.
6. C.I.E. (Central Institute of Education) test of intelligence by *Shri Udayashankar*.

II. Verbal Group Tests

1. Dr. J. Moray's Tests, 1927.
2. The Pasrur group intelligence tests (Urdu) by Prof: R.R. Kumria of Central Training College, Lahore.
3. Group Test of Intelligence (Test No: 3) Bureau of Psychology Allahabad.
4. Sohan Lal's test, 1946.
5. *Samuhik Manasik Yogyatha Pareeksha* by Prof. S. Jalota, Banaras Hindu University, 1951.
6. *Budhi Mapak Pareeksha* by Shri. V.G. Thingram, Dharma Samaj College, Aligarh, 1952.
7. C.I.E. Group Test of Intelligence by Prof. Udayshankar of the Central Institute of Education, Delhi, 1953.
8. Jha's Group Tests by R.B. Pandit Lajja Shankar Jha.
9. Kerala University, Verbal Group Test of Intelligence, Dr. N.P. Pillai, A.S. Nair and J. Gourikutty Amma.

III. Non-Verbal Group Test

1. Hindi Adaptation of Dr. R.A.C. Oliver's Test for East Africa by E.A. Menzel, Bisrampur (MP).
2. Non-Verbal Group Test by T.C. Vicary and M. Draper, Union Christian Training College, Orissa.

3. The Kerala Non-Verbal Test of Intelligence for Secondary Schools – A Sukumaran Nair, University of Kerala.

IV. Performance Tests

Dr. C. M. Bhatia's Battery of Performance Tests of Intelligence, 1945: Bhatia's Batery of Performance Test is developed by him contains Koh's Block Design Test, Alexander's Pass Along Test, Pattern. Drawing Test, Picture Construction Test and Immediate Memory Test for digits with an alternative form for the use illiterate subjects.

The Concept Artificial Intelligence

It is specifically concerned with moulding the human mind whereas as 'intelligence' refers to the main aim of replicating mental faculties in the area of problem solving in particular, which in human is regarded as requiring intelligent behaviour. The argument was put forwarded by Turing (1950). During Second World War some psychologists become involved in the design of controls for complex operating systems such as occur in aircraft cockpits. This involved their working along side specialists in ergonomics (the study of the human machine) and cybernetics (automatic control systems for machines), which late led to the development of the fields of cognitive psychology and Artificial Intelligence (AI).

In the future, Artificial Intelligence may be used to improve human thought by training us how to think more clearly. There is some irony here since it is entirely feasible that our computer slaves may ultimately become our master in a way foreseen by science fiction writers for two generations!

Intelligence Tests and their Correlates

(a) Basic characteristics of test scores –
- Stability and
- Factors and Gene.

(b) Test as predictors –
- School performance,
- Years of education,
- Social status and income,
- Job performance, and
- Social outcome.

(c) Test scores and measures of processing speed –
- Social outcome,
- Cognitive correlates,
- Choice reaction time,
- Inspection time,
- Neurological measures, and
- Problems of interpretation.

THE ECLECTIC THEORY OR TWO-FACTOR THEORY

According to the British Psychologist Spearman (1927), there is a fundamental ability underlying all mental functions. He is of the view that every intellectual activity depended up on general ability of 'g' factor and a separate or specific or 's' factor.

The 'g' factor represents the native intelligence and the 's' factor relates to the specific ability of the individual required to achieve in a specific job.

When we respond to any situation or perform an intellectual task, our general mental ability or 'g' factor is responsible for part of our reactions and our specific ability in that particular task is responsible for the rest.

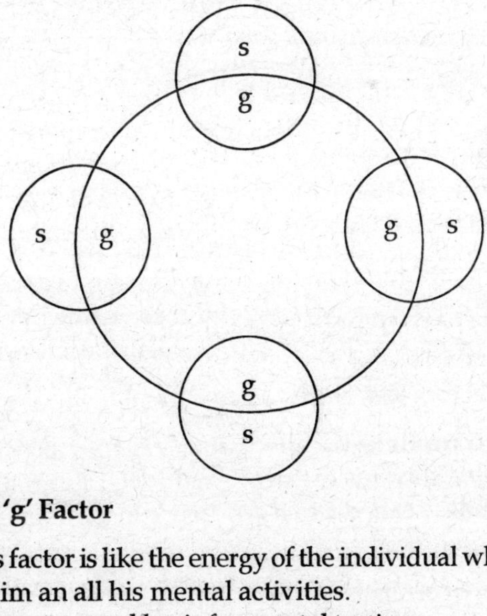

Features of 'g' Factor

1. This factor is like the energy of the individual which is helpful to him an all his mental activities.
2. It serves a good basis for mental testing.

3. This may be explained as human energy working or our nervous system.
4. It is a gift to the individual from nature.
5. It varies from individual to individual.

Features of 's' Factor

1. It comes in to operation when the individual is busy in doing a specific job.
2. The number of there abilities is quite large — verbal ability, numerical ability.
3. There abilities operate only with the help of general ability.
4. An individual can have a number of these abilities.
5. Their capacity of action may also differ.

An individual may have excellent music ability and an ordinary intellectual ability.

Different performance require different—amount of 'g' and 's' in Math's and classics, for instance more of 'g' is required. Where an in music and drawing 's' factor predominates, the latter subjects require a small amount of 'g'. Person having more of 'g' and less of 's' faces well in life. Selection is students for will service based on high score in classics in safer than their selection for such a job based on a good musical ability.

Spearman has established his theory of two factors by shows that there is always a positive correlation in the performance of an individual in any two tasks. It may be concluded that Spearman's theory may loose the battle but it is sure to win the war. This theory has been criticized by Thorndike on various ground.

Spearman, after statistical analysis of test result found correlation between various tests and these tend ended towards a peculiar arrangement, which he expressed, in the following formula:

$$gar \times gbq - gaq \times gbr = 0$$

The above formula is called *tetrad equation* because the test correlation in the formula are deal—with sets of four and value on the left hand side is called *tetrad* difference in the above formula.

gar — means correlation between opposites and completion.
gbq — means correlation between cancellation and disorientation.
gaq — means correlation between discrimination and completion.

Spearman find that the *tetrad* equation holds good for the intercorrelation of all sorts of abilities.

Criticism

According to Spearman each job sequences some specific ability. This view was in tenable as it implied that there in nothing common to different jobs except a general factors and profession such as those of nurse, compounders and doctors could not be put on one group.

The 's' factors are not mutually exclusive. They overlap and give rise to certain common factors. The idea of overlapping and grouping resulted in a new theory called the *group factor theory.*

THORNDIKE'S THEORY OF INTELLIGENCE

The term intelligence covers the abilities associated with all cognitive processes. According to David Wechsler, "Intelligence is the aggregate or global capacity of an individual to act purposefully, to think rationally, and to deal effectively with his environment."

The theories of intelligence propagated by Psychologists from time to time have tried to discover the structure and components of intelligence. These theories can be grouped under two categories, viz., Factor theories and Cognitive theories. Thorndike's theory of intelligence comes under the category of Factor theories.

Multi-factor Theory or Anarchic Theory (1921)

This theory is also is known as the *atomistic theory of intelligence*. It is against the oldest theory of intelligence called the *unitary* or *monarchic* theory which holds that the intelligence consists of one factor, a fund of intellectual competence, which is universal to all activities of the individual.

Thorndike's theory holds that a person's total intelligence is the combination of a numerous separate elements or factors, each one being a minute element of one ability. Then there is no general intelligence (a single factor) and there are only many highly independent specific factors. So on the basis of this theory, knowledge of a person's ability in one area does not help us to understand his ability in other areas.

His theory mentions specific stimuli and specific responses. Intelligence to him is nothing more than a convenient name for an almost infinite number of actual or potential specific connections between these stimuli and responses. Differences of intelligence among people are due to the difference in the number of connections in the neurological system.

Thorndike distinguished four attributes of intelligence.

A. *Level:* This attribute refers to the difficulty of a task that can be solved. If we think of all tasks or test items arranged in sequential order of increasing difficulty then the height that we can attain on this ladder of difficulty determines our level or altitude of intelligence. Level is important factor of the intellect, but we cannot measure it alone.

B. *Range:* Range or width refers to the number of tasks at any given degree of difficulty that we can solve. Theoretically, an individual possessing a given level of intelligence should be able to solve the whole range of tasks at that level. Range is determined not only by level but also by breadth of experience and by opportunity to learn. In intelligence tests, range is represented by items of equal difficulty; we cannot measure altitude without range.

C. *Area:* Area in test means the total number of situations at each level to which the individual is able to respond. Area is summation of all the ranges at each level of intelligence. It is in general highly correlated with altitude level.

D. *Speed:* This is the rapidly with which we respond to test items. Speed and altitude are positively correlated. Speed is much less closely bound up with altitude than the attributes.

Every intelligence test consists these four attributes. When we test a person, we give him a certain number of tasks (area) and these tasks vary in difficulty (altitude) and there is certain number of items at each level of difficulty (range) they are responded in a given time (speed). While preparing the famous CAVD battery of tests with problems of computation, arithmetic, vocabulary and direction, Thorndike laid greater stress upon the degree of difficulty or level.

Based on multi-factor theory we cannot assume that good intelligence is a guarantee of success in all spheres of human life. We can also assume that with certain specific types of abilities and individual would be entirely successful in a particular area and completely unsuccessful in other areas. This explains why a child good at mathematics need not necessarily be good in civics.

Murphy (1968) says: " There is a certain positive relationship between brightness in one field and brightness in other and so on." Thus, there is the necessity of a common factor for intelligence and it gave birth to Spearman's two-factor theory.

THOMPSON'S OLIGARCHIC OR SAMPLING THEORY

This theory was propagated by G.H. Thompson (1939) a British psychologist. It assumes that the mind is made up of several independent bonds or elements. Any specific test or school activity samples some of these bonds. It is possible that two or more tests sample and utilize the same bonds, and a general common factor can be said to exist among them. It is also possible that some other tests sample different bonds, in which case the tests have nothing in common and each of them is specific.

The theory states that intellectual abilities belong to certain groups which are not related to each other has a close relationship between the abilities belonging to the same group. This means that the individual who is intelligent in one group of knowledge may be equally intelligent in the various subjects of that particular group. This theory is based on co-relational techniques. In brief we can say that the individual has got a number of mental abilities. When he has to perform certain type of work, he makes sampling abilities and samples out of certain important abilities, out of the whole world of abilities. Since the individual has to select the abilities through sampling, this theory is called as *Thompson's Sampling* theory of intelligence.

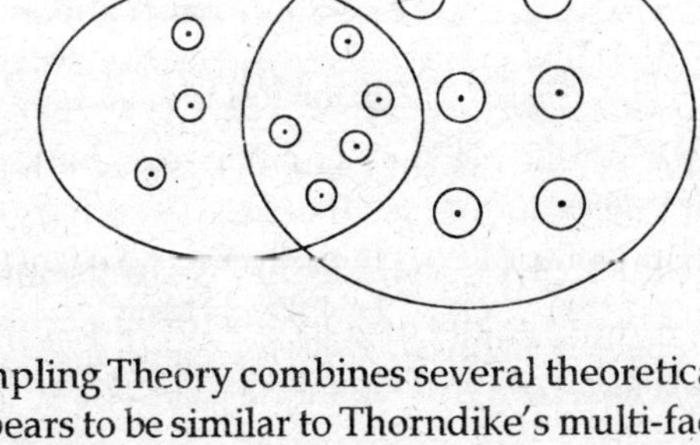

The Sampling Theory combines several theoretical view points in that it appears to be similar to Thorndike's multi-factor theory. In this theory 'g' factor is not considered as important as Spearman's theory. At first, Thompson neglected this factor but later on he realized its importance. His general ability was different from Spearman's theory. He considered it as second order factor. For example, a boy is good in mathematics but poor in English. In spite of this he may be intelligent in allied subjects like physics, statistics etc.

GROUP FACTOR STRUCTURE OF INTELLIGENCE BY L.L. THURSTONE (1938)

Louis Leon Thurstone, American psychologist was prominent among the propagators of Group Factor Theory of Intelligence. Intermediate between the two factor theory of Spearman and multi-factor theory of Thorndike, Thurstone gives the Group factor theory of P.M.A. (Primary Mental Abilities). It was in 1938 that Thurstone gives us this theory after giving 56 types of tests to 240 students of Chicago University. From the result, he conclude that certain mental operations have a common primary factor which gives them psychological and functional unity and, which differentiates them from other mental operations. These mental operations constitute a Group Factor. So there are a number of groups of mental abilities and each of these groups has its own primary factor.

The six primary factors emerged are as follows:

1. Number Factor (N)	–	Ability to do numerical and calculations rapidly and accurately.
2. Verbal Factor (V)	–	Found in test involving Verbal Comprehension.
3. Space Relation Factor (S)	–	Involved in any task in which the subject manipulate a object imaginary in space.
4. Memory Factor (M)	–	Involve the ability to memorize quickly.
5. Reasoning Factor (R)	–	Found in tasks that require the subject to discover a rule or principle.
6. Wordfluency Factor (W)	–	Involved whenever the subject is asked to think of isolated words at rapid rate.

Later Thurstone added three more group factors (Nos. 7-9) to his list making the total the total as nine.

7. Perceptual Ability Factor (p)	–	Capacity perceive things in the physical layout more easily.
8. Deductive Reasoning Factor (RI)	–	Ability to use generalized results correctly
9. Inductive Reasoning Factor (RI)	–	Ability to generalize by taking specific examples.

Thurstone correlation between different primary abilities have been shown as follows:

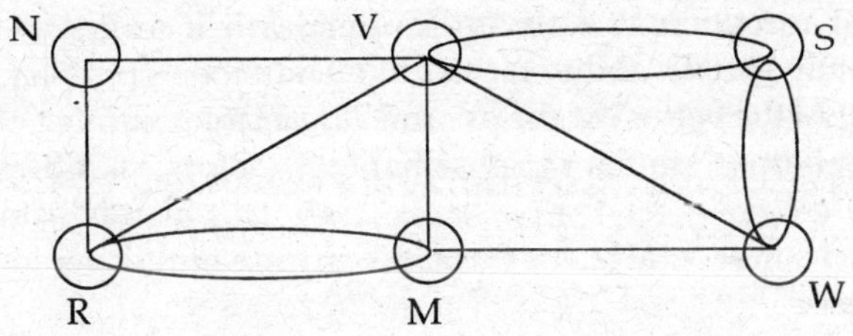

Group Factor Theory

	N	W	V	S	M	R
N	.41					
V	.40	.54				
S	.28	.17	.16			
M	.31	.6	.35	.13		
R	.53	.49	.59	.29	.39	

Some Conclusions

1. Thurstone held that if the individual wants to perform any particular activity one or more of this factors or abilities are involved. Some of them are more important than others. In learning mathematics deductive and numerical factors are involved.
2. He starts with the assumption that these factors are primary and general in nature and play a Vital role in complex intellectual activities. Thus his approach is different from Spearman's—Two factor theory.
3. He also does not agree with the Terman's-View of IQ. He held that the tests according to his theory helps us in forming a profile of abilities which are indicative of a picture of intellect an individual has.

BURT AND VERNON'S HIERARCHICAL THEORY OF INTELLIGENCE

According to Hierarchical Theory, intelligence is pictured as a sort of pyramid. Psychologists like C. Burt and P.E. Vernon, combined the elements of G. factor theory and multi-factor theories and put forward the hierarchical theory of intelligence. At the top of the pyramid is G. General intelligence; which shows up in virtually all kinds of intellectual activity. Underneath it are new several moderately specific ability factors like Thurstone's primary mental abilities. At the bottom of the pyramid are a larger number of highly specific abilities, similar to Spearman's 'S' factors, i.e., abilities that may come to play on one particular task. This hierarchical theory borrows from several factor theories to form a multilayered view of intelligence.

Burt's 5-level Hierarchical Model of Intelligence

Burt in 1940 separated statistically four factors of intellect namely

1. General factors which are common to all traits.
2. Group factors common to some of the traits.
3. Specific factors are limited to each trait whenever, it is measured.
4. Error factors limited to each on each particular occasion it is measured.

He proposed a 5-level hierarchical model which is as follows:

At the lowest level of mental processes are sensations and simple movements. This is known as *Sensory Motor Level* (S.M.).

The second level of hierarchy is that of *Perception* (P) and Co-Ordinated Movement (C).

The 3rd level is known as the *Associative Level* and it is connected with the function of *Memory* (M) and *Habit Formation* (H).

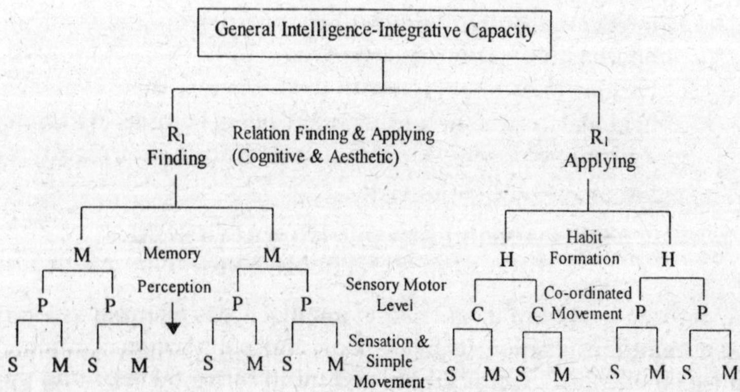

Fig. 7.2: Burt's 5-level Hierarchical Model of Intelligence.

The 4th and highest level in this hierarchy is that of relation finding. It refers to cognitive aesthetic aspects of intelligence.

Burt regards intelligence as the integrative capacity of the mind.

This hierarchical theory of mental structure has been found useful in test construction. According to peel, "It is not easy to get a battery of tests which reveal Burt's hierarchy exactly, but whenever a mixed battery of tests verbal, non verbal, performance etc, is analysis into its factors a hierarchy is found, after going along the fines'.

VERNON'S HIERARCHICAL THEORY

The British psychologist P.E. Vernon (1950) suggested a hierarchical structure for the organization of intelligence.

According to him, the mind is a kind of hierarchy in which 'G' is the most prominent mental ability i.e., an overall factor measured through intelligence tests. Under 'G', are have two major group factors, termed as Ved and KM, representing two main kinds of mental abilities.

The 1st major group factor Ved is concerned with the verbal, numerical and educational abilities.

The 2nd major group factor KM is connected with practical, mechanical, spatial and physical abilities.

These two major factors can be divided into minor group factors and ultimately these minor factors may be further sub-divided into various specific factors related with minute specific mental abilities.

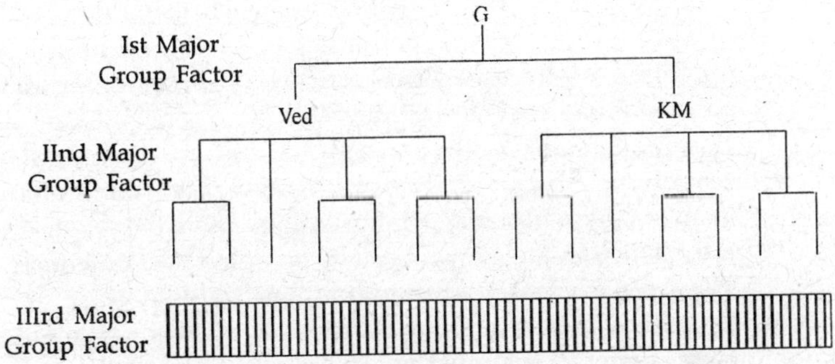

Fig. 7.3: Vernon' Hierarchical Structure of Human Intelligence.

STRUCTURE OF INTELLECT (SOI) BY GUILFORD

Structure of intellect was developed by Dr. J.P. Guilford and his associates in the psychological laboratory at the University of Southern California in 1966 on the basis of factor analysis of many tests. The idea of structure of intellect model was formulated in fifties, following the factor analysis of many tests. It was successively refined and modified until the present model was finally developed in the year 1966. He suggests that the mind is composed of at least three dimensions, instead of unidimensional model of intellect which permeated earlier writing. The model is a three-way classification of intellectual activities namely operation, contents and products. According to Guilford, each dimension of intellect is sufficiently distinct which may be detected by factor analysis. Every intellectual ability, in the structure is characterized in terms of the type of operation, the content and sort of product which results.

In recent years, it has been apparent that three dimensions of intellect can be classified because of the elements of resemblance among themselves. The three dimensions of intellect are given below:

(A) Operations

The kind of classification on the basis of operations gives five major groups intellectual abilities: (1) Cognition, (2) Memory, (3) Divergent thinking, (4) Convergent thinking and (5) Evaluation.

1. *Cognition*: It is the most important fundamental operation in the learning process.
2. *Memory*: It is a primary mental process. It means retention of what is recognized.
3. *Divergent Thinking*: This operation is most clearly involved in aptitude of creative potential. In divergent thinking operation, we think in difference directions, searching and seeking some variety and novelty. Divergent thinking is closely associated with creativity.
4. *Convergent Thinking*: Convergent thinking is the generation of information from given information, where the emphasis is upon achieving conventionally accepted best outcomes. The given information fully determines the response.
5. *Evaluation*: It means taking decisions or making judgments concerning criterion satisfaction of information. In evaluation we reach conclusions and decisions as to

goodness, correctness, suitability or adequacy of what we know, what we remember and what we produce in productive thinking.

(B) Content

A second way of classifying the intellectual factor is according to the kind of material or content involved. The factors known thus far involve four kinds of material content. The content may be (1) Figural, (2) Symbolic, or (3) Semantic and (4) Behavioural.

1. *Figural Content*: It is concrete material such as perceived through the senses. It does not represent anything except itself. Visual material has properties as size, form and colour etc. Things we hear or feel, provide other figural material.
2. *Symbolic Content*: It is composed of letters; digits and other conventional signs usually organized in general patterns such as the alphabet or the number system.
3. *Semantic Content*: It is in the form of verbal meanings or idea for which no examples are necessary.
4. *Behavioural Content*: It means the social behaviour in society.

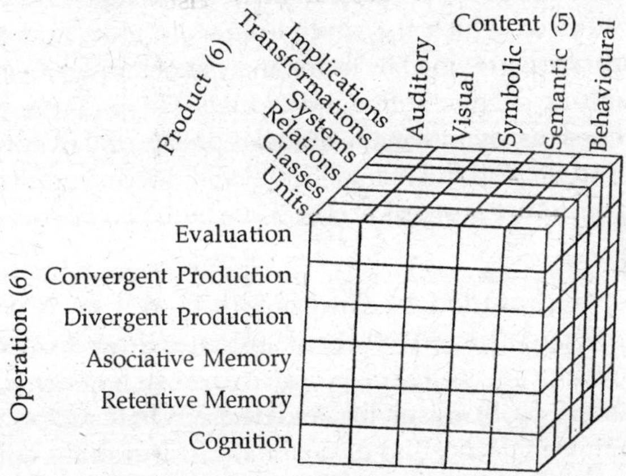

Fig. 7.4: Structure of Intellect (SOI) Model of Guilford.

(C) Products

When a certain operation is applied to certain kind of content, as many as six general kinds of products may be involved. There is enough evidence available to suggest that, regardless of the combinations of operations and contents, the same six types of products may be found associated. The six types of products are:

(1) Units, (2) classes, (3) relation, (4) systems, (5) transformations, and (6) implications on the basis of factor analysis. These are the only fundamental kinds of products.

The three kinds of classification of the factors can be represented by means on a single solid model which is called the *Structure of Intellect Model* (SOI).

Some Implications of Structure of Intellect Model (SOI)

The structure of intellect model developed by Guilford has briefly been explained above with its three dimensions representing ways in which the intellectual abilities differ from one another: 5 basic kinds of operations, 4 kinds of contents and 6 formal kinds of products. Here, we will describe major implications for psychological theory for educational and vocational testing and for education. A brief description of each is given below:

(a) For Psychological Theory

The SOI model is very useful in constructing the tests of various types for different age groups. Factor analysis discovers traits and finds out the ways in which the individuals are alike and also differ. The information provided by factor analysis of human abilities gives understanding of functioning individuals. For example, five kinds of operations discovered in the model represent the five ways of functioning and the six kind of intellectual abilities distinguished on the basis of product suggest a classification of basic form of information.

The concepts provided by Guilford in model by way of distinctions among the intellectual abilities and by their classifications well prove useful in our future research in the areas of learning, memory problem-solving, and decision-making etc. The model is taxonomic in nature and discovered many abilities which were not known before. The model provides a sound basis for new psychological theory.

(b) For Vocational Testing

The Structure of Intellect (SOI) is a theoretical model which predicts that there are 120 intellectual abilities, if every cell of the model contains a factor. We know that two cells contain two or more factors each and there may be other cells of this type.

The implication for the assessment of intelligent is that to know an individual's intellectual abilities thoroughly we need a large number of scores.

Therefore in vocational testing, a multiple score approach will be needed in future.

The model predicts four kinds of mental abilities classified as content which means that there are four kinds of intelligence that need different types of test items in vocational tests.

The first type of content is figural. The mental abilities involving the use of figural information may be regarded as concrete intelligence. The people who depend upon these abilities deal with concrete objects and their properties, for examples, mechanics, operators, engineers, artists, musicians, etc.

The symbolic and semantic mental abilities involve two kinds of abstract, intelligence. Symbolic abilities are important in learning to recognize words, to spell and to operate with numbers. Language and mathematics (except Geometry) depend very much on symbolic abilities. Semantic intelligence is very important for understanding things in terms of verbal concepts and hence is important in all courses where the learning of facts and ideas is essential.

The last content in the model is behavioural which may be described as social intelligence. Which involves the mental abilities to understand the behaviour of others and ourselves in the society. Understanding the behaviour of others in the society is largely non-verbal in character.

The social intelligence is very important for those who deal with other people: teachers, politicians, social workers, statesmen, agents of companies and leaders of other kinds need a good amount of social intelligence.

(c) For Education

The most fundamental implications of the model are in the field of education. Few of them are given below:

Change in the concept of the learner and the learning process. Traditionally we have been following that learner is a kind of stimulus-response device. You present a stimulus and the learner will respond, much on the order of vending machine on Railway stations. You put a coin of 50 paise and you will get a ticket indicating your weight on it. The machine learns what reaction to put out when a certain coin is put in. But the new conception of the learner in the light of the findings of the SOI model is that of electronic computer who not only stores information but uses that information to generate new information either by divergent or convergent thinking and it also evaluate its own results.

Human learners have advantage over a computer. The human learner can seek and discover information from sources outside itself and the steps of programming itself. The concept learner leads to the idea that learning is discovery of information and merely the information of associations (S – R Bondage). The model suggest that in order to under stand human learning and higher mental process of thinking, Moslem saluting and creative etc, some drastic modifications are to be mode in our theory of curriculum construction and methodology of instruction.

The traditional idea that education is the training of mind or of the intellect has lost ground the light of the recent findings of the factor analysis of intellectual abilities. Now the main emphasis in education is given to the learning of specific habits or skills.

The most learning has both specific and general aspects. The general aspects may be along the lines of factors of intellect. This is not to say that the individual's status in each factor is entirely determined by learning. We do not know to what extent each factor is determined by heredity and to what extent by learning. The educators may take the view that every intellectual factor can be developed at least to some extent by learning.

If we believe that the general objective of education is to develop the intellectual abilities of students then we should plan our curriculum in such a way that a certain combination of content, operation and product is made for the improvement of intellectual abilities. We have to develop teaching methods to accomplish the goal of education.

The method of intellect has explored 120 intellectual abilities, which enabled us to find out if any of the general intellectual skill is being neglected in our curriculum. The model is very helpful to device enrichment programmes for gifted and creative children.

CATTEL'S THEORY OF INTELLIGENCE

In our day-to-day conversations we often commend that a particular individual is very intelligent or not intelligent. Such comments are based on our observation of the perfo.mance or behaviour of the individual concerned in comparison to others of his group. David Wechler has given a comprehensive definition as "intelligence is the aggregate on global capacity of an individual to act purposefully, to think rationally and to deal effectively with his environment."

The theories of intelligence propagated by Psychologists from time-to-time have try to uncover the components or elements of intelligence. These theories are grouped into two namely – Factor theories and Cognitive theories.

Cognitive theories of intelligence tried to analyze and describe intelligence in terms of certain fundamental cognitive processes. One of the important theory falling under this category is *Cattel's Theory of Intelligence.*

Raymond, B. Cattel along with Horn proposed a theory of intelligence by distinguishing between two types of intelligence that is Fluid Intelligence and Crystallised Intelligence although both these are distinct they are interacted and intermingled to produce overall intelligence.

Fluid Intelligence and Crystallized Intelligence

Fluid Intelligence is considered to be the mental capacity of an individual which is required for learning and problem-solving. It is dependent on neurological development in other words, it is influenced by biological and genetic factors rather than training and experience. Fluid intelligence is formless and independent of previous experience. This includes inductive reasoning, figural relations, memory and speed problem-solving. Inductive reasoning allows a person to discover a general rule by observing particular instances. Figural relation is the component of Fluid intelligence that allows people to perceive partial relationship, to use maps effectively and to develop a sense of direction. It allows us to see patterns and detect the relationship among objects.

Crystallized Intelligence is not a function of one's neurological development and therefore is not innate like Fluid intelligence. It is specially learned and is therefore dependent on one's education and culture. It can be identified through one's fund of vocabulary, general knowledge of world affairs, knowledge of custom, traditions and the rituals, manner of behaving in the society etc. which requires knowledge experience and practice. This is found to continue to increase through out one's life span.

Important Implications of the Theory

Among children who are similar in cultural and educational background, crystallized and fluid intelligence are highly correlated and it is difficult to distinguish down. In these instances in strong relationship are probably because children who are high in fluid intelligence acquire specific information with greater ease.

But when children who differ in cultural and educational experience are tested the two abilities are easy to identify, children with same fluid capacity may perform quite differently on test that emphasis crystallized task. As these findings suggest Cattel's theory, have important implications for the issue of cultural bias in intelligence testing.

Crystallized intelligence corresponds roughly to verbal IQ and fluid intelligence corresponding roughly to non-verbal IQ reasoning.

Conclusion

Today most psychologists believe that intelligence involves but the general ability to handle a wide range of cognitive task problems and number of more specific abilities. In a sense, though modern thinking about the nature of intelligence has largely moved beyond modern thinking about the nature of intelligence has largely moved beyond the unitary V/s multi-faceted issue and now addresses very differently questions relating to information processing, neural functioning and culture.

INFORMATION PROCESSING VIEW OF INTELLIGENCE OR COGNITIVE THEORIES

Andersons Theory

This theory suggests from differences in the basic possessing mechanism that implements thinking, which in turn yields knowledge.

Sternbergs Triarchic Theory

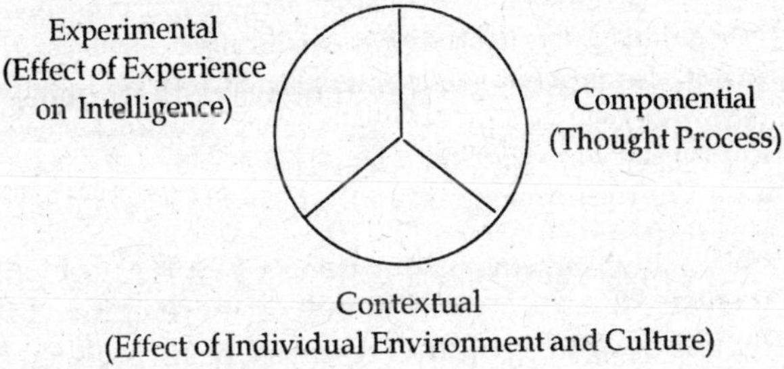

Leci's Bio-Ecological Theory

Everyday or real world intellectual performance cannot be explained by IQ alone or by some biological notion of general intelligence. Instead it depends on the interaction between multiple cognitive potentials with a rich, well-organised knowledge base.

Piaget's Theory of Intelligence

The best known developmentally based consumption of intelligence. Unlike most of the theories Piaget had relatively little interest in individual differences. Intelligence develops in all children through the continually shifting balance between the assimilation of new information into existing cognitive structure and the accommodation of those structured themselves into new information.

Factors Influencing Intelligence

1. Gene-Sources of intelligence differences.
2. Environment—
   (a) Social variable—occupational, schooling, interventions, family environment.
   (b) Biological variable—nutrition, lead, alcohol, pre-natal factors.
   (c) Individual life experiences.

Racial Factor as a Determinant of Intelligence

Different racial groups perform at different levels on IQ tests, which were designed by and for people from European and American cultures. The early studies of immigrant recruits into American Army during the First World War originally showed this to be so. American Negros at around one standard deviation below whites on the contemporary tests.

MULTIPLE INTELLIGENCE

Meaning

Multiple intelligence are nine different ways that, demonstrate intellectual ability (Gardener).

Definition

Gardner defines intelligence as 'the capacity to solve problems as to fashion products that are valued in one or more cultural setting. Using biological as well as cultured research, he formulated a list of nine intelligences. They are logical mathematical intelligence, linguistic intelligence, spatial intelligence, musical intelligence, interpersonal intelligence, naturalistic intelligence of existential. [Recently has included more like gustatory/olfactory intelligence, touch; hepatic sensory system.]

Gardner's Theory

Gardner is the neurologist of Boston University and the psychologist of Harvard School of Psychology and Piaget's student. Gardner defined intelligence as "to my mind a human intellectual competence must entail a set of skills of problem Solving – enabling the individual to resolve genuine problems or difficulties that he or she encounters, and, when appropriate, to create an effective product – and must also entail the potential for finding or crating problems – their by laying the ground for the acquisition of knowledge" (1983). He believes intelligence is a bio-psychological potential.

According to Gardner all human being possess all nine intelligence in varying amounts, each person has a different cultural composition. We can improve education by addressing the multiple intelligence of our students. These intelligence are located in different areas of the brain and can either work independently or together. These intelligence may define the human species. He urges that there is both biological and cultural basis for multiple intelligence.

Difference between Multiple Intelligence and Traditional Intelligence

Traditional Intelligence

1. Intelligence can be measured by short answer tests.
2. People born with a fixed amount of intelligence.

3. Intelligence level does not change over a life time (Constancy of IQ).
4. Intelligence consists of ability in logic and language.

Multiple Intelligence

1. Assessment of an individual can foster learning and problem-solving styles.
2. Human beings have all of the intelligence but each person has a unique combination or profile.
3. We can improve each of the intelligence.
4. There are many types of intelligence which reflects different ways of interacting with the world.

History of Multiple Intelligence

Introduced by Gardner 1983. Now the movement includes publishers, symposiums, websites, 'how to manuals' and educational consultants.

Gardner's Books

Frame of mind (1983).
The disciplined mind (1999).
Intelligence re-framed (1999).

Criticism

- It is not new.
- It is not well-defined.
- It is culturally embedded.
- It defeats national standard.
- It is impractical.

Educational Implications

It helps students to manage their an learning to value their individual strengths.

While all students may not be verbally or mathematically gifted children may have an expertise in other areas such as music, spatial, or inter personal knowledge.

Education should encourage and teach to be a broader range of talents and skills rather than mere development and use of verbal and authentical intelligence in traditional education.

EMOTIONAL INTELLIGENCE (EI)

Meaning

Emotional intelligence is the ability to use our emotions, to help us to solve problems and live a more effective life. EI without intelligence or intelligence without EI is only a part of solution, which is the head working without heart. EI is a cluster of traits or abilities relating to the emotional side of life—such as recognizing and managing one's own emotions, recognizing and managing others' emotions and handling interpersonal relations in an effective manner.

Definition

EI is the ability to perceive emotions to access and generate emotions so as to assist thought to understand emotions and emotional knowledge and to reflectively regulate emotions so as to promote emotional and intellectual growth (Mayer and Salovey, 1997).

History

1985—Wayne Leon Payne—the term first used in his doctoral theses.

1990—Mayer and Salovey—two tests for measuring EI.

1995 and 1998—Daniel Goleman—published "Emotional Intelligence."

Theory

Daniel Goleman suggests five major parts of EI:

1. *Knowing Our Own Emotions*: Everyone is able to recognize their emotions. The extend of unawareness of the individuals own feelings, they can't make intelligent choices. It is very important. It is associated with Gardner's intra personal intelligence
2. *Managing Our Own Emotions*: Regulate the nature, intensity and expression of emotions. Doing so is very important both for our own mental health and from the point of view of interacting effectively with others.
3. *Motivating Ourselves*: Being able to motivate oneself to work long and hard on a task, remaining enthusiastic and optimistic about the final outcome and being able to delay gratifications.
4. *Recognizing the Emotions of Others*: Ability to read others

accurately-to recognize the mood they are in and what emotions they are experiencing. This skill is valuable in many practical settings. It is associated with interpersonal intelligence of Gardner.

5. *Handling Relationships*: Ability to getting along with others.

Components

1. Perception of emotions.
2. Appraisal of emotions.
3. Expression of emotions.
4. Emotional facilitation of thinking.
5. Understanding emotions.
6. Analyzing emotions.
7. Employing emotional knowledge.
8. Reflective regulation of emotions.
9. Emotional awareness.
10. Empathy.

Characteristics of emotionally intelligent person

- can identify and perceive various types of emotions in others,
- can sense his own feelings and emotions,
- can incorporate perceived emotions in his thought,
- have proper understanding of the nature, intensity and outcomes of his emotions,
- can exercise proper control and regulations over the expressions and use of emotions in dealing with his self and others so as to promote harmony prosperity and peace,
- can control impulse,
- have self-esteem,
- have self-motivation, and
- have the ability to manage mood.

Assessment of Emotional Intelligence

1. Bar- On's EQ-I.
2. Multifactor Emotional Intelligence Scale.
3. Emotional Competence Inventory.
4. EQ Map.

Educational Implications

- Emotional literacy holds the key to effective learning.

- Schools must create settings in which the emotional literacy of their teachers and students are developed.
- Educational system should give importance to the development of emotional competence.

APTITUDE AND INTEREST

The observable fact that people differ from one another and within themselves in their performance in one or other field of human activity such as leadership, music, art, mechanical work, teaching etc. Therefore in a simple way aptitude may be considered a special ability or specific capacity besides the general intellectual ability which helps an individual to acquire a required degree of proficiency or achievement in a special field.

Definitions

"Aptitude refers to those qualities characterizing person's way of behaviour which serve to indicate how well he can learn to meet and solve certain specified kinds of problems" – Bingham.

"An aptitude is a combination of characteristics indicative of an individual capacity to acquire (with training) some specific knowledge, skill, or set of organized responses, such as the ability to speak a language, to become a musician, to do mechanical work" – Freeman.

The aptitude of an individual at a particular moment is in all probability, dependent upon both heredity and environment.

Table-7.3
Difference between Intelligence and Aptitude

	Intelligence		*Aptitude*
1.	It tests the general mental ability of an individual.	1.	Specific abilities.
2.	The knowledge of intelligence of an individual we can predict his success in a number of situations involving mental function or activity.	2.	This ability or capacity to succeed in a specific field or activity.

Measurement of Aptitudes

The aptitude test can be classified into the following types according he specific nature of the aptitude test by them.

Table-7.4
Difference between Aptitude and Interest

	Intelligence		*Aptitude*
1.	Interest can be the cause of an activity and result of participation in the activity.	1.	It is an innate capacity or potentiality that is independent of learning.
2.	A feeling of happiness or satisfaction is an inward sign of interest.	2.	A feeling of happiness or satisfaction is not fully the inward sign of interest.

Mechanical Aptitude Tests

Mechanical Aptitude include a variety of factor such as spatial visualization, perceptual speed, mechanical information and manual dexterity. Two types of tests are commonly used. They are

1. Minnesota Mechanical Assembly Test.
2. Minnesota Paper Form Board Test.

Clerical Aptitude Test

Clerical Aptitude tests measure how much capacity one has for clerical details. Accuracy and speed in reading, writing, and marking are the major functions to be tested. The commonly used tests are:

1. Minnesota Clerical Test.
2. General Clerical Test.

Musical Aptitudes

In musical aptitude, a major component is the ability to master the patterns of action required to play an instrument. Measures of Musical Aptitude Tests are

1. Seashore Measures of Musical Talents.
2. The Musical Aptitude Test.
4. Aptitude Test Batteries.

The Differential Aptitude Test

It includes

1. Verbal Reasoning,
2. Numerical Ability,
3. Abstract Reasoning,
4. Space Relations,

5. Mechanical Comprehension,
6. Clerical Speed and Accuracy, and
7. Language Usage.

General Aptitude Test Battery

1. Intelligence,
2. Verbal Ability,
3. Numerical Ability,
4. Spatial Ability,
5. From perception, and
6. Clerical dexterity etc.

Teacher Aptitude Test

For the prediction of performance in teacher training courses the most valid indicators have proved to be previous academic grades, general scholastic aptitude tests and academic achievement etc.

1. Coxe—Or leans prognostic test of teaching.
2. The national teacher examinations.

Aptitude Tests and the Gifted Child

Traditionally, the gifted child was identified primarily by tests of abstract intelligence. There is an increased tendency to think of a gifted child as one whose performance, in a potentially value able line of human activities. The standardized mental and educational tests are used for screening and examining children of high ability, with a toward enrichment of their school programmes. Aptitude tests can aid in identifying giftedness in areas other than the abstract intelligence.

INTEREST

A feeling of happiness or satisfaction is an inward sign of interest. Interest lead to effort and as stimulant for effort, interest is an important aspect in the process of education. Writers have defined interests as of pre-occupation, objectives, likes and dislikes and motives.

According to them the verbal expression of interests is an activity or occupation is *expressed interest*. Interest as evidenced by participation in an activity or profession is *manifested interest*. Interest as measured by objective tests or other information is *tested interest* and in those which are measured by lists of activities or occupation to which the students responds by an expression of linking or preference is termed a *inventory interest*.

Vocational Interest is depend upon knowledge, attitude, values, physical characteristics and environmental influences.

Interest and the Curriculum

A teacher should know the interests of each pupil early in the school year. Instruction should begin at the point of interest of the child, and this cannot be accomplished unless these interests are known. The curriculum should be prepared according to the needs of children.

How to Make Children Interested in a Particular Learning Activity

The important factors in learning/teaching process are the:

1. learners,
2. learning Material,
3. learning environment,
4. method of teaching,
5. teacher, and
6. fatigue etc.

Definitions

L. Russel, describes interest as organismic conditions lead to continuing stimulation of concern about particular object, persons and activities.

Drives say, "An interest is a disposition in its dynamic aspect."

Crow and Crow state, "Interest may refer to the motivating force that impels us to attend to a person, a thing, or an activity, or it may be the affective experience that has been stimulated by the activity itself."

Kinds of Interest

- *Natural Interests*: Natural interests are interests arising from natural tendencies like instincts and emotions.
- *Acquired Interests*: Acquired interests are due to acquired disposition like sentiments, habits, character, ideals and tastes.

- *Intrinsic Interest*: It is the deep-rooted interest. A mother has intrinsic interest in her son.
- *Extrinsic Interest*: Extrinsic interest is motivated by some temporary external force. A pupil has extrinsic interest in the examination.

Growth and Development of Interests

1. During Infancy, there are no marked interests except attraction by colours, souds and moving objects.
2. Upto the age of three some likes and dislike are developed.
3. From three to five, children are interested in toys of various kinds, especially those that represent moving objects (train, aeroplane, etc).
4. From five to ten, the interests of boys and girls separate. Girls are interested sewing, embroidery, drawing, etc. Boys are interested in outdoor games of various kinds, collection of the stamps etc.
5. During pre-adolescence, boys like muscular roles and girls like feminine roles. Boys prefer mathematics and science and girls prefer, languages, social studies, music and home craft.
6. During adolescence, the interests of boys and girls are clearly marked out.

Major Types of Interests

1. Play Interest.
2. Conversion.
3. Reading.
4. Vocational Interest.

Factors in the Development of the Interest

1. Sex.
2. Physical Development.
3. Intelligence.
4. Environment.

Educational Implications of Interest

1. *Interest as the Basis of Attention*: The pupils do not attend to a lesson unless they are attracted towards or feel interested in it. If the lesson is not interesting, attention suffers and the

pupils remain restless. In the absence of attention, the lesson fails.

2. *Need for Knowledge of Interests of Pupil*: The teachers should have a clear understanding of the growth and development of interests of children at successive stages of their mental development, the variety of interest, sex-differences in interests and the effect of various socio-economic factors upon this interests of the children.
3. *Need for Motivation for Instruction*: The teachers should not begin any new lesson unless and until he creates sufficient motivation and interest among the pupils, so as to catch their attention.
4. *Justification to Audio-Visual Aids*: The doctrine of interest is duly justifies the use audio-visual aids and presenting of concrete experiences.
5. *Methods of Making Lessons Interesting*: The teacher should arouse interest not through artificial stimuli, but through intrinsic motives engendered in the minds of the pupils. He should exploit the instincts and arouse natural interests.
6. *How to Avoid Dullness*: Much of the school programme today is dull and boring to the child. The basic factors of dullness are:
   (a) Stress on theoretical knowledge,
   (b) lack of activities,
   (c) lack of novelty (d),
   (d) lack of variety of co-curricular activities, and
   (e) lack of individual attention.

Improvement in the above situations can help in avoiding dullness and boredom. It is the total organization of the school that can create intrinsic interest among the pupils towards the instructional work.

In short, interesting objects and experiences are those which have satisfied or which promise to satisfy motives. Interest are there inter-related with incentive and motives or goals.

APTITUDE

Definition

Aptitude is a condition, a quality or a set of qualities in an individual which is indicative of the probable extent to which he will be able to acquire under suitable training, some knowledge, skills or composite of knowledge, understanding and skill, such as ability to contribute to art or music, much crucial ability, mathematical ability or ability to read and speak a foreign language.

How Aptitude Differs from Ability and Achievement

- Aptitude has a future reference.
- Aptitude tries to predict the degree of attainment in an area of activity.
- Ability concerns only the present condition.
- Achievement is part oriented.
- Achievement reflects on past and indicates what an individual has learned in a particular field.
- Aptitudes are innate ability but abilities and achievements are acquired.

Intelligence and Aptitude

- Intelligence test measures the general mental ability.
- Aptitude measures specific abilities.
- Knowledge of intelligence helps to predict the success in a number of situations.
- Knowledge of aptitude gives us specific abilities and capacities by succeed in a particular field of activity.
- Both are innate potentialities.

Aptitude and Interest

- A person may be interested in a particular activity job or training but may not have the aptitude for it.
- Both are essential for the success of an individual in a given activity, job or course of instruction.

Measurement of Aptitude

- Aptitude tests measures or assess the degree or level of ones special bent or flair.
- They are economically used to estimate the extent to which an individual would profit from a specific course training.

Aptitude Tests

A. Specialised Aptitude Test

Mechanical Aptitude Tests

- Minnesota Mechanical assembly list.

- Minnesota special relation list.
- Minnesota power form board.
- A battery of mechanical aptitude test battery.

Musical Aptitude Tests

Seashore measure of musical taken.

Art Judgment Test

The Meier art Judgement Test

Professional Aptitude Tests

Teaching,, Clerical, Medicine, Law, Engineering.

Scholastic Aptitude Test

The American Council of Education Scholastic Aptitude Test.

B. General Aptitude Test

- General Aptitude Test Battery.
- Differential Aptitude Test.

ATTITUDE

The main aim of education is to modify the behaviour of the child according to the needs and expectancy of the society. Behaviour is composed of so many attitudes. One of these important attributes is attitude. One's behaviour, to a great extent depends upon one's attitude toward the things—idea, person, or object, in this environment. The entire personality and development of the child is influenced by the nature of his attitude.

Meaning of Attitude

Attitudes, the effective by-products of an individual's experience, have their bases in his inner urges, acquired habits, and the environmental influences by which he is surrounded. In other words, an attitude results from personal desires and group stimulation. They actually are a part of an individuals own personality by are affected by the attitudes and behaviour of the group or groups with which he associates.

Attitudes can exert a potent influence upon an individual. They act as causes as well as results of behaviour. They are personal and are associated with the feeling tones connected with the individual's experiences. Attitudes operate in specific behaviour patterns and are associated vary in intensity with the strength of the stimulation and the physical, mental, or emotional state of person himself. Individual is not born with his attitudes, but develop them as accompaniments of experience.

Definitions of Attitude

1. The term 'Attitude' is defined by Freeman as a "dispositional readiness of respond to certain situations, persons, objects or ideas in a consistent manners, which has been learned and has become one's typical mode of response."
2. It is "a tendency to react favourably or unfavourably towards a designated class of stimuli such as a national or racial group, a custom of an institution" – Anastasi.
3. "The degree of positive or negative effect associated with some psychological object like any symbol phrase, slogan, person, institution, ideal or idea" – Thurstone.
4. It is "a personality disposition or derive which determines behaviour towards, or opinion and beliefs about a certain type of person, object, situation, institution or concept" – Vernon.
5. "Attitudes are pre-disposition to react negatively or positively in some degree towards an object, institution or class of persons" – Nunnally.

Characteristics of Attitudes

1. Attitudes have a subject-object relationship.
2. Attitudes are learned.
3. Attitudes are relatively enduring states of readiness.
4. Attitudes have motivational-affective characteristics.
5. Attitudes are numerous and varied as the stimuli to which they refer.
6. It range from strongly positive to strongly negative.

Dimensions of an Attitude

An attitude is a psychological structure inferred from observable responses to stimuli. Attitudes are tendencies with respect to learned stimuli, which are described as goals, to approach or avoid them, to regard them favourably or unfavourably, and to experience pleasant or unpleasant emotions with regard to them. Attitudes may be inferred from preferences and choice implicit in overt behaviour and from expressions of opinions.

Attitudes have four dimensions –

1. Intensity,
2. Duration,
3. Extensity, and
4. Direction.

It can be studies by observation of overt behaviour. Intensity of an attitude can be known from the intensity of motivation. The greater the intensity the greater is the persistence of the individual in his behaviour. Attitudes may be stable and enduring or they may be transient, lasting only a short while because they have not been strengthened or reinforced. Extensity of attitudes is known from the degree of generalized pattern of attitudes. The direction of an attitude is indicated by attraction, repulsion or indifference of an individual.

Components of Attitude

Broadly viewed attitudes are reflected in behaviour. Behaviour has three components:

1. The cognitive component.
2. Feeling element.
3. Action element.

The cognitive component consists of knowledge and beliefs. Attitude always arouses one's feelings and emotions. Both 'feeling' and 'knowledge' urge an individual to act. This action tendency in an attitude enables others to infer the feelings and understanding.

Factors Influencing the Formation OR Development of Attitudes

The factors influencing the formation and development of attitudes can be divided into two parts as follows:

I. Factors within the Individual Himself

1. Physical growth and development.
2. Intellectual Development.
3. Emotional Development.
4. Social Development.
5. Ethical and Moral Development.

II. Factors within the Individual's Environment

1. Home and Family.
2. Social Environment.

Importance of Attitude

The significance of attitudes is very great. They permeate our whole life and our self-concept is essentially the some total of the attitudes by which we live. The cultivation of favourable attitudes toward those valued and ideals which society cherishes and appreciates is the best way of promoting behaviour consistent with the accepted codes and mores of the social order. Promoting favourable attitudes towards work is to encourage students to work better and harder and promoting favourable attitude toward a subject of study is to encourage him to pursue the study of that subject still further. Healthy favourable attitudes in any individual are an asset of both to him and society and their development should be the major task of every school. From the point of view of learning attitudes are important in as much as they facilitate further learning and thus contain within themselves the source of further motivation.

Attitude Theories

A number of psychological theories have been suggested to explain how attitudes form and why they change. The theories most frequently employed can be categorized as either.

1. Learning theories.
2. Consistency theories.
3. Cognitive-response theories.

Learning Theories

One of the first investigators to suggest that learning principles could be applied to attitudes was Doob (1947). He proposed that the principles of classical and instrumental conditioning could be used to explain the formation and change of attitudes in much the same way that they have been applied to overt behaviours. Consider classical conditioning. On successive occasions, a neutral stimulus is paired with an unconditioned stimulus. Over time, the previously neutral stimulus may begin to dicit a response similar to that produced by the unconditioned stimulus. Objects, people or events associated with pleasant experiences may take on favourable evaluations, while those associated with unpleasant experiences may be evaluated negatively.

Instrumental conditioning, in which the reward consequences of any behaviour shape its subsequent enactment, is obviously relevant to attitude formation and change.

Cognitive-Response Approaches

Cognitive-response approach focus on the fact that the recipient does more than react to the external information. The recipient also generates thoughts about the information. These thoughts can increase, neutralize, or even reverse the indented impact of the information. It also emphasize the role of the person's cognitive organization in determining how information interpreted, remembered, and retrieved. This approach appears to be extremely promising in adding to our understanding of attitude processes.

Consistency Theories

A second group of attitude theories focuses on the individual's attempt to maintain consistency among the numerous attitudes he or she holds. Perhaps the most influential of these theories is balance theory (Heides, 1958).

Balance Theory

In its simplest form, balance theory involves the relation between a person and two attitude objects. The three elements are connected by either favourable (good, liking, or positive) attitudes or unfavourable attitudes (bad, disliking, or negative). The structure formed by the relations among the elements may be balanced or unbalanced. The basic tenet of balance theory is that there is a tendency to maintain or restore balance in one's attitude structures. Unbalanced structures are some how uncomfortable or unpleasant.

Cognitive Dissonance

In 1957, Leon Festinger published his theory of cognitive dissonance. Like balance theory the focus of cognitive dissonance theory is on individuals, who are assumed to strive for harmony (consonance) among the elements in their cognitive, or thought structures. The creation of dissonance, similar to the creation of imbalance, is thought to be distressful and to motivate the person to restore consonance.

Evaluating Attitudes

One approach to studying attitudes is to observe them as they are manifested in behaviour. Teachers could have enough opportunities in the laboratories, play grounds, libraries, and extracurricular activities to observe attitudes of pupils. Analyzing expressed opinions in another procedure suggested. Either direct expression of attitudes can be obtained or questionnaires and inventories may be framed to which the testee will respond to, which in turn reveal his attitudes. An attitude scale is a better substitute for these. To develop an attitude scale a series of statements representing different degrees of we and we attitudes have to be formulated. The statements have to be based on the result of interviewing a representative sample of subjects or analyzing statements of attitude written by such a representative group. This will ensure content validity for the scale.

1. *The Bell School Inventory*

This inventory measures the attitude of high school students towards school. Yes or No and Responses are to be encircled by the testee to express his attitude. This scale is widely used in western countries.

2. *Remmers Attitude Scale*

Attitude towards disciplinary procedure, national or racial group, school subject, vocation, teacher or play are measured through different scales published by the Purdue University. The student has to indicate his agreement with a series of phrases or sentences.

3. *The Thurstone Method*

Thurstone's technique of scaling attitude test is known as the method of equal appearing intervals. The first step is to gather a number of statements which seem to express various degree of positive and negative attitudes towards the class of persons or groups being studied. These statements have to be mimeographed on separate strips of paper. The entire collection of statement should then be handed over to a number of selected judges who would sort the statements by the method of "equal appearing intervals."

Indices of variability for each term have to be compute next. The final step is to select from the statements a group that evenly represents and that divides the scale into equal identical forms. The weak point is the absence of any direct procedure for determining whether of not there is only one attitude involved in each statement.

4. The Likert Method

The method starts with the collection of a large number of positive and negative statements about an object or opinion. The terms are rated on a five point scale ranging from strongly agree to strongly disagree. Internal consistency is the only criterion for ten selections. The responses are weighted 5, 4, 3, 2 and 1. It is more empirical because it deals directly with the respondent's scores rather than employing judges. But there is no justification in providing a five point scale. The Minnesota Teacher Attitude Inventory is a modified type of the Likert Scale.

Teacher-Made Techniques of Evaluating Attitudes

Observational method and paper and pencil tests are the two types of techniques that a teacher can use in evaluating attitudes whether it be towards the text, the subject-matter or teachers, or towards reading. The anecodotal record, the interview, the checklist etc., are some of these methods obtaining the co-operation of the students is a major requisite of measuring attitudes.

Uses of Attitude Measurement

One of the major aims of education is to shape and develop correct attitudes in children. Negative attitudes will have to be modified to positive and weak positive attitude will have to be made strong positive ones. In this process attitude test is of great use. Further, attitude tests can be used to find the student's attitude to political, social, moral and religious situations, to schools, teachers, parents etc., so that appropriate corrective experience may be provided to modify their attitude.

Limitations

1. Most of attitude tests are subjective.
2. The measurement of attitude is very difficult due to individual differences.
3. Almost all attitude tests are time consuming.

VALUES

Though the terms attitude and values are used inter-changeably and almost the same type of psychological processes are involved in the development and acquisition of attitudes and values, a destination is drawn between them. Both are generalized orientation or states of readiness, both involved preferences, and choices, and both have emotional components. But while preferences involved in values are based on what is desirable, attitudes have no such basis. It may be said that attitudes refers to likes and dislikes while values are linked to good and bad aspects of behaviour. Values represent objects toward which we direct our desires and attitudes and through or process of socialization they assume a moral or ethical tone. In seeking to mould and influence the behaviour of young people the values inherent in culture provide the guide-posts, and a 'glad' person is one who accepts such values.

Definition of Value

A popular definition of values in the Behavioural Sciences is that of Harward study group which suggested;

"A value is conception, explicitor, implicit, distinctive of an individual or characteristics of a group, of the desirable which influences the selection from variable modes, means and ends of action."

Origin of Values

Values are not simply derived from needs, appetites or interests, but come into play when a choice must be made, which is not decided simply on the basis of a need but is influenced by the ego-deal. Values reflect needs and interests, but are neither of these.

Values are not the same as goals. Values appear as the "criteria" against which goals one chosen, and as the 'implications', which these goals have in the situation. Value is not the same as a belief. Value involves more than mere belief alone and necessitates some degree of commitment to the belief. Belief is a mere affirmation of possibility, whereas value involves commitment to action.

Development of Values

Values are developed and acquired in the same manner as interests and attitudes through need-satisfying experiences and identifications. The child learns certain types of responses because they are rewarding and abstains from others because they involve unpleasant experiences. Such rewards specifically involve social praise and commendation as punishments include social disapproval and ridicule.

Through identification the child adopts the attitudes and values of another individual, parent or teacher to begin with. What things the parent or the teacher holds dear, appreciates and values are internalized through introjections i.e., he adopts them from him into his self so as to have a sense of oneness with them and to feel personally affected by what happens to them.

In the development of values 'interiolization' process is very crucial. Unless values, rules or ideals are made a past of one self, one's mental and moral make up i.e, are interiorized they cannot be said to have been accepted by the individual. When that happen the individual tries to live up to and according to them. The catalytic agent in this process is the teacher whose warmth, affection and sympathy are helpful is producing changes there are integrative and through whose example and percept children's personality is enriched. Each individual has his own system of values which he cherishes and up to which he tries to live and behave.

Classroom Approach to Values that Includes the Important Points

They are given below:

1. The values to be discussed should be related to the interests, needs and experiences of the group.
2. Basic knowledge that performs to the value under consideration should be made available to pupils.
3. Learning should be organized around a particular situation as realistic and close to pupil needs as possible.
4. The problem that is presented should involve conflicting values.
5. Free expression of present and future consequences of values should be encouraged.

Test of Values

A test of values, by contrast with one of attitudes, purports to measure generalized and dominant interests. "The study of values" designed by Allport, Vernon and Lindzey, is based upon six types of values as classified by spranger. Their items are intended to measure the relative prominence of the subjects interests, for the purpose of classifying his values. The six types are:

1. Theoretical,
2. Economic,

3. Aesthetic,
4. Social,
5. Political, and
6. Religious.

According to this classification, the dominant interest of the theoretical man is discovery of truth, the economic man is interested in what is useful, the aesthetic man values most form and harmony; social type is love of people; political man is interested in power. Religious man places highest values in an effort to component the cosmos as a whole.

A different approach to the study of values of high-school and college students and adults is found in the sems SCI occupational Rating Scale. This scale is devised "to level the level in our social structure i.e., the social class – with which a person unconsciously identifies himself."

Check lists are also serve to indicate the subjects values and his attitudes towards persons, institutions, and other aspects of his environment.

Conclude

Validity of tests of Attitudes, Interests, and values is extremely difficult to determine in a statistical manner, since the only behavioural criterion is people's action. Obviously, it is practically impossible to obtain objective- behavioural dates with regard to such matters as attitude toward religion, caste, etc.

Overt behaviour need not always be correlated with attitude scorer. The fact that attitudes and overt behaviour need not correspond makes validation a near impossibility.

CREATIVITY

A great deal of attention has been devoted to creativity in the past several decades particularly following the work of J.P. Guilford. However, the question remains unsolved that what is exactly meant by creativity? Let us peep into certain definitions.

Definition

- "Creativity is an activity resulting in new products of a definite social value" – Zbignition Pietrzinki.

- "Creativity is the forming of associative element in to new combinations which either meet new specific requirements or are in some ways useful. The more mutually remote elements of the new combinations, the more creative the process of solution" – Mednick.

Characteristics

1. Courageous in convictions,
2. Curious,
3. Independent in judgment,
4. Independent in thinking,
5. Becomes pre-occupied with tasks,
6. Intuitive,
7. Unwilling to accept say so,
8. Willing to take risk, and
9. Visionary.

Developmental Stages

1. *Stage of Preparation*: Here he focuses attention on the problem organizing data, defining the problem, and producing relevant ideas towards the end. There is an innate urge to create.
2. *Stage of Incubation*: Here person organizes and recognizes and test his ideas. Flashes of insight and trial judgement occurs.
3. *Stage of Illumination*: This is so-called eureka when he perceives the theme and relationship among various components of the problem.
4. *Revision*: This is the last stage. When individual reflects evaluates and submits to critical appraisal.

Dimensions of Creativity

1. *Creativity and Intelligence:* Getzels and Jakson. They found that the creative children were not necessarily most intelligent, despite the fact that they achieved as well as those how were more intelligent. Another study of Wallace and Kogan, why highly creative but less intelligent students are more frustrated with school and highly intelligent but less creative students are addicted to school and they were when liked by their teachers. However, a number of

investigations maintain that creative children are maintaining considerable intelligence but intelligent one is not always with considerable creativeness.

2. *Guilford's model of intelligence.* (Illuminating the process involved in both intelligence and creativity – there are three main aspects behind the intelligence and creativity. They are, Operations, Content and Product.
3. Two operations mostly related with creativity and intelligence – convergent thinking and divergent thinking.

Types of Creativity

There are several classifications

1. *Hot Creativity:* This is related with art and literature, you are inspired, you will write a poem immediately getting a theme.
2. *Cold Creativity:* It is slow process. You take years to develop an atom bomb and are related with science.
3. There are high order and low order creativity also.

Components of Creativity

There are three important components:

1. *Fluency*: It means frequency with which relevant and unrepeated ideas comes to one's mind after a question is put.
2. *Flexibility*: It represents by a person's ability to produce ideas, which differ in approval or thought trend.
3. *Originality*: It is uniqueness of response. This is the production of unusual fore fetched remote or clever responses among the members of certain population that is culturally homogenous.

Factors Affecting Creativity

There are four important factors affecting creativity; they are

1. Demographic factors like ethnicity, age and sex.
2. Psychological factors like personality traits, interest, drives, self-concept etc.
3. Locus of control (generalized expectancy concerning the relationship between behaviour and outcome.
4. Home environment.

Fostering and Guiding Creative Children

1. By providing ample opportunities for freedom of thought and taking positive attitude.
2. The method of brain storming in the classroom.
3. Elaboration of reasoning, thinking and problem-solving abilities.
4. Providing full freedom for imagination.
5. Creative expression and arts.
6. Use of analogy.
7. By encouraging thinking on consequence of an action.
8. Encouraging divergent thinking.

Conditions Helpful for Creative Work in School

1. Teacher should encourage student be confident in work.
2. Opportunity to express.
3. Mental health of the children should be sound so that they may devote their time in creative activities.
4. Self-evaluation—The teacher should encourage students to evaluate their performance by themselves.
5. Spontaneity—The teacher should encourage spontaneous activities of the children.
6. Conducting some special programmes in productive thinking and in divergent thinking ability.
7. Apply brain storming in the classroom
8. Develop self-concept in the children.

Measurement of Creativity

A number of tests have been evolved to asses creativity. Most important are as follows:

1. Guilford method—in 1955 when Bureau of Educational Research of University of Minnesota attempted to adopt Guilford's materials with the objective to develop a set of tasks to measure creativity among students from Kindergarten to graduate school.
   Guilford's theory concerning measurements of creative ability observed with the following factors such as flexibility, fluency an originality.
2. Torrance test of creative thinking—this is based on Guilford's method. Torrance test of creative thinking is based on areas

of fluency, flexibility, originality and elaboration with respect to verbal and non-verbal activities performed by the subject.

Verbal Test

1. *Ask and Guess Type:* The subjects are asked questions to reveal their abilities for developing hypotheses in terms of consequences.
2. *Productive Improvement Type:* Subjects are asked to suggest the ways and means to improve a toy or a machine or such other products.
3. *Unusual Uses Type:* These are meant to test the divergence about the ways of using a product.
4. *Unusual Question Type:* Here for a particular object or verbal descriptions, the subjects are required to ask as many unusual questions as they can.
5. *Just Suppose Type:*The subjects are required to predict outcomes for unusual situations.

Non-Verbal Activities

The non-verbal activities include activities like picture construction, picture composition and repeated figures.

All the above mentioned activities are evaluated in terms of related creative abilities like fluency, flexibility, originality and elaboration. A high score on this creative test increases the probability of creating the subject as creative.

Contesting Devices

The creative aspects in the child can also be assessed through some contesting devices like natural observation method, situational technique, rating scales, checklists, interviews, personality inventories, interest inventories attitude scales, aptitude tests, value schedules and projective techniques.

Nature and Characteristics of Creativity

1. Creativity as a unique and novel personal experience.
2. Creativity is universal.
3. Creativity is innate as well as acquired.
4. Creativity produces something new or novel.
5. Creativity is adventures and open thinking.

Table-7.5
Characteristics of Creativity

Definition	*Divergent Thinking and Creativity*	*Characteristics of Creative Individuals*	*Stages in Creativity*	*Steps to Develop Creativity*
■ The ability to produce novel and socially valued ideas and solutions is a distinct talent that requires divergent rather than convergent thinking. ■ The ability to find out new relationship & to innovate. ■ Creativity is the capacity or ability of an individual to create discover or produce a new or novel idea or object, including the rearrangement or reshaping of what is already known to him which proves to be a unique experience	■ Divergent thinking is the kind of intelligence most closely associated with creativity. ■ Divergent thinking is often accompanied by divergent behaviour. It enable to find new relationships ■ Divergent thinking is an intellectual operation leads to creativity.	■ Fluency ■ Flexibility ■ Divergent thinking ■ Persistence ■ Tolerance ■ Sense Humour ■ Imagination ■ Originality ■ Elaborating ■ Inquisitiveness	■ Preparation ■ Incubation ■ Illumination ■ Verification	■ Freedom to respond. ■ Opportunity for ego involvement. ■ Encouraging originality and flexibility. ■ Provide rewards ■ Discourage rote learning ■ Removal of hesitation and fear. ■ Provide opportunities for creative expression. ■ Developing healthy habits. ■ Avoid block/accept responses irrespective of feasibility ■ Use creative resources. ■ Encourage fantasy. ■ Brainstorming. ■ Synectics ■ Lateral thinking.

(Contd.)

Definition	*Divergent Thinking and Creativity*	*Characteristics of Creative Individuals*	*Stages in Creativity*	*Steps to Develop Creativity*
				■ Using of teaching model. ■ Gaming technique. ■ Teach with examples. ■ Encourage students to be more reflective. ■ Accept and encourage divergent thinking. ■ Tolerate dissent ■ Encourage students to trust their on judgement and intuition. ■ Assure acceptance ■ Be a stimulus for creative thinking

6. Creativity is a means as well as end in itself.
7. Creativity carries ego involvement.
8. Creating has a wide scope.
9. Creativity and intelligence do not necessarily go hand-in-hand.
10. Creativity rests more on divergent thinking than convergent thinking.
11. Creativity cannot be separated from intelligence.

12. Creativity and school achievement are not correlated.
13. Sociability and creativity are negatively correlated.
14. Creativity and anxiety go together.

REFERENCES

1. A. Antony. *Educational Psychology.*
2. B. Kuppuswami. *Advanced Educational Psychology.*
3. B.D. Bhatia and R.N. Sataya. *Educational Psychology and Guidance.*
4. Berk, E.L. *Child Development* (3rd Edn.)
5. Bhatia & Bhatia (1996). *A Textbook of Educational Psychology.* New Delhi: Doaba Publications.
6. Charles E. Skinner. *Educational Psychology.*
7. Chauhan, S.S. (1978). *Advanced Educational Psychology,* New Delhi: Vikas Publishing House.
8. Child Development (III edition), Laura E. Berk.
9. Chouhan, S.S. (2002). *Advanced Educational Psychology.* New Delhi: Vikas Publishing House Pvt. Ltd.
10. Codaty, Jostna Understanding Emotional IQ, Pustak Mahal, Delhi, 2002.
11. Dandapani. *Advanced Educational Psychology.*
12. Developmental Psychology: Childhood and Adolescence 4th edition-David R. Shaffer: Cole Publishing Company.
13. Dr. K.S. Pillai. *Educational Psychology.*
14. Dr. K.S. Pillai. *Educational Psychology.*
15. E—Paul Torrence 'Guiding Creative Talent' : Engelwood Cliffs - N.J Prentice Hall 1962.
16. J.C. Aggarwal: *Essentials of Educational Psycology.*
17. J.S. Walia: *Foundations of Educational Psychology.*
18. Gardner, H.: *Frames of Mind.*
19. Frank S. Freeman. *Psychological Testing.*
20. S.K. Mangal—*General Psychology.*
21. Good, T.L. & Brophy J. E.: 'Educational Psychology—A Realistic Approach": Holt Rine Hart and Winston 1980.
22. Haimowits N.R and Haimowits M.L 'Human Development ' New York Thomas & Crowel 1973.
23. Hans Raj Bhatia. *A Text Book of Educational Psychology.*
24. *Human Development,* 9th edition—Diane E. Papalia Sally Wend K. Olds, Ruthdeskin Feld Man, Tata McGraw Hill.
25. *Introduction to Psychology,* 4th edition, Atkinson and Hillgard, Thomson, Wardsworth.
26. *Introduction to Psychology,* Munn, A.I.T.B.S. Publishers and Distributors.
27. Jayaswal Sitaram, *Advanced Educational Psychology,* Agra: Vinod Pustak Mandir.
28. John, R., Weisz. *Introduction to Psychology.*

29. Kakkar, S.B. (1993). *Education Psychology*, New Delhi: Prentice Hall of India Private Ltd.
30. Kochar, S.K. Guidance and Counselling in Colleges and University.
31. Kochar, S.K. *Guidance and Counselling in Colleges and Universities*, New Delhi: Sterling Publishers (P) Ltd.
32. Kulshetra, S.P. (1979). *Educational Psychology*, Meerut International Publishing House.
33. Kuppuswamy, B. (1991). *Advanced Educational Psychology*, New Delhi: Terling Publishers.
34. Lefrancois, R. Gay (1988). *Psychology of Teaching*. Belmont: Wadsworth Publishing Company.
35. Lester, D. Crow and Alice Crow. *Educational Psychology*.
36. Mangal, S.K. (1999). *Advanced Educational Psychology*, New Delhi: Prentice Hall of India Pvt. Ltd.
37. Mangal, S.K. (2002). *Advanced Educational Psychology*, New Delhi: Prentice Hall of India.
38. Morgan T. Clifford, (1993). *Introduction to Psychology*, New Delhi: Tata McGraw Hill Publishing Co. Ltd.
39. Osborne, A.F., applied imagination, principles and procedures of creative problem solving' Charles Scrbners Sons, New York 1963.
40. Pandey, K.P. (1988). *Advanced Educational Psychology*, New Delhi: Konark Publishers Pvt. Ltd.
41. Psychology 5th edition, Robert. A. Barol, Pearson Education.
42. Rama, S., Anandan, Anil, R. and Nambiar, B. (2005, July). *Psycho-pedagogy*. Paper presented at the seminar on Psychological Foundations of Education, DAMTEC, Calicut.
43. Serebriakpoff, V. (1988). *A Guide to Intelligence and Personality-Testing*. USA: The Parthenon Publishing Group.
44. Shankar, U. (1984). *Advanced Educational Psychology*, New Delhi: Oxonian Press Pvt. Ltd.
45. Sharma, R.N. *Advanced Educational Psychology*, Delhi: Surjeet Publications.
46. Torrance, E.P. *Experiments in Classroom Creativity*, Engelwood Cliffs— N.J. Prentice Hall, 1962.

Web Resources

http://eqi.org/
http://eqi.org/sphest1.htm
http://www.antidote.org.uk/
http://www.ei consortium.org/
http://www.eq parenting. com/

MODEL QUESTIONS

1. Define Multiple Intelligence.
2. List different types of intelligence according to Hawred Gardner.

3. What is meant by multiple intelligence?
4. What kind of intelligence do you perceive in your students?
5. Which intelligences do you feel are most highly developed in teachers in general?
6. Is intelligence a single or multiple entity? Justify your answer.
7. Is IQ determined by heredity or environment? Justify your answer.
8. Is IQ fixed or changeable? Justify your answer.
9. What does IQ tests measure?
10. How should we define intelligence?
11. What is the connection between intelligence and rationality?
12. Are all intelligences—human, chimpanzee, dolphin, machine, etc., the same? Explain.
13. What, if any are the intrinsic limits of intelligence?
14. How do social changes influence the development of intelligence and vice versa?
15. What is the biological basis or substrate of intelligence?
16. How is the existence of an intelligent being differ from that of a non-intelligent being?
17. If a child who celebrated his 10th birthday can successfully take a test of intelligence standardised for 12 years old. What is his IQ?
18. Differentiate between culture free and culture fare test of intelligence.
19. Differentiate between psychometric and information processing approach of intelligence.
20. Explain Gardners theory of multiple intelligence.
21. Differentiate between multiple intelligence and traditional intelligence.
22. What are the educational implications of multiple intelligence?
23. Critically evaluate our school curriculum in the light of multiple intelligence.
24. How are your areas of intelligence nurtured as a child and as an adult?
25. Are there any difference between intelligence used in your personal and professional life? Justify your answer.
26. Define creativity.
27. How will you enhance divergent thinking to foster creativity?
28. List the characteristics of creative students.
29. How will you identify creative thinking?
30. Briefly explain stages in creativity?
31. What do you understand by the term 'Synectics'?
32. Suggest a problem for brainstorming that can be used in your subject.
33. Explain the characteristics of creativity.
34. Explain the steps in creativity.
35. Define creativity. Explain the stages of creativity and steps to fostering creativity.
36. Define Emotional Intelligence.
37. What do you mean by EQ?

38. Differentiate between EQ and IQ.
39. List the components of EI according to Goleman.
40. Explain importance of EI for success in career and life.
41. Explain Goleman's theory of EI.
42. Explain the characteristics of an emotionally intelligent person.
43. Define EI . Illustrate Goleman's contribution to EI and its educational implications.
44. Define multiple intelligence. Explain multiple intelligence theory and its educational implications.
45. What is Gardner's definition of intelligence and what criteria he use to determine whether or not a specific talent or ability is in fact an intelligence?
46. How many intelligences have been identified by Gardner, what distinguishing characteristics do they possess and do all human beings have these abilities?
47. If implemented into our classroom, how will the theory of multiple intelligence affect the ways in which you evaluate your students?
48. Do you feel the theory of multiple intelligence has influenced the way in which the teacher present material to their students? If so why do you believe to be true?
49. Define aptitude.
50. Differentiate intelligence and aptitude.
51. Why all individuals cannot perform equally in a profession?
52. Differentiate GATB & DAT.

8
Group Dynamics

Group Dynamics is the study of group processes, their objective analysis and measurement, and the effect of group membership on individual members.

- Study of individual's psychology imperfect without reference to his social background.
- learning – an individual behaviour in a social setting.
- Group Dynamics corrects over emphasis of educational psychology on the individual learner.

Dynamics stands for a force. Therefore, the term 'group dynamics' refers to the forces that regulate the working of the group. It is the study of the forces exerted by the group on the individual or by the individual on the group.

Group dynamics is the branch of social psychology which deals with interplay of forces within a group and consequent change of behaviour of the members of the group.

Group dynamics studies the forces exerted by the individual on the group or by the group on the individual. It studies the structure of the group and other phenomena which emerge out of group interaction.

According to Kretch and Crutch field, Group dynamics implies changes that take place within groups. It deals with group processes, their objective analysis and measurement and the effect of group membership on individual members.

FACTORS AFFECTING GROUP DYNAMICS

Sympathy

It influences the group behaviour by arousing collective feelings. It enables an individual to perceive the physiological state of another person. He begins to feels as others feel without caring to know why others are feeling in such a way. Politician play this factor during elections highly.

Suggestions

It influences the behaviour of the group by making the individual members to think collectively. Suggestion makes the individual think as others think. In a group the members share the thought with each other. The group norms and rules of conduct and behaviour are enforced through the phenomenon of suggestion.

Imitation

It influences the behaviour of the group by making the individual members to act collectively. The acts of a leader are imitated blindly and thus individuals in the group exhibit uniformity in their behaviour.

Group Goals

The behaviour of the group is influenced by its goal. The extend of group interaction, the degree of group-feeling, interpersonal relationship, quality of group work etc depends upon the goal that the group striving to achieve. The revolutionary organizations attract common man highly with their utopian ideas.

Cohesiveness

The group dynamics is influenced by the degree to which the members of a group wish to remain in a group. The group loyalty, group mind etc., are found to be decided by the cohesiveness of the group which in turn influences group behaviour.

PSYCHOLOGICAL GROUP

"A social unit consisting of a number of individuals who stand in role or status relationship to one another, stabilized in some degree at the time and who possess a set of values or norms of their own regulating their behaviour at least in matters of consequence to the group." —*Sheriff and Sheriff.*

A psychological group has been defined as "two or more people who bear an explicit psychological relationship to one another."

General Properties of a Group

- *Interaction*: The members are related to each other and dependent in some way. A positive relationship among members.
- *Structure*: It depends on the size. In big groups, sub-groups in a certain hierarchical position exist.
- *Cohesiveness*: A strong we feeling out of positive interaction among members.
- *Common Goals*: Group goals regardless of the individual goal motivate each member to engage in activities to attain them.
- *Group Norms*: They regulate the behaviour of individuals in the group and make the behaviour of all members uniform in accordance with the goals.
- *Role Relationship:* Each member has to play a role such as leader, follower etc.

TYPES OF GROUP

C.H Cooley's classification based on the degree of intimacy among group members.

Primary Group

Very closely related individuals who very strongly influence the behaviour of others in the group. e.g., family, peer group etc.

Characteristics

- Small size,
- Stability,
- Similarity of background,
- Limited self-interest,
- Dominance of face to face relationship, and
- Relationship is personal.

In primary group relationship disappears of the particular person disappears from it. The relationship is non-transferable and irreplaceable. For example, relationship between husband and wife, no third person can't replace the roles.

Intensity of Shared Interests

The common interest is share by every member and by being shared by all, the interest acquired a new significance, a new emphasize and a new valuation.

Identity of Ends

Members more or less identical desires and attitudes. They work together for the attainment of common ends without disagreement. Every member of the group strives for the welfare of the other.

The Relationships is an End in Itself

It is neither utilization nor motivated by any economic gain. It is intrinsically enjoyable. For example, true love between couples, genuine friendship between two individuals. In the above examples the relationship between the pairs are beyond the construction of any selfish motive.

The Relationship is Inclusive

As the members know each other very well, different sides of members personality are know to all the other members.

The Relationship is Spontaneous

In the primary group the relationship is voluntary. It is not planned and not based on any contract. The relationship between members are natural and spontaneous.

Quick and Effective Communication

The direct or face to face contact helps easy communication between the members.

Direct Co-Operation

They do not act independently, they sharing a common experience.

Importance of Primary Group for the Individual

- Socializing/humanizing agent.
- Development of personality.
- Satisfaction of psychological needs.
- Strengthens the democratic spirit.

(b) Secondary Group

Not always face to face. Less intimacy and less influence of behaviour on other members. But the group is organized with some specific goals. For example, School, clubs etc.

"Secondary groups are those that are relatively casual and impersonal in their relationship. Relationship in them are usually competitive rather than mutually helpful" – P.H. Lamdls, e.g., trade unions, social organizations.

Characteristics

- Formal and impersonal relationship.
- "Touch and go" type.
- Large in size.
- Option for membership, not compulsory.
- Active and inactive members.
- Indirect communication, hardly meet face to face.
- Group structure.
- Formal rules.
- Status to each individual, status depends upon his role e.g., president, secretary, treasurer, etc.
- Limited influence on personality, compared to primary group.
- Goal oriented, e.g., trade unions are functioning for their better working conditions, school functioning for education.
- No physical basis, the members are scattered over a vast area.
- Nature of group control, formal means of social control such as Law, Legislation, Police, Court, etc.

(c) Tertiary Group

A group in which most of the members remain independent and unrelated. Very minimal interaction among members, e.g., passengers in a railway station, people in a cinema hall etc.

OTHER CLASSIFICATION OF GROUPS

1. W.G. Sumner divided into two groups –
   In Group: Sense of loyalty, friendliness, co-operation.
   Out Group: Sense of indifference, avoidance, disgust, competition.

2. *Permanent Groups*: School, family –
   Temporary Groups: Accidental crowds.
3. *Open Group*: Everybody can become a member.
   Closed Group: Secret society, membership is not open to all.
4. *Organized Groups*: Formed as a result of previous planning and these exist for some specific purposes.
   Spontaneous Group: The individuals come together naturally without specific purpose or previous planning.
5. *Formal Group*: Members are bound to observe certain pre-determined rules.
   Informal Group: No such rules and code of conduct.

SOME PSYCHOLOGICAL GROUPS

1. Family

The most important primary group which influences the personality development of the child.

- The basic values, ideals, attitudes and interest of the individual are developed in the family.
- Very important in emotional development.
- The first social setting where the child learns the first lesson of social behaviour.
- Responsible for development positive and negative social mind.
- Roots of maladjustment from family problems.
- Instances of overprotected child, neglected child, the child crushed between the egos of parents, children in the broken family etc.

2. Peer Group

A group of same aged playmates. It is a informal primary group. It is a collection of individuals more or less the same age, same maturity and same prestige. They bound together by strong 'we feeling.'

- Social cohesion is very strong.
- No distinction of caste, colour, creed.
- We feeling and friendly bondage.
- Development of co-operation, tolerance, accommodation, team spirit and competition.
- Leadership and loyalty.

- Groups formed in different stages – Early Play, Solitary Play, Parallel Play.
- Very intimate relationship.
- Very next social unit where child learns the basic group norms.
- Very important place in the socialization of the child.
- Basic lessons of emotional tolerance in it.
- Sense of group cohesion begins to develop here.

Some time undesirable peer group, can spoil the members by developing anti-social tendencies, unhealthy interests and attitudes and bad behavioural patterns, e.g., smoking, alcoholism, etc.

3. Gangs

Any grouping often male adolescents or youth which sees to control a territory and operates on margins of legality:

- It is a psychological group in the sense that members interact within the group maintain a cohesion.
- Most often labelled as anti-social.
- It has its own sub-cultural rules and status systems.
- Teachers may prevent the formation of gangs with necessary precaution.
- Special training may give to students to take decisions of their own and to escape from joining gangs.

4. Cliques

A network of maximum three or four individual in any organization (Burns):

- A minority sub-group with firm friendship and mutual support.
- Cliques–not desirable in a group.
- may endanger group cohesiveness and group morale.
- Identified with the sociometric Technique developed by J. L. Moreno (1934).
- Teachers should take steps to reduce the possibility of cliques in the Class.

5. Classroom Group

- A typical psychological group with its all essential features.
- All members are directed to certain common goals.

- Interaction more positive.
- An organized structure with a democratic leader.
- Though formed involuntarily, members are interdependent and highly cohesive.
- All members more or less of same age – a formal peer group
- The most important group of a learner.
- Develop the mental processes through intellectual activities.
- Motivates learner to achieve higher goals in his future life.

ROLE OF TEACHERS IN A CLASSROOM GROUP

Teacher in a classroom group should be democratic leader:

- An initiator of all purposeful activities.
- Create confidence in children.
- Enhance pupils' aspirations.
- Develop positive feelings in them.
- Develop their commun icative skills.
- Support moral and emotional development.
- Give them chances of social responsibility.

Formation of Groups

The tendency to form association is universal and is essential for the survival of the individual in a civilized society. Human beings form groups out of natural needs. Group characteristics like cohesiveness, morale, structure, common interests, group norms, conformity with the group and the group mind. Different groups will differ in the number of their members, their needs, interests and cohesiveness.

MOST ESSENTIAL CHARACTERISTICS OF A PSYCHOLOGICAL GROUP

1. Group Cohesiveness –

Due to the interaction of members develops a we-feeling towards the group

- Indicates the degree to which the members stick together so that there is unity in the group.
- Produces a collective energy called 'Synergy' which leads to a loyalty of members to the group.

Cohesiveness is the extent of intimacy of the members of a group and may be said to be the sticking force in a group. The degree to which the members of a group wish to remain in the group because of a feeling of belonging is called group cohesiveness.

Cohesive Factors

- Sense of belongingness.
- We feeling.
- Favourable attitude towards membership in a group.
- Freedom of action.
- Self-expression and communication.

But, cohesiveness however is affected by the nature of the members as well as their status in the group.

Example, if the group is divided into sub-groups based on status and if it provides no opportunity for mobility then naturally each sub-group will develop hostility to the others and this may destroy group cohesiveness.

Factors Affecting Group Cohesiveness

1. Attraction towards the group and satisfaction of psychological needs.
2. Spirit of interpersonal positive competition.
3. Leadership.
4. Size and structure of the group.
5. Motivation.
6. Commonly accepted goals.
7. Co-operation.

2. Group Morale

Unity and Solidarity of the Group—a team spirit caused by aims, activities and leadership. Group morale is the basis to determine the standard of activities of the group.

Morale refers to the level of group functioning, as well as the unity and solidarity of the group. It stands for team spirit, loyalty, among its members, devotion to the ideals of the group and desire to perform at the highest pitch of endeavour.

Determinants of Group Morale

- Positive goals.
- Asense of advancement towards the goal.
- Satisfaction of felt needs.

- Understanding of the present activities and the goal.
- Feeling of security.
- Capable leadership.

Indications of Group Morale

Strong structure, high cohesiveness, less disintegrating tendencies, Positive attitude towards group, clearly defined goals. Unity in opinion, and Criticism only in the group are the indications of group morale.

3. Group Conscience

In a psychological group an individual looses his identity and a group conscience (a group psyche) develops. He becomes part of the group and assimilates the synergy of the group. The behaviour of individual is affected by the group conscience.

4. Group Structure

An examination of the dynamics of groups must start with an examination of the basic structural characteristics of groups. They are:

(*a*) size of the groups,
(*b*) individual roles within the groups, and
(*c*) group relations.

(a) Size of the Groups

The smallest group is made up of two people with a membership of three the group significantly increases its potential complexity. With a group of four people, the possibility of interrelationship becomes enormously complicated. For example, in fives foot ball, each players are more chance to get ball, but in elevens football they are less chance.

But number is not the only factor of affecting inter relationship. The group relations will depend upon the nature of the group, its morale, the kind of leadership characteristics of the groups etc.

The size of the many groups is determined by the operation of arbitrary external factors.

(b) Individual Roles within the Groups

When a man takes a new job his relations to his superiors, inferiors, and associates are to a very considerable, extent, pre-determined for him. How an individual behaves toward other members of the group depends partially up on the personality of the individual and partially up on the nature of the group structure and his role within that structure.

Similarly, how the individual in perceived and reacted to by the others also partially depend upon his role. Who fills a certain role in a group may quite often be entirely arbitrary and bear no relation to the personality / abilities / interests of the individual.

In formal social organizations there is a marked tendency to channel interpersonal relations among routnized lines. Whereas in psychological groups the dynamic interactions among people have much more significance in determining the role of the individual.

(c) *Group Relations*

A very obvious fact about most groups is that they are made up of sub-groups. Groups are not usually homogenous within but are characteristically divided into sub-groups each of which is relatively homogenous but tends to differ from other sub-groups. There are both horizontal and vertical relationship among sub-groups. For example, in a school the teachers are a subgroup and students are another sub-group.

That is some sub-groups are on an equal level, having equivalent power and status. Others are parts of a hierarchy, some being superior to others and thus, having more power and status. The difference sub-groups vary in the closeness and remoteness of relationship to one another.

Change in Group Structure

Some groups use more stable than others. Their structure tends to remain unchanged over a period of time. The unstable group, on contrary, undergoes progressive changes even the absence of significant variation in the external situation.

Change in Group Structure as a Result of Internal Imbalances

Instability arises out of conflict among individual members and among sub-groups, within the whole group. Several sub-groups may seeking to increase their power at the expense of the others; the leader of the group may be trying to broaden his authority and other members may be trying to displace him. Contradiction between the attitude and believes of members and group objectives also leads to changes.

As a result of such conflicts in the lack of balance among internal forces, changes in group structure occurs. In general these changes tend to move in the direction of a reduction of tensions, a balancing of the forces, hence a more stable group structure. These may be temporary expedients in tension reduction. One *scapegoating*. *Scapegoating*, in which the internal group tensions become manifested through aggressions centred on certain individuals or subgroups within the group.

External aggression, in which group tensions become expressed in attacks upon individuals and groups outside the group. The most extreme consequence of intra group tensions is complete dissolution of the group. For example, marital divorce, demise of a political committee, etc.

Change in Group Structure as a Result of External Influences

Group differ in the degree to which they respond to such external influences. Some groups have very rigid structure that resist changes. Others are more flexible. As the environmental circumstances in which a group exists undergoes changes, there are likely to be significant changes in the group structure, itself. Threats or attack against the group arising from outside the group has often been observed to induce important changes in group structure. Under external dangers group unity often seems to be increased and inner differences are found to diminish.

LEADERSHIP

An interpersonal influence exercised in a situation and directed through communication process, towards the attainment of a specified goal or goals – a personal quality – the ability to influence the behaviour of others.

A leader is the person who can exercise control over the behaviour of other members of the group.

Characteristics of a Good Leader

(*a*) Possesses a vision.
(*b*) Shows a route to reach the dream or vision.
(*c*) Gives extra meaning to the goals.

Other Qualities

(i) High levels of confidence.
(ii) A high degree of concern for the followers' needs.
(iii) An excellent communication Style.
(iv) Self-sacrifice.
(v) Creativity.
(vi) Intellectual superiority and honesty.
(vii) Patience, endurance and greatness of mind.
(viii) Courage to recognize his own short coming.
(ix) Emotional stability.
(x) Receptive to public opinion.

Functions of Leadership

(a) Formulate policies and plans.
(b) Organize activities to carry out plans.
(c) Develop group morale.
(d) Facilitate communication.
(e) Reconcile individual goals with Group goals.
(f) Performance evaluation.
(g) Initiation.
(h) Interaction.
(i) Co-ordination.
(j) Maintain team spirit.

Types of Leadership

1. Autocratic (Authoritarian) leadership.
2. Democratic leadership.
3. Leissez-faire leadership.

Out of these three types the worse is Autocratic leadership but it is better than Leissez-faire leadership. Training should be given in the school for development of democratic leadership.

REFERENCES

1. Barron, A. Robert. (1996). *Psychology*. New Jersey: Prentice Hall.
2. Good Thomas, L. and Brophy Jere, E. (1990). *Educational Psychology – A Realistic Approach*. New York: Longman.
3. Mangal, S.K. (1999). *Advanced Educational Psychology*. New Delhi: Prentice Hall of India Pvt. Ltd.
4. Rama, S., Anandan, Anil, R. & Nambiar, B. (2005, July). *Psycho-*

pedagogy. Paper presented at the seminar on Psychological Foundations of Education, DAMTEC, Calicut.

MODEL QUESTIONS

1. What you mean by Group Dynamics?
2. What are the factors affecting group dynamics?
3. What are the general properties of a group?
4. What are the types of groups?
5. How family influence the personality development of the individual?
6. What are the characteristics of a good leader?
7. What is the importance of 'gang life' in the social development of children?

9

Guidance and Counselling

GUIDANCE

Guidance is a personalised assistance made readily available by a sympathetic, mature, experienced and personally qualified person to a needy person.

Definitions

Moris—"Guidance is a process of helping individual's through his own efforts to discover and develop their potentialities for personal happiness and social usefulness."

Jones—"Guidance as kinds of help given by one person to another in developing ability, making adjustments and problems that confront him in attainment of his goals."

Guidance is an 'umbrella term' involving several functions such as publications, information, institutions, testing, counselling services, etc. Guidance is not carrying others burden, but enabling them to carry their burden themselves.

COUNSELLING

Counselling is a process of enabling the individual to know himself and his present and possible future situations in order that he may make substantial contributions to the society and to solve his own problems through a face to face personal relationship with the counsellor.

Definitions

Ruth Strang, "It is a face to face relationship in which growth takes place in the counsellor as well as the counsellee."

Webster's Dictionary, "Counselling is a consultation, mutual interchange of opinions deliberating together."

Counselling is a face to face session meant for rendering guidance.

Scope of Guidance and Counselling

1. Intended to help the individual to realize his potentialities.
2. It helps the persons to solve his problems.
3. It provides assistance to teachers.
4. Aimed at enabling students to acquire abilities which promote self direction and self-realisation.
5. It is a centred round the needs and aspiratior of students.

Principles of Guidance and Counselling

1. It is unique to an individual.
2. Concerned with total individual.
3. Meant for all those who need help.
4. It is a continues process.
5. Not specific to any stage of development.
6. Should be based on reliable data.
7. Should have a flexible approach.

Relation between Guidance and Counselling

1. Counselling is a part of guidance, not of all it.
2. All counselling involves guidance but all guidance is not counselling.
3. Counselling is the centre of the whole guidance programme.
4. Counselling is a technical programme which enlightens the client.
5. Guidance and counselling are complementary.

TYPES OF GUIDANCE

Educational Guidance

Educational guidance is aimed to help students to solve their problems related to education at different levels of education – from primary to university. Its functions are to help.

(a) Selection of course.
(b) Adjustment with the institution and course.
(c) Ensuring achievement in the course.

Definition

"Dictionary of education" regards educational guidance as 'guidance concerned principally with matters relating to schools, courses, curricular and school life, rather than vocational social or personal matter" —Good C. V.

Vocational Guidance

Vocational guidance is the process of helping the individual to chose an occupation that fits him best. Its functions are to help.

(*a*) To select a career.
(*b*) To adjust with the career.
(*c*) To enhance and fulfil his potentiality in the career.

"It is to help fix square pegs in square hooks and round pegs in round hooks, and not square pegs in round holes."

Definition

The General Conference of International Labour (GCILO) defines, it as "Assistance given to an individual in solving problems related to occupational choice and progress with due regard for the individual's characteristics and the relations to occupational opportunity."

Personal Guidance

Personal guidance refers to the guidance to students to enable them to adjust themselves to their environment. So that they become efficient citizens. Its functions are to help in solving:

(*a*) Personal problems.
(*b*) Familial problems.
(*c*) Occupational problems.
(*d*) Problems in attaining fulfilment and success.

Definition

"As the phase of guidance that aims to assist an individual in respect to personal habits, attitudes and intimate personal problems"— Good C.V.

TYPES OF COUNSELLING

Directive/Prescriptive/Counsellor Centred Counselling

Propound by E.G. Williamson, "Here the counsellor plays the major or pivotal role in initiating the process of counselling." Decisions are imposed by counsellor.

Non-Directive/Permissive/Client Centred Counselling

Developed by Carl Rogers, "Here the client voluntarily approaches the counsellor where he receives friendly and positive attitude." Decisions are taken by counsellee.

Eclectic Counselling

Chief exponent is F.C Throne, "It is the synthesis and combination of directive and non-directive counselling."

Qualities of a Good Counsellor

1. Patient listener.
2. Accepting attitude.
3. Ability to elicit.
4. Ability to establish rapport.
5. Theoretical knowledge about the various problems.
6. Insight about individual differences.
7. Ability to judge body language.
8. Ability to interpret verbal and non-verbal cues.
9. Excellent communication.
10. Ability to convinces.
11. Ability to analyse response.
12. Respecting the individuality and rights of a client.
13. Approving freedom of the client to descent.
14. Tolerating ambiguity.
15. Professional skills.
16. Ability to Empathise.

Method of Educational and Vocational Guidance

Educational and vocational information may be disseminated through the following techniques:

1. Talks by teachers and visitors.
2. Audio-visual aids.
3. Group activities – arts club, music club, world affairs form, etc.
4. Visit to work sites – industrial and related establishments.
5. Normal classroom work.

6. Career conference.
7. Career corners/talks in schools.

Steps in the Organisation of Guidance Programme

1. Formulation of a guidance committee.
2. Organisation of the guidance bureau.

Guidance Bureau Organises the following programmes:

(a) Career Corner – availed periodicals, employment news and bulletins.
(b) Career Talks – on teaching, banking, Indian defence services, Indian administrative forces, etc.
(c) Career Conference – supplementing information. A number of successful persons explains the vocations in which they work and answer questions about their job.
Occupational orientation cover the following points:
  (i) Nature and importance of work.
  (ii) Conditions of work.
  (iii) Minimum qualification necessary for receiving training.
  (iv) Different aspects of training.

(d) Placement programme – provide help to secure a grade, a place or a job.
(e) Testing programme – administration of tests or assessing traits and aptitude of peoples.
(f) Film show – arranged to give educational and vocational informations.
(g) Visits – visit to institutions relevant to occupational choices.
(h) Exhibitions-organised to disseminate information regarding modern courses and occupation.
(i) Diagnostic programmes – for identifying physical disabilities, mental ill health and mal-adjustment.
(j) Guidance service centres – like employment guidance bureaus – Employment news bulletins.
(k) Career guidance academics and institutions.

REFERENCES

1. S. Narayana Rao, *Counselling and Guidance.*
2. Dr. Dalaganjan Naik, *Fundamentals of Guidance and Counselling.*
3. B. G. Barki & B. Mukhopadhyay, *Guidance and Counselling.*
4. S.S. Chauhan, *Principles and Techniques of Guidance.*

5. Dennis Child, *Psychology and the Teacher*.
6. Rama, S., Anandan, Anil, R. & Nambiar, B. (2005, July). *Psycho-pedagogy*. Paper presented at the Seminar on Psychological Foundations of Education, DAMTEC, Calicut.

MODEL QUESTIONS

1. Differentiate between career talk and career conference.
2. What are the relevance of guidance and counselling with respect the current changes in the society? Explain different measures for rendering guidance and counselling in schools.
3. Differentiate between guidance and counselling.
4. Define educational guidance. Write its functions.
5. Define vocational guidance. Write its functions.
6. Define personal guidance. Write its functions.
7. Explain difference types of guidance.
8. Explain difference types of counselling.
9. What are the qualities of a good counsellor?

Appendix

CASE DATA SCHEDULE

PERSONAL DATA

1. Name of the pupil :
2. Name of school :
3. Age and date of birth :
4. Religions and caste :
5. Boy or girl :
6. Permanent address :
7. Mother tongue :
8. Rank or position of the child in the family :

FAMILY BACKGROUND

FATHER

9. Name of the father :
10. Age :
11. Education :
12. Father's occupation :
13. Monthly income :
14. Father's attitude towards the child :
15. Father's ambition about the child :

MOTHER

16. Name of mother :
17. Age :
18. Education :
19. Mother's occupation :
20. Monthly income :
21. Mother's attitude towards the child :
22. Mother's ambition about the child :

BROTHERS AND SISTERS

23. Number of brothers :
24. Are they studying or employed? :
25. If employed, monthly income :
26. Number of brothers married :
27. Number of sisters :
28. Are they studying or employed? :
29. If employed, monthly income :
30. Number of sisters married :
31. Total monthly income of the family :
32. Has there been untimely death of father or mother or both? :
33. Guardian, if parents are not alive :
34. Are the parents divorced? :
35. If yes, are they remarried? :
36. Joint family, or Nuclear family :
37. If joint family the members residing in the house :
38. Is the relationship with the members friendly, hostile or withdrawn? :
39. Child's affection towards the father :
40. Child's affection towards the mother :

41. Child's attitude towards the brothers :

42. Child's attitude towards the sisters :

HOME ENVIRONMENT

43. House whether own or rented :

44. Does the child own a separate room for study? :

45. If no, is there shortage of space at home? :

46. Does the child feel insecure? :

47. Is this over protection or under protection? :

48. Is the child compelled to do any work at home? :

49. Discipline exercised by parents, very harsh or lenient :

50. In their discriminatory treatment towards the child :

51. Is there quarrel among the parents? :

52. Is there quarrel among brothers? and sisters? :

53. Is the child's father a gambler or drunkard? :

54. The person the child likes most :

55. Is there electric supply in the house? :

56. Is the house provided with a T.V.? :

57. Does the child watch T.V. programmes ?:

58. How many hours spent on watching T.V. programmes? :

59. Do all the inmate watch the programmes sitting together? :

60. Does the child get newspaper/ periodical to read? :

61. Which type of news does the child like most? :

SOCIAL BACKGROUND

62. Social status of the family :
63. Type of neighbourhood :
64. Does the child mingle freely with other children in the neighbourhood? :
65. If no, what reason does the child accounts for it :
66. Is the child well liked by all his classmates? :
67. Does the child like the school atmosphere? :
68. How many friends does the child have? :
69. Does the child experience difficulty in making friends? :
70. Does the child willingly take the lead? :
71. Is the child neglected by his classmates? :
72. Is the child humiliated or mocked by any of the friends? :
73. Does the child participate in social activities? :
74. Extent of participation in social activities :
75. Social activities in which the child usually engages :
76. Does the child quarrel with other children (put a mark against the appropriate word)? :
77. Is there any physical defect in Vision/Hearing/Speech?
78. Any other physical deformity :
79. Any serious illness in the past? :

80. Any serious injuries or accidents :
81. Any mental deformity :
82. Any present ailment? :
83. The child's attitude towards health :
84. General health condition whether good, satisfactory or poor :

SCHOOL RECORD

ACADEMIC

85. Number of schools previously attended :
86. Medium of instruction :
87. Past achievements in studies :
88. The child's rank in the class :
89. Does the child feel sad or satisfied on the present achievement? :
90. Does the child ask doubts in the class? :
91. Does the child listen carefully in the class? :
92. Time spent on studies after school hours :
93. Does the child study the daily lessons? :
94. Does he often feel lazy? :
95. At what time does the child begin studying at night? :
96. The subject the child like most :
97. Why does the child like it? :
98. The subject, the child like least :
99. Whey does the child like least :
100. Is the child always late at school? :
101. Does the child have private tuition? :
102. Is the child punctual in home work? :

103. Is the child frequently punished for his faults? :

104. Specify the faults :

105. Educational plans of the child :

106. Child's study habits according to the parents :

107. To whom does the child ask doubts?:

108. Report of the class teacher regarding the intellectual efficiency :

CO-CURRICULAR ACTIVITIES

Arts, Sports, Literacy Activity Science Clubs

109. Types of activities liked most :

110. Does the child enjoy reading books, magazines and newspapers? :

111. Does the child like to browse in a library? :

112. Which type of book is preferred? :

113. Does the child often go for movies? :

114. With whom does the child go? :

115. The Co-Curricular activities the child takes parts in :

116. Does the child participate in sports? :

117. Does the child play during the interval? :

118. Achievements in Co-Curricular activities :

119. What are the child's special abilities? :

120. What are the child's favourite hobby?:

121. Does the school provide proper encouragement to these activities? :

122. Has the child at any time represented the school in competitions ? :

123. Is the children courage at home to participate in the activities? :

124. Has the child won any prize at school level? :

125. Has the child won any prize in state level? :

126. Is the child :

(*a*) self-confident
(*b*) shy or bold when answering a question
(*c*) co-operative or not co-operative
(*d*) systematic or careless or average
(*e*) always attentive or restless
(*f*) neat in personal appearance
(*g*) honest
(*h*) a good leader
(*i*) courteous in speech and manners
(*j*) responsible
(*k*) disturbed by criticism
(*l*) aggressive or submissive
(*m*) sociable or unsociable co-operative.

Bibliography

Adler, A. (1921). *The Neurotic Constitution.* London: Kegan Paul.

Adler, A. (1928). *Understanding Human Nature.* London: Allen and Unwin.

Adler, A. (1930). *The Education of Children.* New York: Greeberg.

Adler, A. (1937). *What Life Should Mean You.* New York: Grossett and Dunlop.

Adler, A. (1968). *The Practice and Theory of Individual Psychology.* New Jersey: Little Field Adams.

Adler, A., Hall, C.S. *et al.* (1978). *Theories of Personality,* 3rd ed. New York: Wiley.

Aggarwal, J.C. (2002). *Essentials of Educational Psychology.* New Delhi: Vikas Publishing House Pvt. Ltd.

Antony, *Educational Psychology.*

Arnowitting, *Introduction to Psychology.*

Atkilson & Hilgard, *Introduction to Psychology.*

Ausubel, D. P. and Fitzgerald, D.(1962). Organizer, general background, and antecedent learning variables in sequential verbal learning. *Journal of Educational Psychology.*

Ausubel, D.P. (1962). A Subsumption Theory of Meaningful Verbal Learning and Retention. *The Journal of General Psychology.*

B.D. Bhatia and R.N. Sataya. *Educational Psychology and Guidance.*

Barron, A. Robert, (1996). *Psychology.* New Jersey: Prentice Hall.

Barrone. F. David and Michel Hersen *et. al.* (1998). *Advanced Personality.* New York: Plenum Press.

Benjamin, B. Lahey (1998). *Psychology—An Introduction.* McGraw Hill

Benjamin, B. Lahey, *Introduction to Psychology.*

Berk, E. Laura (1997). *Child Development,* Allyn and Bacon, Boston, London.

Berk—*Development Psychology.*

Berkely Calif and Mc Cutchan (1977). *Learning and Instruction.*

Bhatia and Bhatia (1996). *A Textbook of Educational Psychology.* New Delhi: Doaba Publications.

Biggie, Morris. *Learning Theories for Teachers* (IV Edition).

Borrone, F. David and Michel Herson (1998). *Advanced Personality*. New York: Plenum Press.

Bower, G.H & Milgard – *Theories of Learning* (1982).

Brainerd, C. (1978). *Piaget's Theory of Intelligence*. Englewood Cliffs, NJ:

Braner, *The Process of Education*.

Braner, *Towards a Theory of Education*.

Charles Catania (1992). *Learning*, 3rd Ed. New Jersey: Prentice Hall, Engle Wood Cliffs, 1.

Charles E. Skinner. *Educational Psychology*.

Chauhan, S.S. (1978). *Advanced Educational Psychology*. New Delhi: Vikas Publishing House.

Chauhan, S.S. (2000). *Advanced Educational Psychology*. New Delhi: Vikas Publishing House.

Chauhan, S.S. (2002). *Advanced Educational Psychology*. New Delhi: Vikas Publishing House (P.) Ltd.

Chauhan, S.S. (2003). *Advanced Educational Psychology*. New Delhi: Vikas Publishing House (P) Ltd.

Clifford, T. Morgan, Richard. A. King, John R. Weisz and John Schopler (1993). *Introduction to Psychology*, 7th Ed. New Delhi: Tata McGraw Hill Pub. Co. Ltd., 140.

Clifford, T. Morgan, *Introduction to Psychology*.

Codaty, Jostna Understanding Emotional IQ, Pustak Mahal, Delhi, 2002.

Counselling and Guidance, S. Narayana Rao.

Crow, LDT Crow Alice (1964). *Human Development and Learning*.

Dandapani, S. (2000). *Advanced Educational Psychology*, New Delhi: Anmol Publications Pvt. Ltd.

David, A. Lieberman (2000). *Learning Behaviour and Cognition* 3rd Ed. Woods Worth, a Division of Thomon Learning. USA, 328-365.

De Cecco. P. John & Crowford William, R. (1988). *The Psychology of Learning and Instruction-Educational Psychology* (2nd Ed). New Delhi: Prentice Hall Ltd.

De Cecco. P. John and Crawford R. William (1988). *The Psychology of Learning and Instruction*, New Delhi: Prentice Hall of India Pvt. Ltd.

Dennis Coon (1998). *Introduction to Psychology: Exploration and Application*. Brooks/Cole Publishing Company; ITP.

Developmental Psychology – Childhood and Adolescence 4th edition – David R. Shaffer – Cole Publishing Company.

Dr. Grewal, J. S. (1984). Early Childhood Education, National Psychological Corporation, Agra.

Dr. K. Shivarajan (2000). *Educational Psychology*. Calicut: Calicut University Co-operative Press, 170-183.

Dr. K.S. Pillai (1991). *Educational Psychology*. Trivandrum: Kalaniketan, 188-200.

Dr. Sitaram Jayaswal (1974). *Advanced Educational Psychology*. Agra: Vinod Putak Mandir, 336-342.

Driscoll, Mercy P. (1994). *Psychology of Learning for Instruction – Needham,* Ma: Allgn & Bacon.

E. Paul Torrence . 'Guiding Creative Talent' : Engelwood Cliffs - N.J Prentice Hall, 1962.

Edward, E. Smith—*Introduction to Psychology.*

Emeralled, V. Dechant and Henry P. Smith (1977). *Psychology in Teaching Reading* 2nd ed. New Jersey: Prentice Hall Inc., 50-52.

Feist and Leist (2002)—*Theories of Personality*—Mc Grawhill—Higher Education.

Fernald/Fernald (2001). *Introduction to Psychology* (V Edition).

Flavell, J.H.(1963). *The Developmental Psychology of Jean Piaget*. New York.

Frank S. Freeman. *Psychological Testing.*

Fredeubeirgh Fraz, A. (1971). *The Psychology of Personality and Adjustment.* California: Cunnings Publishing Co.

Freud, S. (1986). The Essentials of Psycho Analysis. England: Penguin Books.

Fundamentals of guidance and counselling – Dr. Dalaganjan Naik.

Gagne. R.M. (1970). *The Conditions of Learning* (II Edition) New York 1970.

Gardner, H., *Frames of Mind.*

Gari. R. *The Psychology of Learning.*

General Psychology—S.K. Mangal

Good T. L. & Brophy J. E – 'Educational Psychology – A realistic approach" – Holt Rine Hart and Winston 1980.

Good Thomas, L. and Brophy Jere, E. (1990). *Educational Psychology- A Realistic Approach,* New York: Longman.

Guidance and Counselling – B. G. Barki & B. Mukhopadhyay

Guilford, J.P. (1959). *Personality*. Mc Graw Hill.

Haimowits N.R. and Haimowits M.L 'Human Development ' New York Thomas & Crowel 1973.

Hall, C.S. (1978). *Theories of Personality,* 3rd ed., New York: John Wiley.

Hans Raj Bhatia. *A Textbook of Educational Psychology.*

Hansfather, Samuel. J. (1996). *Vygotsky and Schooling: Creating a School Concept for Learning.*

Hilgard, R. (1956). *Theories of Learning.*

Hizard & Bower. *Theories of Learning.*

Human Development 9th edition—Diane E. Papalia Sally Wend K. Olds, Ruthdeskin Feld Man Tata McGraw Hill.

Hurlock, Elizabeth B. *Child Development*. New Delhi: Mc Graw. Hill International Book Company.

Introduction to Psychology, 4th edition—Atkinson and Hillgard—Thomson, Wardsworth.

Introduction to Psychology, Munn—A.I.T BS Publishers and Distributors.

Ivie, Stanley D.(1998). Ausubel's Learning Theory: An Approach to Teaching Higher Order Thinking Skills. *High School Journal.*

J.C. Aggarwal. Essentials of Educational Psycology.

J.S. Walia. *Foundations of Educational Psychology.*

James, W. Kalat (1993). *Biological Psychology,* V Edn. Books & Cole.

Jayaswal Sitaram, *Advanced Educational Psychology,* Agra: Vinod Pustak Mandir.

John W. Best & James V. Khan. *Research in Education.*

John, R., Weisz. *Introduction to Psychology.*

Joyce and Weil (1997). *Models of Teaching.* New Delhi: Prentice Hall of India Pvt. Ltd., 110001.

Joyce Bruce, Weil Marcha & Showers Beverly (1992). *Models of Teaching.* New Delhi: Prentice Hall of India (P) Ltd.

K.G. Rastogy (1983). *Educational Psychology.* New Delhi: Rastogi Publications, 161-178.

Kakkar, S.B. (1993). *Education Psychology.* New Delhi: Prentice Hall of India Private Ltd.

Kakkar, S.B. (1995). *Educational Psychology.* New Delhi: Prentice Hall of India (P) Ltd.

Kochar, S.K. *Guidance and Counselling in Colleges and Universities.* New Delhi: Sterling Publishers (P) Ltd.

Kulshetra, S.P. (1979). *Educational Psychology.* Meerut International Publishing House.

Kuppuswami (1994). *Advanced Educational Psychology.* New Delhi: Sterling Publishers (P) Ltd., 111-114.

Kuppuswamy, B. (1991). *Advanced Educational Psychology.* New Delhi: Sterling Publishers.

L. Bodge Fernald and Peter, S. Fernald (2004). *Introduction to Psychology.* AITBS Publishers and Distributors.

L.S. Vygotsky. *Educational Psychology.*

Lefrancois, R. Gay (1988). *Psychology of Teaching.* Belmont: Wadsworth Publishing Company.

Lester, A. (1983). Lefton and Lalra Valvatine (1983). Mastering Psychology, 2nd ed. USA: Allyn and Bacon Inc., 22.

Lester, D. Crow and Alice Crow. *Educational Psychology.*

Lewin, K. (1935). *A Dynamic Theory of Personality.* New York.

Lewin, K. (1936). *Principles of Topological Psychology.*

Lewin, K. (1948). *Resolving Social Conflicts: Selected Papers on Group Dynamics.* Gertrude W.

Lewin, K. (1951). *Field Theory in Social Science; Selected Theoretical Papers.* D. Cartwright (ed). New York.

Lyle E. Bourne, Jr. Nancy Felipe Russo. *Psychology Behaviour in Context.* New York: NW Norton.

Madhavan Nair, S. (1998). *Educational Psychology.* Ottapalam: Breeze Publications.

Mangal, S.K. (1999). *Advanced Educational Psychology*, New Delhi: Prentice Hall of India Pvt. Ltd.

Mangal, S.K. (2000). *Advanced Educational Psychology*, New Delhi: Prentice Hall of India (P) Ltd.

Mangal, S.K. (2002). *Advanced Educational Psychology*, New Delhi: Prentice Hall of India.

Mangal, S.K. (2003). *Advanced Educational Psychology*, Prentice Hall of India Pvt. Ltd., New Delhi.

Dr. R. N. Sharma, *Methodology of Educational Research.*

Miller, P.H. (1999). *Theories of Developmental Psychology* U.S.A.—W.H. Freeman and Company.

Minsky, R. (1996). *Psycho Analysis and Gender*. New York: Routledge.

Morgan T. Clifford, (1993). *Introduction to Psychology*; New Delhi: Tata McGraw Hill Publishing Co. Ltd.

Morgan, C.T. *et al.* (1994). *Introduction to Psychology*. New Delhi: Tata Mc Graw Hill Publishing Company Ltd.

Morrison, George S. (1997). *Fundamentals of Early Childhood Education*. New Jersey: Prentice Hall, Inc.

Munn, N.L. *et al.* (1967). *Introduction to Psychology*. New Delhi: Oxford and IBH Publishing Company (P) Ltd.

N.L. Munn. *Introduction to Psychology.*

Osborne, A.F. applied imagination, principles and procedures of creative problem solving' Charles Scrbners Sons – New York 1963.

Pandey, K.P. (1988). *Advanced Educational Psychology*. New Delhi: Konark Publishers Pvt. Ltd.

Paul Greenhalgh (1994). London: Routledge, 11-13.

Pervin Lawrance, A. (1984). *Personality*. New York: Wiley.

Peter. D. Spear, Stephen, D. Penrod and Timothy B. Baker (1998). *Psychology: Perspectives on Behaviour*. New York: John Willey and Sons, 239-289.

Piaget, J. & Inhelder, B. (1969). *The Psychology of the Child*. New York.

Piaget, J. & Inhelder, B. (1973). *Memory and Intelligence.*

Piaget, J. (1929). *The Child's Conception of the World*, New York.

Piaget, J. (1932). *The Moral Judgement of the Child*, New York.

Piaget, J. (1969). *The Mechanisms of Perception*, London.

Piaget, J. (1970). *The Science of Education and the Psychology of the Child.*

Previn, Lawrence, A. (1984). *Personality*. New York: Wiley.

Prof. Dandapani, '*A Textbook on Advanced Educational Psychology*'.

Psychology 5th edition, Robert. A. Barol—Pearson Education.

Psychology and the Teacher, Dennis Child.

Psychology, Robert. F. Biehler.

Rama, S., Anandan, Anil, R. & Nambiar, B. (2005, July). *Psycho-pedagogy.* Paper presented at the Seminar on Psychological Foundations of Education, DAMTEC, Calicut.

Rober. A. Baron. *Psychology* (V Edition).

Robert, A. Baron (2001). *Psychology, Pearson*—Education.

Robert, S. Feldman (1993). *Understanding Psychology*, 3rd ed. USA: Mc Graw Hill Inc.

Robert. S. Feldman (2002). *Understanding Psychology*. Tata McGraw Hill Publishing Company Ltd.

Robert. S. Feldman. *Understanding Psychology* (IV Edition).

Ross, T.A. (1921). *Introduction to Analytical Psychotherapy*. London: Arnold.

S. S. Chauhan. *Techniques and Principles of Guidance*.

S.B. Kakkar. *Reading in Educational Psychology*.

S.K. Mangal (2000). *Advanced Education Psychology*, 6th Ed. New Delhi: Prentice Hall of India (P) Ltd., 143-45.

S.K. Mangal. *Advanced Educational Psychology*.

S.S. Chauhan. *Advanced Educational Psychology*.

SCERT, *Psychological Foundations of Early Childhood Education*, Vidyabhavan, Poojappura, Trivandrum, 12.

Serebriakpoff, V. (1988). A Guide to Intelligence and Personality- Testing. USA: The Parthenon Publishing Group.

Shankar, U. (1984). *Advanced Educational Psychology*, New Delhi: Oxonian Press Pvt. Ltd.

Sharma, R.N. (1992). *Advanced Educational Psychology*, New Delhi: Surjeet Publications.

Sharma, R.N. (1999). *Advanced Educational Psychology*, New Delhi: Surjeet Publications.

Smith K. Peter, Cowie Helen and Blades Mark (1998). *Understanding Children's Development*. Blackwell Publishers, Oxford.

Southwell, E.A. and Merbaum, M. (1964). *Personality, Readings in Theory and Research*, Wadsworth Publishing House.

Stagner, (1974). *Psychology of Personality*. New York: McGraw Hill.

Thope J. and L.P. Schmuller (1958). *Personality: An Interdisciplinary Approach*. D. Van Nostrand Company.

Torrance E.P., Experiments in Classroom Creativity' Engelwood Cliffs, N.J. Prentice Hall 1962.

Valentine (1951). *The Psychology Audit bearing on Education*. Herne Hill Great Britain.

Vygotsky, L.S. (1978). *Mind and Society. The Development of Higher Psychological Process*. Cambridge; Harward University Press.

Wertsch, James. V. Sohmer, Richard (1995). *Vygotsky on Learning and Development*. Human Development.

Willam S. Sahakian. *Theory of Learning*.

Worth, R.S.W. (1965). *Contemporary Schools of Psychology (rev. ed)*. London: Methuen.

WEB RESOURCES

http://eqi.org/
http://eqi.org/sphest1.htm
http://www.antidote.org.uk/
http://www.ei consortium.org/
http://www.eq parenting. com.

Index